# Akratic Compatibilism and All Too Human Psychology

# Akratic Compatibilism and All Too Human Psychology

## Almost Enough Is Free
## Will Enough

J. Christopher Maloney

LEXINGTON BOOKS

*Lanham • Boulder • New York • London*

Published by Lexington Books
An imprint of The Rowman & Littlefield Publishing Group, Inc.
4501 Forbes Boulevard, Suite 200, Lanham, Maryland 20706
www.rowman.com

86-90 Paul Street, London EC2A 4NE

British Library Cataloguing in Publication Information Available

**Library of Congress Cataloging-in-Publication Data**

Names: Maloney, J. Christopher, author.
Title: Akratic compatibilism and all too human psychology : almost enough is free will enough / J. Christopher Maloney.
Description: Lanham : Lexington Books, [2023] | Includes bibliographical references and index. | Summary: "J. Christopher Maloney argues that free will is compatible with necessary laws of science and immutable history. For free will emerges from an akratic will that asymptotically approaches the ability to choose to act otherwise than it willfully does"— Provided by publisher.
Identifiers: LCCN 2023004326 (print) | LCCN 2023004327 (ebook) | ISBN 9781666919486 (cloth) | ISBN 9781666919493 (epub)
Subjects: LCSH: Free will and determinism. | Akrasia.
Classification: LCC BJ1468.5 .M35 2023 (print) | LCC BJ1468.5 (ebook) | DDC 123/.5—dc23/eng/20230324
LC record available at https://lccn.loc.gov/2023004326
LC ebook record available at https://lccn.loc.gov/2023004327

# Contents

# Acknowledgments

I am deeply grateful to John Fischer, Michael McKenna, Al Mele, Carolina Sartorio, and Wesley Holliday for their wise criticism and generous counsel regarding free will. Were it not for what they have written, I would be both blind and deaf to much of what matters most in this arena of philosophical inquiry and unrelenting debate. Each kindly and patiently read a bit of my badly limping and primordial scribblings that evolved into this book. They are all entirely innocent of the crimes against right reason that my pen has committed in the following pages. From among my long-time colleagues, I shall always be grateful to (the sadly late) Jerry Gaus and David Schmidtz respectively for the friendships we shared fueled by the best philosophy available on cold tap or awaiting high ahead on an ascending mountain trail. But for the many always enriching philosophical discussions I have enjoyed with Keith Lehrer for the last three decades— often over lunch on the shaded patio of the historic Arizona Inn—I would have less than a nickel's worth of thoughts about free will. Each time I re-read something which that Regents Professor put down on paper I snatch a gem brighter than those of his I've previously pilfered. But he too is immunized against my downstream mistakes. So, my kind readers will not be surprised that, with his permission, my references in chapter 1 to the big dog literature bristle with pointers to Keith's forthcoming book. *Ultimate Freedom: Beyond Free Will.* Do read it!

My admiration of Romane Clark, too soon and too long deceased, escapes my powers of calculation and estimation. Bo directed my dissertation and, by his example and papers, showed me what a real philosopher should be. He and I never discussed free will, but he taught me how intertwined is the philosophy of mind with the philosophy of just about anything in the local light cone. Would that I could repay him by approximating the standard he set!

Although I am an atheist, I am compelled to conclude that the poet was right: "God moves in a mysterious way / His wonders to perform." For it is certainly a miracle that for most of my career I was blessed to be a member of the University of Arizona's Department of Philosophy and Cognitive Science Program. There is not enough ink in a full barrel to record what my dazzling colleagues—past and present—and our successive cohorts of sparkling graduate students here in the beautiful Sonoran Desert have taught me about the questions that have always gnawed on my philosophical neurons. None of these brilliant thinkers is complicit in any of my many errors ahead, or worse, to be saddled with my views. Still, their benign influence saturates what is on offer here wherever, if ever, I manage to get things right or nearly so.

Sandra Kimble sacrificed her big box of sharp blue pencils on my manuscript in her efforts to save me from the fate of Mrs. Malaprop. And Debbie Jackson's management of departmental matters made possible many of the hours I sat at my keyboard instead of feigning competence as Department Head. I thank them both for our joyful years of co-conspiracy. I am guilty; they are not. Well, mostly.

I thank Thomas Christiano—now Arizona's Philosophy Department Head—for generously funding both the proofing of the text and also its index by Arc Indexing Inc.

My gratitude extends to an anonymous referee whose wisdom I hope was not wasted on me. And, damn! I should have bought a lottery ticket the lucky day Jana Hodges-Kluck became my editor.

Yes, I am a fortunate—wildly fortunate—guy. For I have loved Judy Nantell every day since that subtle autumn evening in 1970 when first we kissed, and she vanished behind her dormitory door like a whisper in the wind. Together we have two beyond precious daughters, Maura and Brigid. This book is dedicated to that lovely and loving trinity with all the love that this man might muster.

# Introduction

*Human freedom implies that a person could have done otherwise, and so compatibilism implies that a person could have done otherwise even though the person was causally determined to do what she did.*

Keith Lehrer[1]

*In a world with deterministic laws of nature, at any time there is only one future evolution of the world that is possible given the laws and the state of the world at that time. Determinism is the thesis that the laws of our world are deterministic. If determinism is true, then the laws of nature and the initial conditions of the Big Bang determined a unique future for our world; every movement you will ever make is part of that unique future, determined eons ago. . . . For those who regard the traditional debate about the freedom to do otherwise as resolved in favor of incompatibilism, it is time to consider the other kinds of control that we wield over the natural world, including ourselves as parts of it. We may yet find a form of inner freedom that is possible even in a deterministic world.*

Wesley H. Holliday[2]

Moral responsibility presupposes freedom of the will. Let that be our guiding axiom. If true, it would link morality for materialized mortals of our imperfectly rational and often conflicted sort to our materializing matter. But what, if anything, is the will and its putative freedom? Moreover, and central to our concerns here, if the will should prove to be real and recognized by scientific psychology, both cognitive and social, is its freedom compatible with determinism? Is freedom of the will, once properly understood, consistent with how successful science should represent the way in which the principles of nature settle and rule the entire range of reality? Consider epistemology's golden age when science is to be satiated with knowledge of all the universally binding laws of nature. How exactly do the laws of this complete and compelling legal lore govern their domain? In what manner do they determine all the events involving things like us that roam the settled supraatomic levels floating above the subatomic dicey depths stochastically bubbling below? How precisely do the definite regularities that science shall ultimately confirm forever fix and unerringly forecast the events, including our actions, that exhaustively sum to the causal history of time?

It is my humble hunch that when ethics, metaphysics, and the philosophy of mind have the wisdom to welcome advice from the galloping psychological sciences, their intersection may promise plausible—though not uniquely credible—answers to our interwoven collection of perennially recalcitrant questions. So, in the following I look to that converging cadre of mutually informative disciplines to discern how, surprisingly, a rookie conception of free will *might* comport with determinism of the decidedly most devilish sort.

We begin our compatibilist project with a familiar but controversial assumption to complement our initial axiom: An agent's free will requires as a necessary, though perhaps insufficient, condition the deliberative ability—the psychic power—to choose and act otherwise than she actually does (Chisholm 1989). She may have done what she did, but—if free—she presumably could have done otherwise had she so chosen. Had she normally opted for such a foregone action, her vote and its candidate action would have emerged from the nearly rational psychology characteristic of the kind we sometime sinners against logic and coherence turn out to be. A deliberator so free but fallible would have the cherished chance to peer into her future to cherry-pick from a range of mere—but genuine—possibilities an open action. Ideally, she would, because she could, fictively represent in her mind a bit of yet unrealized intentional behavior poised to precipitate within the rain of events that pour down as the vanishing present into the headwater of the henceforth. However, mature science may seem hostile to our assumed ability to choose and act otherwise. For gold-standard science evidently demands determinism. Roughly put, determinism dictates that every macroscopic event, state, and object bobbing in time—including each physically implemented choice and action—is when, where, and as it is in virtue of being so implied by the conjunctive conspiracy of the laws of nature and the history of what's afloat. So strict is this potent conjunct's implicative warrant that, regardless of what agents may anticipate, only one array of future possibilities is consistent with the steadfast laws conjoined with the evaporated past. If, as we here assume, determinism—once fully and properly formulated—should be right, then the finely sieved future is perhaps most naturally, though maybe naively, conceived as a uniquely exhaustive and asymmetric straight stream of events cascading ahead in the course of causation. So represented, the future would be a single channel forward without latitude or leeway, full bank to bank with the laws' exclusively allotted shimmering shoal of real things and events. Our passage through time, if so determined, would be a voyage down unrelenting chronology's event-full river, a course unrelieved by wayward distributaries of alternative possibilities forgone and without the chance to throw action's rudder to starboard or port. But does the current so carry us that our specific course is necessary and unalterable? Or does the flow permit or enable us to veer off the actual line to which we deterministically hew?

Hoping to square morality's freedom occasionally to veer with science's charted straight sail through time, compatibilism, in its various tussling incarnations, affirms and aspires to explicate the consistency of free will and determinism. The typical compatibilist tacks by refining at least one of the provisional, but arguably problematic, concepts of the will—freedom, or determinism. Compatibilists are a heterogenous lot though, disjoined primarily by disputes regarding exactly what the will, if ever free, is and precisely how it comports with determinism once properly presented. But prominent compatibilists who would navigate the straits with either Lewis or Lehrer at the helm try to secure free will's presumed open alternative possibilities of choice and action by tempering the concept of determinism. With their sextant on Hume, they recommend an empiricist conception of the laws of nature that would scour away from them any stain of necessity, whether logical or natural. Humean scientific laws would be the finally adopted pragmatically warranted—if not correct—predictive universal principles happily embedded in the optimally entrenched explanatory systems in the fabled golden age of rational inquiry. The laws ensconced in such systems collectively reveal why, but in no way make, events temporally tumble just as they do. Hume's laws merely legislate the sequence in which events occur but do not—because they cannot—necessitate or enforce compliance. The benighted thought that the laws of nature are inescapable necessary truths is, for Humeans, a vestigial cognitive illusion triggered by our inveterate epistemic or psychological habit of calling upon them in our explanations of why things happen as they do. Hume's adherents portray nature's norms as reliable but merely contingent regularities. Presumably, nature's lawful regulations differ from other but merely accidental universal regularities by epistemically supporting subjunctive, if not counterfactual, reasoning. Such laws are simply to be general presumptive truths content to supervene upon the prevailing physically realized objects, facts, and events that, by being splayed across time, happen collectively to constitute the universe (Horgan 1993; Davidson 2001b). Humeans would have the laws of nature—including the principles of psychology—asymmetrically depend on what there is and, hence, in part upon what we do. Thus, Hume's laws take their cue from our actions rather than our actions being in any way necessitated or otherwise established by those laws. The populist laws that empiricists posit are beholden to the countless things, including events and actions, of whatever kinds adrift in time's canal. As Humeans would have it, natural laws owe their legal status to all things chronologically arrayed. Mosaics neatly model the Humean picture. For Hume's laws take their shape just as a mosaic's emergent image owes its character and content to the plenitude of autonomous tesserae of different shape, stain, and stuff individually positioned in stone within the art's fixed frame. Hume's never-necessitating and only efflorescent laws would predict and specify—but neither compel, govern, nor regulate—what there is. When cited in explanations, these pattern-dependent principles only implicate what happens and what we do without saddling either their reports or implicants with constricting modality. Since Humean principles necessitate nothing, they would, by their modal silence, permit possible alternatives not only to what there actually is or happens but also, thereby, to what we sometimes do. The tesserae within the frame of nature's mosaic simply are what, where, and as they are because their alternates are not. In an empiricist-approved predictable world Hume's way concedes the possibility of those foregone leeway-licensed alternative actions that free will may require. Humean laws chart our sail ahead down time's river by simply foreseeing or forecasting each event in the stream while being blind to those that would have been were they not excluded by those that are.[3] Partnered with history, Hume's indulgent laws completely imply what each of our actions *will* be without ever implying what any *must* be. Whatever we will do, we shall do, without this secure trivial truth entailing that any of our doings be nomically necessary. So, if Humeans have the laws their way, then to the cheers of compatibilists we can unproblematically act otherwise than we do. Compatibilism is quick and clean if the laws of nature are as compliant as Hume would have them (Lehrer forthcoming, ch. 4).

Nevertheless, would-be compatibilists need not, and perhaps should not, pledge allegiance to all the dogmas of reigning empiricism (Quine 1951). For party loyalty should tolerate dalliance with tempered rationalism. Without default expulsion from their clan, card-carrying compatibilists might dare to dally with the necessitarian tradition of nature's laws historically exemplified by Spinoza, variously described these days by Carroll, and most prominently—though not uniformly—represented in our modern vernacular by Armstrong, Dretske, Tooley, and Holliday.[4] Spinozans doubt the gentle Humean conception of modally innocent nomic regularities. Instead, they countenance, if not affirm, the (natural, if not logical,) necessity of scientific laws and their implicants, including all actions. By allowing for the contingency of some actions courtesy of their modally muted laws, Humeans are at liberty to elect compatibilism's presumption of possible open but foregone alternative actions. In contrast, Spinozans are apt—too hastily, I think—to despair of the will's freedom and instead to settle for incompatibilism. Thus, those intimidated by the long shadows of van Inwagen or Pereboom may be inclined prematurely to relinquish compatibilism's requirement on leeway in action. In their despondence, some may needlessly urge rescission or revision of our opening axiom tethering morality to free will. And others might take an imprudent libertarian leap of faith by avowing freedom's mysterious persistence in the strong jaws of modally fortified determinism.

Although most philosophers at the altar of compatibilism may genuflect to Humean commandments, it remains a contested—perhaps finally unanswerable—question whether the mundane laws deserving our devotion are Humean or Spinozan. And so, I urge unblinkered but hopeful compatibilists cautiously to pause to wonder with me whether Spinoza rather than Hume may have been right. Provisionally supposing the Dutch heretic correct, circumspect compatibilists then ought to ask whether, *pace* Spinoza, we may nevertheless enjoy the ability to act otherwise. As Holliday's above epigram suggests, might it be that "we may yet find a form of inner freedom that is possible even in a deterministic world" of the draconian sort that the severest of Spinozans posit? Indeed, they might. That, anyway, is what I shall argue.

I welcome all patient ears to consider the reassuring compatibilist sermon I preach in the context of debatable assumptions to come. My ecumenical homily is tuned in some ways both to compatibilists whose catechism calls for *leeway* in free action as well as to those whose doctrine would *source* an action's freedom in the character of its cognitive spring. I admit to advancing a new and untested edition of compatibilism. Yet, since it takes to heart a conception of the laws of nature toward which the strictest incompatibilists may be apt to endorse, perhaps they too might glance this way. And I do recognize that zealous Humeans—who would excommunicate Spinozans from the commune of the righteous—might by now elect not to read further. Still, I confess to hoping that my few words might find their way to anyone who has paused with a freshly opened mind to wonder, if not for the first time, about free will. However, if that good fortune fails me, I am content to speak to the too few chary but inquisitive wannabe compatibilists willing simply to consider whether the laws may be, as Spinoza would have it, iron necessities rather than plastic contingencies.

I invite these would-be cautious compatibilists to assume with me that free will does require the ability or leeway to act otherwise, where the act arises from a cognitive source to be described in chapters to come. But I advise them against prematurely despairing of action's leeway should the laws be Spinozan-iron. For I argue—conditionally—that even *if* determinism should be as dictatorial as Spinoza might say, free will's leeway to act otherwise than actual nevertheless may have a place in a world so inflexibly determined and strictly governed. Admittedly, mine is a revisionist rendition of the concept of freedom. Like other versions of compatibilism on the historical occasions of their introduction, mine is an abductive hypothesis rather than a soundly deduced certainty immune to all fanciful counterexamples. I recommend a particular but contestable conception of the will hatched in a nest woven from hunches borrowed from cognitive psychology and feathered with ideas favored in social psychology. If my fledgling hypothesis merits a name before it takes wing, then call it "Akratic Compatibilism." It would fiddle with how we should conceive of free will's presumed ability to act otherwise under the provisional concession of Spinozan determinism. For free action, surprisingly but properly understood, may be a remarkable—though not universal—sporadic human achievement against the odds won by some—and maybe for others—by a kind of oddly akratic action. Such an action is famously illustrated by the plight of the tormented young Augustine. St. Augustine's autobiographical *Confessions* portrays a passionate youth who struggles mightily—but unsuccessfully— to do what is right. Augustine confesses both his sin and—importantly for our purposes—his sincere, determined, but finally doomed effort to do otherwise. He wills at first not to sin. But he also wills— ultimately and decisively—to sin. His cognitively peculiar transgression is intentional, purposeful, preferred, and willed. He initially resists temptation, but finally and perhaps necessarily succumbs. Free will, I say, is born of just such an internal and characteristically human psychological conflict. That is the idea that animates akratic compatibilism. I wager that an action, if free, may prove to be intentional behavior contrary to a conflicted agent's superseded will, a weak will embedded, but defeated, within her prevailing conflicted regime of practical thinking (Davidson 1980, 22; Mele 2012; Holton 2009a and 2009b). Our paradigmatic akratic actor—Augustine—would be of two competing contrary wills: one weak and defeated, the other strong and victorious. Evidently, he knowingly does what he judges to be wrong. Psychology is, of course, the natural logos of the psyche. So, if the laws of nature, including psychology, are Spinozan, Augustine's philosophically puzzling akratic action would be the culmination of optimally resisted but ultimately irresistible—because necessary—psychological processes unfolding within such an *ambi-volent* incarnate agent.[5] Our conflicted double-willed free agent may too weakly want, and thus unsuccessfully will, to act one way while he quite strongly wants, and thus successfully wills, to act in another way. What is crucial in the case Augustine exemplifies is not that his action is sinful, wrong, or bad. No, its moral character is irrelevant here. What matters from the perspective of akratic compatibilism is that the action is the culmination of internal cognitive conflict where the actor psychologically resists doing what, because of the inescapable governance of Spinozan psychology, she actually and inexorably does. Recall that under the provisional assumption that the laws of nature, including psychology, are Spinozan, psychological laws dictate the ways we reason and act with necessity. Certainly, cognitive psychology casts us as deliberators that rely upon typically complex—often partially unconscious and introspectively inaccessible—psychological processes to launch our actions. Our efficacious psychic currents stream within and—*per* our provisional assumption—with the natural inevitability ensured by necessitarian laws of thought, Spinozan psychology. As actors in the firm grip of such psychology, we act exactly as, and of the necessity with which, our inescapable—often messy, sometimes too quick, frequently dirty, and somewhat modular—psychology mandates (Fodor 1983 and 2001; Carruthers 2006).[6] On some occasions psychology so governs an agent as to ensure that, in the cognitive run-up to her action, she initially and necessarily wills to act one way but nonetheless, in ultimate deliberative conclusion, necessarily wills to act otherwise.

Who hasn't once wanted desperately to do one thing, perhaps the right thing, while—like Augustine—finally regretfully, but willfully, doing the contrary? If we are sometimes internally conflicted and Spinozan determinism is true, that is because our psychology legislates just so. And if such damning determinism prevails, that psychic legislation applies with necessity, rendering it impossible on such occasions ultimately to do what, in a too weak way, one wills, wants, or prefers. When these kinds of circumstances obtain, an agent's actually induced and ultimately willed action fails, as it must, to fulfill that indecisive agent's early frail and, hence, annulled will. Her delicate vernal sprout of volition emergent in the agent's best laid plans and good intentions loses, as it must, in a take-no-prisoners psychic competition.[7] The fragile sprig is trampled in the stampede of conflicting practical attitudes that constitute the agent's competitive deliberative process from which the winning willed action emerges victorious. That overall incoherent tussling sum of mental contestants constitutes the agent's occurrent conclusive practical reasoning, the rough and tumble prevailing psychological process that culminates in her action. When in this peculiarly akratic way we fail to do what we too weakly, but perhaps intensely, will to do, we might well realize a law-abiding psychological process that *asymptotically approaches* its weakly willed goal. If the approach is indeed asymptotic, it cannot produce—but must *almost* produce—the weakly willed action. That willed but unrealized action is other than what actually occurs. If so, then by riding the asymptotic cognitive curve, we are *almost able to act otherwise* than we do upon that occasion. So, we are *almost free to act otherwise* in the elusive asymptote. And that, I shall argue—by considering the logic of "almost"—is just enough, maybe only barely enough, to be free. Usually, of course, almost achieving a goal is failure to achieve that goal. But sometimes and relative to some circumstances, almost achieving an elusive goal is enough actually to achieve the prize. Almost enough is sometimes enough. If that is right, then we are free enough to be responsible even *if* Spinoza, rather than Hume, should be right. I would have free will square with even Spinozan determinism in scientific psychology. But you'll be the fair judge of that.

## NOTES

1. Keith Lehrer, *Metamind*, p. 4: Oxford University Press (1990-06-14)) Retrieved 28 Mar. 2022, from +https://oxford.universitypressscholarship.com/view/10.1093 /acprof:oso/9780198248507.001.0001/acprof-9780198248507-chapter-1. © Keith Lehrer 1990; Oxford University Press Copyright © 2022. All rights reserved. Reproduced with permission of the Licensor through PLSclear.

2. Wesley H. Holliday, "Freedom and the Fixity of the Past," in *The Philosophical Review* vol. 121, no. 2, pp. 179–207. Copyright 2012, Cornell University. All rights reserved. Republished by permission of the copyright holder and the present publisher, Duke University Press. www.dukeupress.edu.

3. Equivalently, the actual world, if Humean, is situated among many possible worlds, each individuated by its distinctive ontic population, a population upon which the local—and thus perhaps distinctive—laws supervene.

4. Among Spinoza's credible cohort I number those who have variously defended necessitarian-like conceptions of the laws of nature as naturally necessary governing regularities inclusive of universal truths, facts, or conditions. See Kneale 1950; Dretske 1977; Tooley 1977; Kripke 1980; Armstrong 1983; Fales 1990 and 1993; Carroll 1987 and 1994; Swoyer 1982; Sydney Shoemaker 1998; Fine 2002; Bigelow, Ellis and Lieres 2004; and Holliday 2012. Necessitarian governing laws are to be represented by modally modified statements appropriate for inclusion in the sort of systematic explanations ultimately to be confirmed by mature successful sciences that are alert to the role of modality in competing systematizations of the principles of nature. See Schaffer (2005) and Wilson (2013) for their contrary assessments of some editions of necessitarianism.

5. Holton (2009a, 118–19) contends that an adequate theory of how agents persist in their resolutions when subject to conflicting desires requires reference to the will and its powers to supplement the roles of propositional and practical attitudes. He remarks, "The central point is this. If accounts [appealing only to beliefs, desires, and intentions] were right, then sticking to a resolution would consist in the triumph of one desire (the stronger) over another. But that isn't what it feels like. It typically feels as though there is a *struggle*. One maintains one's resolution by dint of effort in the face of the contrary desire. Perhaps not every case of maintaining strength of will is like that. . . . But, by and large, maintaining strength of will requires effort. Moreover, the empirical evidence bears this out . . . consider just the most straightforward, which comes from simple measures of the physical arousal to which the exercise of willpower gives rise. Ask agents to regulate themselves in ways which involve acting

against contrary inclinations—to regulate their emotions, for instance, the expression of their emotions, their attention or their thoughts—and they will show the standard signs of physiological arousal that accompany effort: increased blood pressure and pulse, with changed skin conductance, etc." Holton cites the interesting empirical work of Muraven and his colleagues regarding the depletable power of a cognitive faculty subserving difficult self-regulation (Muraven, Tice, and Baumeister 1998; Muraven and Baumeister 2000).

6. Some compatibilists who endorse Spinozan psychology and consider that all of an agent's practical reasoning occurs of necessity may want to opt out of Moore's subjunctive conditional analysis of "could have done otherwise" in favor of agental causation. See Chisholm (1989, 7–8).

7. Models of competitive cognitive processes operating within various psychological domains are common in cognitive neuroscience. See, for example, Desimone and Duncan 1995; and Moore and Zirnsak 2017. Milner and Goodale's landmark work on dual stream visual processing (with one stream contributing to a subject's informationally guided movements and the other stream feeding her conscious visual experience) demonstrates one way in which the behavior and experience of cognitive agents can be subject to control by different and sometimes mutually uncooperative processes (Goodale and Milner 2013). Then, too, various models of processes underlying subjects' decisions to opt for one rather than other alternatives in selection tasks indicate that differences in attention and various other factors influence or determine the selection of an alternative (Smith and Krajbich 2019; Busemeyer and Diederich 2002). For accounts of decision-making inspired by the notion of bounded rationality, see the essays by various authors collected in Gigerenzer and Selten 2001, especially Gigerenzer 2001a and 2001b.

# Chapter 1

# Determinism and Compatibilism Redux

*CAVEAT LECTOR!*

I am gratefully influenced by the instructive quarrels among compatibilists in history's unending free will debate. But I must confess that I've not learned quite the lessons any of the many sages would teach. I realize that I risk exile to the classroom's corner and the capping shame of Duns Scotus's hat. Still, mindful of Chisholm's admirable humility when entering the quarrel, I ask your temporary tolerance for yet another but, I think, entirely fresh rendition of compatibilism: Grant the strongest version of determinism.[1] Assume that whatever we do *must* be done (G. Strawson 2005). Still, despite the stern necessity under which we would thus toil, those who recoil may be free. That, anyway, is the uncertain compatibilist hunch at which I aim. I do fondly wish that the question of free will in a deterministic world could be answered *a priori* by wits wiser than mine. A snappy deduction from incontrovertible certainties or fail-safe intuitions would be reassuring. But with an eye on the literature's long-fraught past, I am not inclined to wager much on my wish. Neither does it seem likely that the competition between free will and determinism is likely to be won by endless volleys in conceptual analysis tennis in which each credible concept successively served is bandied right back by an increasingly incredible counterexample. If that is how a cautious gamble goes, then the odds might favor that we would-be compatibilists put down some, though not all, of our money on what philosophy, at its sub-certainty abductive best, is best at: exploring why what *might* be so *may* be so (Graham and Horgan 1994; Papineau 2009; Jackson 2000; Haug 2014).[2] Here goes.

## A WORD ABOUT THE WILL

En route to examining its freedom, let's discern and then, without defense, endorse a particular conception of the will. Ears tuned to philosophy's saga from centuries past anticipate that talk of freedom of will aims to draw attention to the workings of our psychological faculty or power to cause our actions—that is our intentional behavior. However, reference to the will, as such a potent but perhaps occult faculty, is a bit scarce in the contemporary literature.[3] This may strike some as surprising in light of Kane's laudable efforts to update and ensure the credentials of the concept of the will delivered to us by historically influential authors (Kane 1999-03-18, chap. 2). Nevertheless, contemporary parlance tends to replace talk of the will with verbiage pertaining simply to intentional action. Better, we are told, to ask whether our actions might be free than to fret about the occult will's freedom when we consider the implications of determinism.[4] Nevertheless, I think that attending to the will need not hobble consideration of compatibilism if we employ the palate of contemporary cognitive psychology to paint a picture of the will. Consider, then, the familiar functionalist scheme of mentation generally favored by cognitivists. Though not without its own shortcomings and sharp critics, functionalism has held hegemony over its rivals in the contest to characterize the nature of mental states since it superseded behaviorism more than 60 years ago. The endurance of functionalism is largely due to its plausible claim to be the best available—but admittedly imperfect—working hypothesis designed to accommodate the requirements of psychology with the demands of physicalism characteristic of more fundamental natural sciences (Turing 1950; Putnam 1960 and 1967; Block and Fodor 1972; Fodor 1975 and 1983; Block 1980a, 1980b, 1998, 2001; Shoemaker, 1981; Lewis 1983a; Pylyshyn 1984). Some alternative traditional conceptions of the mind, perhaps best exemplified by Brentano's *act psychology*, posit potent mental *acts* among the basic elements critical to an adequate psychology (Tassone 2012, pt. II).[5] However, contemporary functionalist accounts of human psychology generally replace talk of empowered mental acts with reference to networks of mental *states* with various causal dispositions. Such states are to include a wide range of propositional, practical, and conative attitudes, paradigmatically but not exhaustively including beliefs, desires, preferences, and decisions. These states are to be multiply realizable physical structures with rich causal connections to one another and, perhaps in some cases, to the likes of the hosting agent's stimuli and behaviors whether past, present, or possible. Their myriad interrelations arguably enable a cognitive agent's psychological states to be tied together in the manner of semantically endowed representations with conceptual—that is, inferential—roles.[6] So connected, an agent's stream of contentful mental states deployed on an occasion would constitute her then prevailing cognitive process. Thus, to think is in one way or another to reason in virtue of instantiating a sort of inference, either theoretical or practical.[7] Why not, then, identify the will with the aptitude or disposition to reason practically, to issue mental representations forming practical inferences culminating in psychic imperatives disposed to cause the actions they mandate?

While all functionalists suppose that mental states are relationally defined and type identified, these theorists are—in principle—at liberty to disagree as to whether such relata are restricted to states whose spatio-temporal addresses or locations are bound to fall within the skins or skulls of the agents to whom they are correctly attributed. Steeped in the Cartesian tradition that treats mental states as covert and private to cognizers, conservatively inclined *short-arm functionalists* would situate mental states entirely within the corporeal boundaries of an individual agent. As such, mental states would enjoy a sort of ontological autonomy permitting the possibility of their persistence regardless of the status of an agent's environment. But *long-arm functionalists* would enumerate among an agent's mental states or their determinants some of the physical states external to her embodied mind including—but perhaps not limited to—her parochially construed sensory stimuli and bodily maneuvers (Putnam 1975; Burge 1979; Fodor 1980; Harman 1982; Block 1986; Clark and Chalmers 1998; Rupert 2009; Rowlands 2010; Menary 2010; Maloney 2018). Most long-arm functionalists may be inclined to limit an agent's exogenous mental states and cognitive relata to only those involving stimuli nearby and responses to what is on the thinker's side of her moving body's boundaries. However, let us note here—since it will be relevant later—that it is in an empirically open question just how far into the natural and social world a system of long-arm mental states may reach for relata suited for inclusion within the system's possibly far-flung network of inputs, outputs, and mediators. For functionalists who are most radically inclined do in fact cast cognition's net far enough to capture among one's percepts remotely located properties and objects. Thus, even the ocean's property of being blue stretching from your toes in the surf to the distant horizon and also the pompano leaping out of the surf at the end of your taut long line may figure in the constitution of your perceptually conscious, and hence, cognitive states (Gibson 1966 and 2015; Tye 2009; Brewer 2011; Clark and Chalmers 1998; Byrne and Logue 2009; Chemero 2009; Maloney 2018). If so, then—in your natural cognitive reaction to my action that you've witnessed—might not the hue of *my* mood and quality of *my* will also be within *your* long-arm psychological reach? For like much that is mental, my moods and willings are just physically realized representational states. Hence, they enjoy rich dispositions causally to interact with other material states such as your mental representations. So, my moods and willings—as well as other of my mental states—are candidates for membership in your conceptual network if it should extend as widely as the longest arm functionalists would allow.

So, one way or the other, functionally characterized mental states and their relations find their way into psychological science as theoretical posits with just the sort of ordinary causal powers—perhaps exposed as dispositions—permitted or tolerated throughout the empirically credentialed natural sciences (Lewis 1987b). When fussy, long-arm functionalists are apt differentially to designate internal and external mental states, they join their short-arm cronies in calling internal mental states "representations." However, they may also opt to label external states "referents" or "satisfaction conditions" of the representations registered within. But all functionalists concur that, regardless of their labels and thanks to their conceptual roles, semantically endowed efficacious mental states mediate or subserve the processes, conscious or not, that constitute thought and experience generally and practical reason particularly (Putnam 1975; Burge 1979; Fodor 1980, 1984 and 1987; Stich 1983; Baker 1987). These streaming states thereby enable our theoretical and practical defeasible reasoning, whether rationally laudable or lamentable. As they flow, they may form nonmonotonic inferences subject to either the salutary influence or corrupting interference of representations occurrent in sensation, perception, affect, and emotion (Gigerenzer and Selten 2001).

Let's simplify the functionalist picture with a helpful, but not entirely innocent, sketch that will prove useful later. With a nod to disputes internal to functionalism about mental representations and the manner of their connectivity, let's adopt—if only for heuristic purposes—the common practice of designating a mental representation by nominalizing its content in italicized caps. And then, with more than a pinch of salt seasoned with a taste of dogma, we can sample the controversial hypothesis that mental representations occur within a covert language of thought, Mentalese (Fodor 1975 and 2008; Rumelhart and McClelland 1986; Maloney 1987 and 2018; Smolensky 1988; Rey 1995 and 1997; Greenberg 2013).[8] Our conjecture would depict an agent as instantiating a propositional attitude—say, believing that snow is white— by tokening *SNOW IS WHITE*. That tokening would be doxastic by dint of the token's embodying a disposition to occur in causally connected streams of the agent's representations as if it were an element in an inference or a process of reasoning sensitive to truth preservation or amplification. Used in that fashion by a student doing her logic homework, *SNOW IS WHITE* would be apt to precede *SNOW IS WHITE OR GRASS IS GREEN* and to succeed *SNOW IS WHITE AND GRASS IS GREEN*. Were our student's attitude decisively practical rather than doxastically propositional, she would tend to use *SNOW IS WHITE* differently, in the manner of a representation in an action-enabling practical inference concerned with satisfying preference rather than seeking truth. But in any case, the functionalist theme is that mental representations have causal powers of the merely ho-hum sort countenanced by good-faith empiricists. For these supposed psychological workhorses are just realizers of everyday dispositions to occur in networks of things with similar dispositions. Once networked, such representations form a cognitive economy enabling the sort of intelligent mediation that cyclically transforms an agent's reactions to stimuli into appropriate responses, themselves ready for feedback as stimuli. Mental representations are, then, the stuff of which dreams are made, plans laid, and deeds decided.

Now that we are on the functionalist path, we can find our way to a rough conception of the will couched within a cognitivist conception of thought and action. Let's think, then, of psychology as a science nicely nested among the sciences and all within an orderly, if not reductive, framework for theories generally perhaps in the fashion Carnap once proposed and which Thomasson has profitably adapted (Carnap 1950; Fodor 1974; Thomasson 2014). We start our way down history's heavily trafficked route to the nature of the will by following Locke's tracks. We can acknowledge and put into enriched current jargon his early declaration that the will, if real, is a kind of psychologically realized power.[9] As such, an agent's Lockean will on a typical occasion of action would be that stream of her then prevailing practical attitudes that constitute her practical inference. That action-inducing inference would be a sequence of Mentalese representations that is normally apt to cause her intentionally to act in accord with its imperatival conclusion. Her willing—say to get ice cream—is a bit of practical reasoning. Idealized, it starts with a selected ensemble of her mental representations encoding her relevant beliefs, desires, and preference and ends with a self-directed imperative. To wit: *I WANT ICE CREAM; IT'S IN THE FRIDGE; I, WILL TO FETCH IT FROM THE FRIDGE AND TO EAT IT!* Her reasoning concludes with a directive in the first-person singular, a mandating representation tokened by and to herself that causes her to act as that imperative directs. If things are normal, by fulfilling the concluding imperative the agent attempts to get what she wants and, world permitting, gets the goods. Such effective but multiply realizable thinking may be more or less complex depending upon how an agent's practical attitudes—including, but not limited to, the likes of wants and desires, preferences and plans, and intentions and decisions—coalesce and perhaps cohere so as normally to cause her purposefully to act (Frankfurt 1971; Lehrer 1980 and 1990; Kane 1999-03-18, chap. 2, 196; Bratman 2000 and 2007; Davidson 2002, 83; Ekstrom 2010). In virtue of the various practical attitudes of which it is complexly and variably composed upon an occasion, the will foresees, selects, and—unless abnormally blocked, trumped, or diverted by circumstances beyond the agent's control—normally suffices for successfully acting. The will is a power, albeit blasé, because, as a potent practical inference, it is prone to cause intended action. If its potency is mysterious, it is only as mystifying as other dispositions and causes casually countenanced by sound science.

Upon reaching the part of the functionalist path where it turns contemporary, we find ourselves at a well-known but foggy junction. To the radical left runs the trifecta of ways eliminativism would repudiate or diminish the will and its power. To the conservative right lies the track to realism's several ways of preserving the will (Horgan and Graham 1991). Below I briefly scout the signed alternative passageways in order to illumine the partisan route I shall tendentiously trek. Since I hesitantly trust to the critical literature's warnings against the several ways left, throughout I will march right, with Locke, toward a realistic way of preserving the will.

The most radical of eliminativists on our left say that functionalism writ large is itself just a desperate theoretical scam to salvage what should be shed. They complain that talk of the will, as part of the babel about opaque propositional and practical attitudes, is all fictious hooey best buried with the entire body of terminally ill folk psychology by which it has been irredeemably infected (Paul Churchland 1979 and 1992; P. S. Churchland 1989). Perhaps, though I doubt it, these critics of intentional explanations of behavior and action will be vindicated in the golden age of the sciences on which they bet. That is certainly an open possibility. But the resolution of the issue awaits the maturation of the sciences and meanwhile remains contested by the impressive continuous successes of cognitive psychology. So, I pray that your kind prudence will forgive me for forsaking the leftmost eliminativist turn on the trail. Instead, let us temper our talk of the will with the terms in which the cognitive sciences trust (Horgan and Woodward 1985; Baker 1987; Fodor 2008).

Although the most radical of the three eliminativist routes might best be avoided, two other more temperate eliminativist ways remain. Instrumentalism would not entirely slash all of folk psychology from correct explanations of action. Instead of scoffing at intentional explanation, instrumentalism recommends its selective adoption with a dash of admonition. While instrumentalists do concede the truth and applaud the predictive utility of some common-sense intentional explanations, they nevertheless deny that such trusty truths need refer to anything real. Yes, it may be that an agent did what she did because she wanted what she got and believed so doing would get it. However, for that chestnut to be true of the agent there need not be any such thing as either her belief and want or her believing or wanting. Something else—something deeper, different, and essentially physical—must cryptically be doing the causal work if the honest-to-God truth be totally told. For the ontology ultimately adequate to underwrite intentional explanations that cite episodes of practical reasoning is unlikely to tolerate, much less require, beliefs or believings that really partner with wants or wantings in the production of action. If so, then ditto for the cognitive attitudes generally. Though instrumentalists may commend confirmed folk psychological explanations and their affiliated predictions of behavior, these circumspect eliminativists would slough ontological commitment as a requirement in complement to each verified—but only fictively referential—explanatory expression. After all, "The average senior enrolls in exactly 4.37 courses per semester" might well be a sentence true of the campus this semester. Yet there is certainly no individual student to whom the descriptive phrase within the sentence could refer. And it's impossible to enroll in exactly 4.37 courses anyway. But if, as is reasonable, we do acquiesce in the truth of the statement in question, we should quickly admit that the declaration is nothing but useful shorthand. At most it is merely a handy verbal instrument embedded in a familiar—but ontologically noncommittal—casual linguistic calculus we've been trained to master. We may pragmatically employ this ontologically neutral way of speaking to call out real patterns emergent from the activities of real individual students when we want to compute a measure of central tendency. But it is only as our tipsy talk of the average student tediously— but precisely—yields to sober references to particular people measured and specific algorithms applied that we might finally manage genuinely to refer to any real thing at all. Once we restrict ourselves to ontically laden language, we might refer to this or that student. And maybe, if numbers be real, we might literally mention the exact number of courses some student took. So too for true, but metaphysically hollow, psychological talk of the will and would-be willings. Talk of the will is like dispensable talk of the average student. Really, there is no will and certainly no willings in agents who act on the heels of practically reasoning. Surely, says the instrumentalist, willings are not literally encoded in, or as, real mental representations. If they were, then contrary to fact, one's will would be as easily edited as would be Mentalese terms in a mentally encoded imperative (Dennett 1975 and 1978a). When we want full and deep explanations of what, why, and how we willfully act, we must—instrumentalists say—foreswear the intentional level lingo and turn to the technical vocabulary of an underwriting certified science or technology even if it, in turn, should ride upon the broad shoulders of yet more basic science. Only in terms so sturdy and deep can we expect to fathom the causal depths casually presupposed by facile intentional talk. When we cast our psychological models at the right depth, we probably need to rely on the onerous technical terminology about calculators pitched in the erudite language spoken in the intersection of bioengineering, computational theory, and neuroscience where words are wanting for wills and their wantings. According to the instrumentalist, human agents, when best understood, are most likely bound optimally to be conceived as evolved carbon-based inference machines captured by the conceptual schemes collectively characteristic of nearly fundamental sciences. It is only this faith in the fundamental that sanctions our disciplined credence in the instrument of the intentional idiom (Dennett 1975, 1978a, 1978b, 1984, 1987, 1991, 1992, 2003 and 2006; Davidson 1973). Of course, critics of instrumentalism invariably complain that it struggles to explain why attributions of propositional and practical attitudes could be as accurate and predictive as they regularly are were their would-be referents, once properly reduced, reduced to nothing at all. For suppose that intentional attitude attributions were, as instrumentalists say, merely dispensable instruments in the psychologist's explanatory tool kit vanishingly reducible to their composing particles and the processes thereof. Then, contrary to instrumentalists, would not intentions and their psychological complements be every bit as real as the real-enough scalpel in the surgeon's hand or hammer in the carpenter's belt?

The most tolerant stance in our trio of eliminativist perspectives on the will salutes the progress of cognitive science, to which this permissive position mostly adapts and happily adopts. But the adaption would selectively prune from sound psychology all its vestigial concepts that uselessly sprout below the graft that joins cultivated cognitive science to its gnarly roots of psychic lore. Better, the most tolerant eliminativists specifically recommend, not to reify the vestige of pop psychology's ultimately autonomous and mysteriously potent phantom will as a power that transforms mere thought into real action. These judicious eliminativists would precisely snip reference to the ill-bred will from genteel cognitive theory. Rather, they advise, talk instead of *intentional actions* and trust to progressing contemporary psychology abductively to identify the psychic states that subserve an agent's control over what she purposefully does (Goldman 1970; Fischer 1994, 134ff.; Mele 2006).[10] So, the most tolerant eliminativists advise that in lieu of looking for the will, we investigate planned, intended or otherwise motivated actions when we wonder within the scientific scheme whether actors' actions might ever be free.

I am content not to contest the tolerant eliminativist's preference for action intended over action willed. For that preference seems to be but a matter of taste, a taste for one theoretical concept, *intending*, rather than another, *willing*, although each competitor (but not both together) deserves the available place on psychology's menu. After all, what, besides the label, differentiates intentional from willed action? As an event, each such action is a bit of behavior an agent normally launches by representing it as the terminus of a typical instance of practical reason. Intending and willing are equally intentional; each is about a specific bit of behavior mentally represented under a specific description. And each, if physically realized, packs the causal power to induce the appropriate sequence of physical events that is apt to produce the targeted behavior rather than alternatives in the agent's repertoire. And so, with a grateful nod to Kane's instructive recipe for the ways of the will, I'll take the liberty of retaining it on the menu and ordering it up as the opportunity arises.

Now that we have glanced at conceptions of the will that in one way or another would banish it as bogus, we may turn the corner realists recommend on the functionalist road to the will. As functionalists, realists treat all modes of thought and experience as ways in which mental representations realize dispositionally connected mental states. They are leery of schemes for volition that require an ontology inflated with medieval selves: causal agents *per se*, efficacious actors *qua substances*, or potent persons *as substrates*. In this regard, our realists are like eliminativists of one sort or another. Some functionalists, in league with radical eliminativists, abjure secret selves (Pollock and Ismael 2006), holding that the first-person pronoun is referentially empty and that Descartes's "cogito, ergo sum" is simply unsound. Others ally with moderate eliminativists by allowing casual, but instrumentally tempered, reference to agental selves as a temporary way station on the road to sophisticated genuine reductive reference to selected arrays of mental states. Of course, various philosophers not captivated by functionalist psychology certainly have championed the Cartesian posit of a bare subject or naked particular that, by instantiating them all on their schedule, would unify the conglomeration of properties psychology attributes in explanation of one's actions. However, such a unifier, since distinct from a person's properties, evidently defies conceptualization by whomever may want to conceive of it, unadorned by the properties it collects. And yet, it would be this simple but finally cryptic self that would be the ultimate agental cause of a free or undetermined agent's actions. Functionalists understandably reject the very idea of an efficacious Cartesian self as distinct from the ensemble of properties or states it is abduced to unify. They rhetorically ask what could such a naked substance add to scientific psychology beyond the bounty provided by a theory of systematized efficacious representational states realized by one's perceptible body or brain.[11] For all functionalists, whether realists or not, the will, if mysteriously rooted in the causal efficacy of a covert willful agental substance, should be as taboo as is the notion of an empowering occult substance served up by an otherwise adequate theory of any organized system of states. Our solar system is just such a system, but no one nowadays dares to account for its systematic unity by positing a cryptic substrate. Where there are systems, there are things systematized, but there need not be unified entities distinct from the unified systems and what they systematize.

Nevertheless, nothing in principle precludes a functionalist from reductively identifying an agent's self or her will with some of her theoretically sanctioned representational arrays. Just as Locke would identify one's self with certain of one's conscious mnemonic mental states, so too may functionalists identify an agent's self or will with some of her rightly related mental states. So, if true to their functionalist bearings, realists foreswear identifying an agent's will with any feature that she, as an obscure substance, might have. Rather, if the will is to be real, it must meet muster either as a solo mental representation or as a choir of many.

It is at this juncture where the realist road also splits: soloists going one way, choristers the other. Soloists say that the will is a distinctively engaged and thus empowering type of solo psychological state causally disposed to instigate overt action or effort so aimed. That psychic soloist, when normally summoned and unblocked, would be realized as an isolated Mentalese imperative that, by mandating an action antecedently represented by the agent's prevailing bit of practical thinking, thereby typically causes the action (O'Shaughnessy 1973; Ginet 1990). Or its presumed power might be deployed to resolve occasional conflicts among the conative states of an otherwise indecisive agent (Holton 2009a).[12] Thus, an agent who, as a result of practical reason, wills to flip the switch that lights the room, would issue an effective Mentalese order such as *LET THERE BE LIGHT!* Critics of the soloist line who forget that functionalism supposes that mental representations are causally efficacious might unfairly object with a snide rhetorical flare. For, trusting to rhetoric rather than reason and with tongue in cheek, they might ask whether the remarkable power of that individually efficacious Mentalese mandate is mysteriously miraculous. Is it like the illuminating commandment of Genesis's divine creator of light, an order that turns on the light simply by command?[13]

Choristers, being good functionalists, rightly scoff at the rhetorical question. But unlike the soloists, choristers think of the causal oomph of Mentalese representations as a package deal. Causes generally aggregate multiple conditions to suffice for their effects. It is not only the friction that causes the match to light. Rather, it is the friction teamed with the oxygen and the dehydrated sulfur in the match head that, along with other unmentioned prevailing conditions, coalesce to coax the flame forward. And so too, say the chorists, do the various mental representations arrayed as an instance of practical reason collectively cause the action the complex inference prescribes. That concert of representations, rather than any single voice, is what we ought to identify as an agent's will. To will is to reason, to reason practically toward if not all the way to, an actionable conclusion. If choristers are right, the will takes the form of the sequence—or a proper part thereof—of the psychic elements that constitute the culmination of an agent's prevailing practical thinking.[14] If so, then a typical willing upon a cognitive occasion is a variable heterogenous complex ensemble—whether coherent or not—of beliefs, wants, preferences, evaluations, intentions and plans conspiring toward a conclusion (Frankfurt 1971; Kane 1999-03-18; Bratman 1999, chap. 3, 2000, and 2007).[15] As a temporally evolving process, an instance of willing can be cut short, inter-rupted, and terminated prior to concluding with a Mentalese imperative upon which an attempt to act ensues. Or if the clock permits and interruption slumbers, a willing might reach an imperative with enough oomph to induce an attempt at the action mandated. Chorists deny that a single imperatival mental representation normally suffices for intentional action. For they appreciate that a typical, if not idealized, action, if intended, needs be the result of practical reasoning, the rehearsal of pros and cons in the context of desires tempered by preferences (Lehrer 1990, 2004, 2016, forthcoming). So, if choristers are right about the complexity of the will, it should come as no surprise that we are sometimes indecisive. As we defeasibly reason our way to what we eventually do, we are apt to entertain reasons that cut against the conclusion we finally reach (Pollock 1995). An instance of willing, as an instance of complex inference, may include proper representational parts that would induce us to do what we don't were they not defeated, undercut, or otherwise overridden by the parts that follow. Reasoning pro and con may be like reasoning in the manner of *reductio ad absurdum*. By way of *reductio* one temporarily reasons en route to a contradiction that, once derived, one rejects so as to advance to the argument's downstream conclusion. A river that empties into a lake to the north might flow south for a while but finally find its way north. And so too might one's will wander one way toward one conclusion only later to reverse course to reach its ultimate destination. A reflective person's will is apt to wander its way through a bit of indecision as she carefully reasons first *pro* and then *con*. This fact about the will is critical to its freedom. Or so I shall argue later when we consider how, by wrestling with temptation, the will wins its freedom from determinism's dictates.

Although I think realists regarding the will are free to treat it as a solo or choral element in intentional action, without further argument and I hope with your tolerance, in all that follows I shall adopt the chorister conception of the will. It is, I assume, a complex efficacious array of mental representations (or arrays of mental representations) that, as such, is normally apt to result in action.[16] We shall see that one way to render the will's freedom compatible with the most demanding—and possibly correct—version of determinism trades on an indecisive will's complexity.

## A Word about Freedom of the Will

Equipped with the chorister's realistic conception of the will, we can proceed to ask about its freedom in the context of determinism. To fix the concept of freedom here at work while distinguishing it from rivals in the literature, let us provisionally assume throughout, albeit controversially, that when we consider the implications of determinism, the kind of freedom that intrigues us entails the ability—the leeway—to act otherwise than we actually do. Might we yet be just so free and thus, in coordinate fashion, morally responsible even *if* the storm of the strictest determinism should darken our lives? Still courting controversy but to set the bar high for compatibilism, adopt for the moment the harshest and most challenging conception of determinism. Allow, to a first approximation, that whenever we may be poised to act deliberately, there should be only one possible way to sail from the present into the future. Concede, provisionally, what most may deny but few others plausibly affirm: Admit that any tack we ever take is not only unique but also inevitable. Suppose that determinism so commandeering leaves our hand on action's rudder powerless against nature's necessitating laws to control the line we cut into the future's wind.[17] If the blow of determinism strips from our sails any chance of alternative bearings, might we ever go forward freely and responsibly? Would a determinism so unforgiving infect our actions with a freedom-forbidding fatalism fatal to morality and the leeway it may want? Must such rigidifying determinism deny to us the hope of dignity beyond the grasp of mere mechanisms? Or, despite the apparent hostility of determinism so construed toward freedom thus characterized, might we, as I shall contend, yet steer against the necessity of nature as to sail free into our fraught future's chop?[18]

The ink sacrificed below aspires to answer these hoary questions by appending a novel lyric to compatibilists' familiar reassuring polyphony. The verse I would insert to their popular hymn praises resistance. For it is within our power sometimes and in some ways to resist—even if always unsuccessfully—the necessity that, by *pro tempore* assumption, ultimately determines our actions. By so resisting we may nevertheless approach—and thereby authoritatively secure—the leeway in action that freedom presumably requires. Let us admit that any rebellion against nature's enslaving governing laws may be at once not only necessary but also doomed to fail. That is, let us suppose that generally we simply cannot act otherwise than the inviolable laws of nature dictate, that typically we cannot omit to act in accord with nature's governance. Nonetheless, it is a firm fact that we can, and sometimes do, cognitively resist those of our willings that ultimately cause our inevitable actions. I venture that by akratically contesting irresistible temptations to act contrary to our considered practical attitudes, we do indeed revolt against the inevitability nature's laws impose on our actions. On some such occasions we may, in the elusive asymptote, approximate liberation from prevailing necessity.[19] Indeed, this—I contend—is true even under our provisional assumption that all our decisions, efforts, and actions are necessary. In struggling against the here-assumed necessitation of nature, we may be like an asymptotic function under computation. The function's continuously successive values, tediously crunched, ever more closely approach, but never quite equal, their limit. However, these nearly right numbers serve the practicing engineer full well when she applies them for most purposes for which their evasive target may be hopelessly wanted. So well may the calculations work in the projects in which they are applied that we might discount the negligible difference between approximating and approximated number. That the approximating almost equals the approximated value is enough for the former to fulfill the role of the latter in any context that might matter. When archery is scored, almost a perfect bull's eye is a bull's eye enough. So too, in some contexts and upon some occasions, human agents who—because of their nature—resist nature's governance may be like an electronic calculator heroically computing the successive closing values of an asymptotic function. For an agent unsuccessfully rebelling against the dictates of her psychology may do as well as can be done to do what cannot be done when doing what's not done matters most of all. If so, then for all human purposes, the agent's undone discount may matter not at all. If the rebel against her governing psychology should almost do what she cannot do—if she almost acts otherwise than she necessarily acts by almost omitting to act as she must—then she would be almost free. And, I say, almost free may be free enough to be free. That, anyway, is what I shall argue. Harness buckled? Helmet on? Hang on!

## DETERMINISM, DAINTY OR STERN

Widely endorsed classical compatibilism teaches us that human freedom— understood in one diluted and disputed way or another—is cheerfully compatible with determinism—well, at least a delicate determinism. Dainty determinism presumes frail laws of nature, mere brittle regularities. These patterns that objects always rehearse are the fragile universal contingencies that in the golden age of science we will have entrenched in our best systematic, but ultimately pragmatic, explanatory schemes (Lewis 1973, 73–75, and 1987, postscript C, 121–32).[20] Card-carrying Humeans in the image of Lewis, the likeness of Lehrer, or the reflection of Frankfurt allow flimsy principles of nature. Such pliant prescriptions pretend to legislate to the mundane by the ruse of being, by fortune, forever unbroken although they admit all the while of possible violation. But such lax laws, though they remain ever intact, still shiver with fragility and fear maybe-miraculous fracture. For these permissive laws are threatened throughout time by the various leashed abilities and coiled dispositions they allow with each passing moment in their supervised subjects, whether agents or objects (Lewis 1981; Beebee 2003). After all, agents, if enabled, and objects, if disposed, can, though they don't, do what the laws say that they won't. The contingency of nature's laws does not trouble the friends of Hume. They surmise that nature's prescriptions—if thus wispy—emerge only as explanatory clouds, grateful simply to supervene upon what, fundamentally, happens, here or there, to be, in either this way or that (Horgan 1993; Davidson 2001b; Perry 2004, 237–41). These evaporated legislations depend upon, and hence carry information about—but do not dictate to—the happenstance patterns of actual things and events. For those legislating Rorschach arrays are just how things appear when we turn a scientifically sober eye to matter's innumerable tesserae, individually set as they are within the frame of space-time from the cosmos's initial big bang until its last little whimper. Historians may credit Hume with deposing the would-be necessary laws of nature from their once deific Platonic pretense. But it was Lewis who inimitably distilled the chief empiricist's treatise thus[21]:

> Humean supervenience is named in honor of the greater denier of necessary connections. It is the doctrine that all there is to the world is a vast mosaic of local matters of particular fact, just one little thing and then another. . . . We have geometry: a system of external relations of spatiotemporal distance between points . . . and at those points we have local qualities: perfectly natural intrinsic properties which need nothing bigger than a point at which to be instantiated. For short: we have an arrangement of qualities. And that is all. There is no difference without difference in the arrangement of qualities. All else supervenes on that. [22]

But compatibilism can do better than soft Humeanism on behalf of free will. Human freedom need not rely on a determinism not *al dente* (Pereboom 1995). Rather, as I see it, compatibilism can, and indeed should, aim to accommodate—should it be true—even iron-fisted determinism. I certainly lay no claim to any *a priori* conceptual analysis—whatever that might be— of human free will. But I do aim abductively to argue that freedom of the sort that requires leeway in action is compatible with—though it need not presume—an adamantine determinism in the unflinchingly necessitarian and leeway-less spirit of Spinoza's stern metaphysics stripped of its theistic gargoyles and recast in secular scientific parlance (Carroll 2004, 8).[23] Should Spinoza supersede Hume, then the objective principles properly pursued by science would be absolutely unbreakable, entirely restrictive, and naturally necessary governing laws. Additionally, unlike Lewis's mutable laws, Spinoza's immutable regulations are well-welded to an inflexible history in which every event, from cosmological first to final, would be infused with the same necessity and fixity that saturates the laws (Lewis 1981; Fischer 1994, chap. 4; Holliday 2012).[24] This hardest sort of determinism would, *if true*, impregnate all events and, hence, our actions—past, present and future—with a nomic necessity so harsh as to make their omission or alternation impossible. No matter, I say, that Spinozan determinism on modal steroids implies that, simply and categorically, we cannot act otherwise than we do. Nor does it matter, as some incompatibilists have cogently argued, that such determinism entails that we are powerless over the laws and impotent pertaining to the past.[25] For, as we shall see, should we be governed by Spinozan psychology, that very necessitarian dictation entails that, in a crucial sense, we may remain free to do what we don't in a way that contextually abides the necessity of what we do and the impossibility of what we don't. This is so, if my hypothesis should be right, since the best among us sometimes may act in ways that liberate not only themselves but perhaps also those with whom they collaborate or lead in futile but ennobling revolt against Spinoza's would-be fettering necessity.

## COMPATIBILISM, SOPRANO OR CONTRALTO

A typical first-year philosophy course casually sketches the vexing question of free will posed under the tentative assumption of fuzzily depicted determinism. Upon the unindoctrinated student's hasty first glance, the blurry picture appears to portray every event and, thus, each human action as implied by the conjunction of the already-on the-job laws of nature—including psychology—and up-to-date history. In order for any event, whether mental or material, ever to be, some pair of conjoined true propositions—one securing the laws of nature and the other the history of the relevant event—entails the event's timely occurrence. Let these paired propositions and their implications be represented by corresponding language set within a scientifically ideal system of representation tolerant of covert *ceteris paribus* clauses or implicit reference to unspecified variable conditions to which the laws are tuned.[26] Then idealized reasoners, having mastered the pictured scheme, would be positioned fully to explain—by soundly inferring and accurately predicting—all that ever happens. These divine forecasters would be apt inferentially to foretell not only each flutter of the butterfly's wing but also each of its fluttery effects up until entropic tranquility. Granted the quick sketch, whatever occurs, now or tomorrow, including whatever we do would seem necessary—well, necessary *relative* to the laws and history. The green student's quandary then is whether such relative necessity of a person's action is compatible with her action's being free, with her having the chance to act otherwise.[27]

Survivors of that first foray into philosophy will have heard a discordant chorus of alternative contemporary answers, some compatibilist, others not. With apology to the others neglected here, I consider next only representatives of the two most prominent ranges of compatibilist voices in the contemporary choir, sopranos and contraltos. I cite these two sorts of voices so as to contrast their conceptions of compatibilism with mine. So, from here to this chapter's end, my aim is only exposition, not criticism. In chapter 3 I shall adapt and then adopt what to my ears is most sonorous in the songs of my companion compatibilists, though I suspect that none of these vocalists would bless my appropriation. For with a nod to Spinoza rather than Hume, I would suspend their common conception of the laws of nature.

## Sopranos Cantando con Lewis

The prominent compatibilists voices—some high, others low—that neophyte philosophers typically hear divide over conceptually different stanzas. Singing under Lewis's elegant direction, *soprano* compatibilists cantillate of the unconstrained deliberating agent neither hobbled by manipulation nor under compulsion's gun. Although her actions are all implicatively determined—that is, implied—by the concert of laws and history, she may yet occasionally be *free to act otherwise* and *thus responsibly*. For she may secure her freedom thanks to the posited fragility of the prevailing deterministic Humean laws of nature or the presumed plasticity of her past (Lehrer 1980; Lewis 1981). In order freely to fulfill (whether consciously or not) her exemplary plan to point her finger to the left on cue, the agent need only, on that occasion, be able—have the ability, power, or leeway—to act differently from, alternatively to, or otherwise than the way she then lawfully acts in actually pointing her pinkie left (Pereboom 2001, 2–5; M. Smith 2003; McKenna 2013, 38; Vihvelin 2013). She certainly seems to have this ability. Surely, prior to her episode of pointing left, she was able to point right and able to point left. All the dry matches in a Humean's pocket have the capacity to ignite even if none ever burst into flame. The world, as Hume would have it, is littered with wasted, because forever untapped, dispositions. If the unlit match is able to ignite and also able to persist unlit, then surely our agent was able to point right even as she points left. Though she pointed left, she evidently could have acted otherwise. So, her pointing left seems to have all the leeway that a free action could want. For she would have acted otherwise had she so willed. But, upon consideration, must we not pause to ask, with Lewis, whether the laws of nature conjoined with the agent's history implicationally preclude her ability so to decide and act otherwise? With an eye on the consequences of the engagement of the laws and history, it may at second glance look as if our agent lacks the ability to act otherwise when pointing. For the prevailing laws and history conjointly imply that she raise her finger and, hence, not act otherwise. Evidently, to act contrary to the implication of the laws paired with history, she would need to do what she can't: either break the laws or change the past. Neither anyone nor anything has such power (van Inwagen, 1975). So where in a deterministic world or its near neighbors hides the leeway in action our agent, if free, requires?

Lewis would preserve compatibilism by trading on the presumed contingency of either the past or the laws. In the context of his influential conception of modality, he lucidly explains how it may be the case that it is indeed possible that an agent act otherwise than the partnership of the laws and history implies. Consider our agent who points her finger left by willing to do so. Her action, being actual, is embedded as a particular element among all those particulars—the individual things, events, actions, and properties—that collectively constitute the basic elements from which, throughout all time, the actual world is constructed or on which it depends. It is as if these ontologically basic building blocks, arrayed as they actually are in space-time, form a massive ontic mosaic, $M^{actual}$, of all that fundamentally ever is. For Humeans, each element in $M^{actual}$ is where and as it is only contingently, unburdened by any necessitating existential modality. And the actual laws, since Humean, merely supervene on the patterns and regularities that happen to emerge from the ontic tesserae that make $M^{actual}$. Thus, reference to Humean laws of nature and history is always relative to an associated ontic mosaic or its dependent (possible) world. This is why, by bald default, every element in $M^{actual}$ abides by the laws. For each such element helps to establish both the laws and all of history simply by existing as it does in its place within $M^{actual}$. By the very contingency of our agent's leftward pointing, she does her part not only to make the laws be what they are but also and thereby to ensure that her leftward pointing conforms to those laws. Now, take a deep breath and consider $M^{possible}$. It is to be one from among many alternative ways $M^{actual}$ could be were our agent's pointing left not among the elements of $M^{actual}$. So, $M^{possible}$ may also differ from $M^{actual}$ in various other elements. Some of the distinguishing elements of $M^{possible}$ might lurk in the agent's past while others within that would-be mosaic find their way into her future. In any case, since $M^{actual}$ and $M^{possible}$ differ as the actual and a merely possible world would differ, they respectively enable the supervenience of different laws and histories. The laws and history emergent from $M^{actual}$ constitute the actual laws of nature and history. In contrast, the laws and history spawned by $M^{possible}$ are simply some from among the many sheerly possible ways the laws and history might have been. Of course, our agent actually exists only in the genuine world governed by the genuine—presumably Humean—laws that happen actually to prevail and to which she constantly conforms. But a census of $M^{possible}$ omits her pointing left. So, $M^{possible}$ is one among the many ways in which our agent's past and future can differ from the way they actually are. Whatever our agent does in the possible world of $M^{possible}$ is certainly implied by the conjunction of the laws and history that supervene upon that would-be mosaic. For regardless of the mosaic we conceive the agent to inhabit, we are to find her obeying the laws local to it since such laws supervene upon what she locally does. But if the laws or histories characteristic of the two alternative mosaics differ, then what the agent does in $M^{possible}$ is proscribed by the joint implications of the laws and history of $M^{actual}$. In that case, it would be true of our agent that since she omits to point left in $M^{possible}$, she actually can omit to point left when she actually does point left in $M^{actual}$. Whatever she does in the world of $M^{possible}$, is something that she is able to do in $M^{actual}$. So, if what she should do in $M^{possible}$ is other that what she does in $M^{actual}$, then she is actually able to act otherwise than she does. If, while wearing our comparative goggles, we look at $M^{possible}$ from our perspective in $M^{actual}$, it should be evident that our agent situated within $M^{actual}$ can act contrary to its local laws. Because, goggled, we see that her entirely lawful actions in $M^{possible}$ differ from her equally lawful actions in $M^{actual}$. As a resident of $M^{possible}$, she there unexceptionally obeys its laws while she refrains from pointing left. Her so refraining in the world of $M^{possible}$ is implied by the conjunction of the laws and history local to that world. Thus, the worlds of $M^{actual}$ and $M^{possible}$ differ either by their laws or histories, if not both. If their laws are the same, then it is the difference in their histories that secures the fact that our agent's leftward finger pointing is implied in the actual world but not in its possible cousin. And if the histories of the two worlds prove to be the same, then the implicational difference is due to a difference in the worldly laws. If we should be inclined to speak casually while we think comparatively of the two worlds in our conceptually goggled view, we may be tempted to say, echoing Lewis, that the ways in which $M^{actual}$ and $M^{possible}$ diverge may look miraculous when considered from either alternative. Viewed from $M^{actual}$, the ways in which the elements in $M^{possible}$ differ from the elements in $M^{actual}$ will seem miraculous. For the differences would look like violations of the local laws or amendments of the local history. However, if we persist in such casual talk, we should also add, that in order that things seem to be just so miraculous, it need not appear that any persons or any things within the actual world actually do anything miraculous. From our actual perspective it may appear that our agent's ability to act otherwise requires a miracle. But that appearance would be the illusion induced by noting the fully lawful action of our agent should she exist in a possible world where either the laws or history diverge from their actual cousins. Hence, our agent actually has the ability to choose and act otherwise in the actual world even though she always conforms to the joint implications of the actual laws and history. Thus, if we grant that there exists a possible world, tethered to $M^{possible}$, with its own alternative set of possible laws and history, there, the agent, by constantly conforming to the local laws and history, chooses and acts differently from how she actually does in $M^{actual}$. Although the agent herself, *qua* resident of $M^{actual}$, has no mysterious miraculous power over the actual laws or history, as just such a resident she nevertheless actually does have the leeway to act otherwise than she actually does. To have that leeway she need only exist in an alternative possible world where she obeys the laws she at once creates and obeys.

If Lewis is right and the laws are Humean, compatibilism is secure. However, a dubious Spinozan can be excused for doubtfully asking whether there is a finally mysterious *miracle* concealed in the gospel according to Lewis. For his testament requires belief in merely possible worlds, worlds that both aren't and are. It mandates that we credently quantify existentially over inexistent worlds in order to explain what's possible in the only world that properly submits to such ontologically expensive quantification. Many moons ago Quine advised that to be is to be the value of a bound variable. And yet in order to secure your ability to act otherwise, Lewis advises that you exist in a world that does not exist, where you do what you actually don't. (Lewis 1981; Fischer 1994, chap. 4). Puzzled? Me too.

## Sopranos Cantando con Lehrer

Some sopranos lilt with Lehrer in his duet with Moore (Moore and Shaw 2005; Campbell and Lehrer 2018; Lehrer 1960, 1980, 2004, 2011, 2016, 2020; forthcoming).[28] Lehrerians sing of an agent who, consistent with Humean determinism, has the leeway—albeit only rarely and under demanding psychological conditions—to choose and act otherwise.

In order to appreciate Lehrer's bold compatibilism let's rehearse the most fundamental fact about how explanation works if the laws of nature are Humean. Such laws are to supervene upon the things—including us—that they rule. Thus, Humean psychology supervenes on us. It depends on the patterns our mental states make within the Lewisian mosaic of what happens actually to exist. Hence, whatever the final principles of human psychology might be—including the laws pertaining to reason, preference, and choice—those laws depend upon our episodes of reasoning, preferring, and choosing. So, were it a law of human nature that all people prefer vanilla over chocolate ice cream, its being a law would itself be explained by each of us always preferring vanilla over chocolate. Suppose, then, I catch you preferring vanilla over chocolate and insist upon your explanation. In reply, you correctly cite the vanilla-over-chocolate law and its application to you. I then ask you why does that preference law apply to you, why does *it* explain *your* preference. If you know the law to be Humean, then your right reply would circularly—but not viciously—be that you simply do prefer vanilla. And you ought to add that were you to prefer otherwise—though you don't and never shall—it would not be a law that all humans prefer vanilla over chocolate. The Humean vanilla-over-chocolate law is a law that applies to your preference because you do prefer vanilla over chocolate. It supervenes on your preference together with the preferences of all others. Thus, the ultimate explanation of why you prefer as you do must cite your very preference. Your preference apparently has a kind of power over the preference law. You certainly do not have the power to change that law. Still, by preferring as you do, you do exert a power to shape the law. You have the power to do your part both to make it be a law and to make it be the specific law that it is. The law depends on you; you don't depend on the law.

Much the same applies regarding Humean laws about how humans rationally exploit their information en route to adopting their preferences. Suppose that it should it be a law that all humans who believe that vanilla is salutary and chocolate toxic, prefer vanilla to chocolate. Then, its being a law would itself be explained by each of us always reasoning just so. Perhaps I catch you reasoning just so and insist upon your explanation. In reply, you correctly cite the vanilla-over-chocolate-reasoning law and its application to you. I then ask you why does that law of reasoning apply to you, why does *it* explain *your* reasoning. If you know the law to be Humean, then—once again—your right reply would circularly—but still not viciously—be that you simply do reason just so. And you ought to add that were you to reason otherwise—though you don't and never shall—it would not be a law that all humans reason just so. The Humean vanilla-over-chocolate-reasoning law is a law that applies to your reasoning because you do reason just so. Thus, the ultimate explanation of why you reason just so must cite your very just so reasoning. Your just so reasoning apparently has a kind of power over the vanilla-over-chocolate-reasoning law. You certainly do not have the power to change that law. Still, by reasoning as you do, you do exert a power to shape that law of reasoning. You have the power to do your part both to make it be a law and to make it be the specific law that it is. Once again, the law depends on you; you don't depend on the law.

So, it should come as no surprise that, from Lehrer's perspective, each of us individually, by the way in which we adopt our preferences, exert powers—ultimate power preferences—sufficient for compatibilism. Whether we know it or not, if Lehrer should be right, we are the authors of the laws of thought by which we live. How we think, what we prefer, and the choices we make are all ultimately explained by how we think, what we prefer, and the choices we make. Let's keep this point in mind throughout our discussion of Lehrerian compatibilism.

## Lehrerian Leeway

In what follows within this long section I will aim sympathetically to recount Lehrer's view in moderate detail. But first—compressed and encapsulated—his attractive version of compatibilism sums to this.

It suffices, but need not be necessary, for a normal agent's liberating ability to choose and act otherwise on a specific occasion that her chosen action arise in conformity with the laws of nature from a certain kind of empowering cognitive source. As is sometimes the case, let her choice be completely explained by her prevailing preferences rather than, say, desires. These preferences are to be as characterized within cognitive psychology. They are, then, (perhaps primitive) dispositional mental states or attitudes she adopts regarding the various options or opportunities she presumes. Informed as she happens to be in the moment, she is to rank her considered options from a range or profile of alternative choice-driven actions that she (perhaps correctly) believes presently to be open to her.[29] That ranking establishes her preferences (Tversky and Kahneman, 1974; Hausman, 2011, ch.1). And let her preferences so admit of hierarchical integration or networking such that, once integrated, each preference is itself either preferred or not (Rumelhart and McClelland 1986; Bechtel and Abrahamsen, 2002). Moreover and critically, assume that her preference net includes a—metaphorically crowning or presiding—reflexive preference for both itself and its own embedding structure.[30] Her regal preference would thus prefer itself in concert with its structure because, well, she just so prefers. Call it a power preference. If that preferential hierarchy should be the genuine or *ultimate explanation* of her psychological situation upon the occasion of her particular chosen action, then—according to Lehrer—she would choose and act freely. For by hypothesis, in accordance with psychology she tunes her prevailing preference structure in real time with an eye on her fluctuating available information. So, were she to choose otherwise, she would act otherwise, with this critical fact secured, and itself explained, by her manner of adopting and deploying her preferences. Whatever choice she may make on the variable occasion is to be settled by her then current, but always fluid, crowned preference structure. Consequently, it suffices for her choice and action to be free that their explanation reveal that they owe their occurrence not to being implied by the laws supplemented by history—although they certainly are so implied. And neither would abnormal coercion or manipulation explain her choice. No, rather the genuine explanation would appeal to only the special kind of preference that Lehrer portrays. If she should choose to act as she does because she prefers in the Lehrerian way, then she would choose and act freely while abiding by the laws of nature. For, while obeying the laws, she so fluidly prefers as to ensure that she could choose and act otherwise.

The free agent Lehrer has long described across a stream of publications constantly conforms to the prevailing Humean laws, including psychology. Psychology certainly legislates her choices and action. That is say, but only to say, that conjoined with history, Humean psychology nomologically implies the choices that induce her actions. However, in Lehrer's view, nomological implication does not universally suffice for genuine explanation, including scientific explanation. Citing others, he cautions against confusing nomic deduction with explanation properly understood. Thus, if a Lehrerian agent's chosen action is free, it is not explained by appeal to its secure nomic implicational heritage. Rather, by Lehrer's lights, the explanation of the chosen action—in contrast to its implication from the conjunction of the laws of nature and history—must advert only to her special prevailing efficacious preference structure. That structure is not mysterious; it itself is certainly susceptible to full throated scientific explanation. But regardless of its explanation, since explanation is not generally transitive, the scientifically sound explanation of a preference structure crowned by a power preference need not transitively suffice to explain the preferred choice and action. That choice and action may remain best and solely explained by her regal preference structure. And when all is said and done, if that self-preferring preferential structure should stand alone as the complete explanation of an agent's choice, then her choice and its action would be free. Indeed, an agent's choice so explained is such that, were she to choose otherwise, she would act otherwise. For she is such that whatever her choice might be, it would be as she prefers. Thus, for Lehrer, if a power preference should be the cognitive source of an agent's choice and action—perhaps a source with which the agent herself is identified—that suffices for her having the leeway that lands agental liberty.[31] Let's see why.

## *Lehrerian Preference*

Preference and desire are distinct kinds of dispositional psychological states among those that psychology allows normally, but complexly, to cause choices and their attendant actions. Sometimes one's choice may be caused by one's desires, while other times preferences might pull the trigger. But while desire is monadic and sometimes immune to reason, preference is fundamentally dyadic and apt to be sensitive to a rich host of other kinds of mental states in the light—whether dim or bright—of reason. Put differently, desire and preference arise within an agent from different cognitive processes. An agent might desire chocolate ice cream without ever giving a thought to vanilla or any other luscious treat. However, if she should prefer chocolate, then she must prefer it to something she takes to be an alternative, perhaps vanilla. In other words, in order to prefer chocolate over vanilla, the agent must consider a profile of what she takes to be her options. In our tinker toy example, her presumed options are limited to chocolate over vanilla and vanilla over chocolate. By way of preferring chocolate to vanilla she is attentive to the pair of choices of chocolate over vanilla and vanilla over chocolate. That pair constitutes her profile of preferences on the occasion. Her coming to prefer chocolate over vanilla is to be a cognitive process in which she consults her profile of options while selecting from among them. Leaning on metaphor, we might depict her as first introspecting her profile while reflecting on her reasons pro and con. Upon completing her reflection, she simply mentally ostends one rather than the other of the two in view so as thereby to elect it and, thus, prefer it to the other. And still metaphorically, so long as she should keep her profile in cognitive view and reflect on her reasons, she need only ostend the other so as fluidly to amend her preference. To prefer is to be disposed to vacillate, to be apt to amend—rationally rather than capriciously—election of elected options.

Desires and preferences each admit of ranking. Our agent might desire both chocolate and vanilla while desiring one more than the other without regard for what she might know of each. In contrast, by way of preferring among things, an agent is wont to rank them with an eye on the values she attributes to them given whatever array of her background mental states may bear upon the way in which she culls or ranks her profile. All too obviously, one's desires and preferences can conflict and compete. On some occasions of choice, desire trumps preference; other times, preference holds the ace. Either way, the winner is winnowed as psychology and history conjoined may imply.

Under the assumption that functionalism (as previously characterized) correctly explicates psychological states, preferences are mental representations that physically realize forward-looking dispositions to choose among alternatives. To prefer chocolate over vanilla is to be disposed to choose to take the chocolate over vanilla. However, this forward-looking aptitude, though necessary, is not sufficient for a mental state's being a preference—that is, being a token of that mental type. Given that preferences are alert to reasons (as well as various other types of cognitive states), their type partially depends upon the reason-sensitive cognitive processes from which they spring. Functionalism still presupposed, an agent's preferences are mental states (realized by Mentalese representations) whose type depends upon their causal histories and futures—that is their causal roles within the agent's cognitive system. It is its role that determines not only that a mental state is a preference but also that it is the specific preference it is. Like characters in a play, preferences— realized by mental representations—take their identity from the roles they play in psychology's drama. Thus, assuming that she prefers chocolate to vanilla, our Lehrerian agent's cognitive system of Mentalese representations includes *I PREFER CHOCOLATE OVER VANILLA* among her preferences, with that representation playing just the right sort of cognitive role. This representation must—in the right way—depend upon the agent's reasons and—again in the right way—control her choices and actions. Otherwise, it is off script and not really a preference at all.

In any case, since by hypothesis *I PREFER CHOCOLATE OVER VANILLA* is among our agent's preferences and, thus, conforms to psychology, it is apt to control her choice on a specific "ice cream occasion" of choice rather than of desire. That is simply to assume that on the occasion in question it happens, in accordance with psychology, that her choice is actually settled by preference rather than, say, desire. Thus, *I PREFER CHOCOLATE OVER VANILLA* is her disposition—*ceteris paribus*—to choose chocolate over vanilla. If so, then conditions permitting, her preference, not her desire, would cause her to choose chocolate. In that case, the correct explanation of her selection of chocolate would cite her prevailing preference. Why did she select the chocolate rather than the vanilla? She preferred just so. *I PREFER CHOCOLATE OVER VANILLA* played its role within her cognitive system. Of course, she forms her preference by way of the cognitive process that controls her consideration of her profile of preferences. So, were she to have elected vanilla over chocolate from the profile, she would have chosen vanilla instead—again, because she would prefer just so. In that case, *I PREFER VANILLA OVER CHOCOLATE*, rather than its alternate, would have done its job.

One's desires and preferences can be orthogonal. However, insofar as an agent lamely approximates ideal rationality, her preferences rather than her contrary desires tend to control her actions. Lehrer's agent might, in the moment, intensely desire the vanilla ice cream within reach. But—approximating rationality and believing vanilla to be toxic and chocolate salutary— she might prefer the latter and, always *ceteris paribus*, opt for it instead. Of course, in a bad moment the same agent might wantonly succumb to her desire and, *ceteris non paribus,* find herself eating the vanilla despite her preferences. Sometimes, depending upon the pickles in which we find ourselves, we act on desires, other times on preferences. Nevertheless and as remarked above, given determinism, we always choose and act in accord with psychology. Thus, correct psychological explanations of our choices and actions do point to the right psychic source—maybe desire; maybe preference; maybe something else—whatever it actually happens to be.

While some desires may be brute reactions to seductive stimuli and indifferent to what an agent believes, her preferences, as remarked, are typically sensitive to information at hand and trade upon her operant conceptual scheme—that is her mental representations as subject to the various processes definitive of her cognitive system. (Block 1980a, 1980b; Harman 1973, 1982). Our agent might desire both vanilla and chocolate but desire the vanilla more than the chocolate. Given her desire, she might initially prefer the vanilla to the chocolate. But, perhaps upon learning vanilla's toxic downside, she might nevertheless reasonably amend her preference so as to rank the supposedly healthy chocolate over the suspect vanilla. Since they are apt to resonate with what an agent believes, human preferences evidently tend roughly and wobbly to approximate a logic to the degree to which their rationally imperfect hosting agents individually approach, albeit distantly, ideal rationality (von Wright 1972; Kahneman and Tversky, 1979; Kahneman and Tversky 1982b; Hausman 2011).[32] Although it is not guaranteed, a relatively rational agent's preferences would, for example, appear virtuously to stumble toward transitivity and asymmetry (Broome 2021). Because preference is apt roughly to conform to some such logic while also being tempered by what an agent believes, collections of preferences can approach coherence. Coherence is an elusive cognitive virtue that resists easy description. Nonetheless, we should not be scolded for wagering that coherence runs beyond mere logical consistency (Lehrer 1970; Thagard 2007; Bonjour 1985; Zagzebski 1996; Sosa 2007). Contradictions cannot be true. No geometrical figure can contradictorily be at once both rectangular and not, full stop. Neither can an agent at once contradictorily both prefer, and not prefer, chocolate over vanilla, full stop. Nonetheless, we human agents, even if constrained by such consistency, are yet certainly susceptible to conflicts among our preferences insofar as they form more or less coherent schemes.

## Lehrerian Preferential Hierarchies

Our agent who desires vanilla has reasonably amended her preference so as to prefer chocolate over vanilla. However, her desire unsettlingly persists. But she is capable of self-assessment born of self-awareness. So, she might also prefer that she not prefer chocolate over vanilla. If so, she would instantiate a bi-level hierarchical preferential scheme regarding ice cream. Her scheme seems less than ideally coherent; she is conflicted (Lehrer 1980 and forthcoming, ch. 3). But although she is conflicted, her lower-level preference for chocolate over vanilla retains control over her choice and action. Under the assumption that first-level preferences occasionally do control choice and action, our conflicted agent would choose the chocolate over vanilla when her preferences determine behavior in accordance with psychology. However, since she is conflicted and her desire for vanilla remains unsatisfied, she might regret her choice (Kahneman and Tversky 1982b). Evidently, she might come to dodge, diminish, or otherwise manage disquieting regret by hoisting a third-level preference for her conflicted scheme. That is, she might manage her regret by convincing herself that it is better to be conflicted as she is than not. So convinced, she might then prefer that she not prefer preferring chocolate over vanilla while still preferring chocolate over vanilla. In that case her preferential scheme would be

- *I PREFER THAT I PREFER THAT I NOT PREFER CHOCOLATE OVER VANILLA*
    - *I PREFER THAT I NOT PREFER CHOCOLATE OVER VANILLA*
        - *I PREFER CHOCOLATE OVER VANILLA*

Of course, her situation could be otherwise, less conflictedly and more coherently so. Starting afresh, at her lower preferential level, she might still prefer chocolate to vanilla. But, now at her second level and despite her lingering desire for vanilla, she might reasonably prefer that she prefer chocolate over vanilla. In this latter case her bi-level preferential scheme would be unconflicted and more coherent than above. And, pleased with her coherence, she might again insert into her scheme a third-level preference for her scheme. She might then prefer that she prefer preferring chocolate over vanilla while preferring chocolate over vanilla. Regardless of which hierarchy should control her choice and action, she would be apt to opt for chocolate.

Persistent desires may be prone to resist amendment in response to changes in belief about what's desired. However, preferences are evidently apt more readily to evolve upon rational reflection in light of available relevant information. Presumably, an agent's preferences within her overall cognitive system cluster as representations according to relevance in cognitively penetrable plastic subsystems or modules. The operations and outputs of a penetrable module are variously sensitive in real time to information in play within the agent but beyond the module.[33] The visual system, for example, is evidently cognitively penetrable within certain limits. Upon hearing me say that a camouflaged lizard lurks in your full view on the trail at your feet, you might suddenly recognize the critter to which you had been blind. If so, your plastic visual system would have immediately altered its recognitional output upon penetration by your fresh information. Arguably, preferences within an agent's preferential scheme are similarly sensitive to alteration in the information to which the agent has access. Thus, suppose our agent who prefers chocolate should be surprised to learn that she is allergic to chocolate but not vanilla. She might, with her preference profile cognitively in view, automatically alter her selection from the options profiled so that her operant hierarchy of preferences instantly changes. She would thereby swap her first level *I PREFER CHOCOLATE OVER VANILLA for I PREFER VANILLA OVER CHOCOLATE.* She would then be like you looking at the lizard. Your penetrable visual system lawfully amended its recognitional output as quick as half a wink thanks to its adroit exploitation of your new information. And so too might our agent's penetrable preference system amend its choice-determining preference in response to what she learns.

In agents, such as us, capable of self-awareness, amendment of a preference at one level of a preferential hierarchy can invite revision of preferences at other levels. For an agent aware of revision in her hierarchy is in posses-sion of fresh information of the sort that, as noted above, is grist for the pref-erential mill. Such revisions might increase, decrease, or otherwise temper preferential coherence and conflicts. But in any event, a self-aware agent may instantiate a hierarchical preferential scheme that, once sprouted, can mutate in a moment as appropriate to her stream of incoming information.

## Lehrerian Power preference

Once we allow that agents can instantiate preferential hierarchies, it becomes an open empirical question as to how many levels human agents actually can sustain. And since that same allowance permits preferences regarding preferences, it raises the question as to whether a preference for a preference might be reflexive, namely a preference for itself. Consider "I am in this book, and I precede other sentences in this book." That is a true conjunctive sentence in English. It indexically refers to itself twice over while also conjunctively affirming its relation to other sentences in its book. Preferences, *qua* Mentalese sentences, are analogous. For a prefer-ence might indexically refer to itself twice over while also conjunctively affirming its relation to other preferences in its hierarchy. For example, *I PREFER MYSELF AND I PREFER VANILLA OVER CHOCOLATE* evi-dently realizes a preference that indexically refers to itself twice over. And it conjunctively affirms its relation to another preference, namely *I PRE-FER VANILLA OVER CHOCOLATE.*

Certainly, human preferential hierarchies are finite. And Lehrer's compati-bilism unproblematically supposes—as cognitive psychology permits—that an agent's choice and action can be under the control of a finite preferential hierarchy. But his theory becomes especially intriguing, and perhaps compel-ling, when he adds his distinctive twist: Regardless of the degree to which an effective preferential hierarchy may be coherent or conflicted, it can be crowned by—and so include—a reflexive preference, a *power preference*. A power preference both prefers itself and the hierarchy of preferences it nim-bly comprehends. Should Lehrer be right about this, then it would be as if an agent with such a preferential hierarchy were to have exercised executive control over her hierarchy, including all of her preferences within it.

Think of a power preference this way: As a preference, it arises as the result of an agent's consideration of a profile of options. Let the options now consist of finite alternative (and perhaps conflicted) preference hier-archies. Moreover, suppose that they differ one from the other save for the fact that each includes a preference for itself. Recall our earlier metaphor for how an agent selects from among the candidates in a profile. It is as if—by way of exercising her psychological power rationally to consider a profile of options—she were to introspect her profile, psychically seeing in a glimpse all of her options. But now each candidate in her profile is itself a self-preferring preferential hierarchy. She is poised to prefer how, overall, she shall prefer. Upon rational reflection, she points to one within her profile so as thereby to recognize it as preferred overall. In the manner of demonstrative ostension, she selects a self-preferring preferential hierarchy from among her profiled options. She thus elects it as her choice-controlling hierarchy effective upon an occasion of choice determined by preference. In recognizing the winner in her profile, she would be like you recognizing the lizard on the trail within the full rich visual scene at your feet. Modeled on you—with more than just the lizard in your scene—our agent remains aware of the options in her profile even as she recognizes the winner among them. You can look afresh at your lingering scene and perhaps detect another camouflaged lizard therein. And so too, with her profile constantly available, our agent might be apt to change her vote. For each of the unelected in her lingering profile remains a candidate should she be apt to revise her preferential vote. An agent who, in something like this way, forms a preference for a hierarchy of preferences adopts a hierarchy that prefers itself. For it includes a power preference, a reflexive preference that, by preferring itself thereby prefers the hierarchy it crowns.

Previously we saw that a self-aware agent might aim to manage her regret by preferring at a higher level to prefer as she happens to prefer at a lower level. Such management apparently amounts to an agent's *authorization* of preferences so preferred (Newman 2006; Dennett 1984; Velleman 2006; Fischer 2009, chap. 10; Baker 2016). For it evidently displays an agent's approval and adoption of her preferences upon consideration of her prevailing beliefs and allied attitudes. It is as if she were to whisper to herself, "Given all that I know, this is exactly what I hierarchically prefer. I prefer to prefer this way."

Consider, then, a Lehrerian agent who in fact realizes a power preference that presides over her preferential hierarchy appropriately deployed on an occasion of choice. If there is a way worth salt of authorizing one's operative preferences, then surely instantiating a preferential hierarchy that includes a power preference is sufficiently salty. To appreciate our Lehrerian agent's psychological situation upon her reflective adoption of a power preference, imagine that she introspects. It would be as if she were to peer into her psychological mirror with her profile of all her power preference crowned-preference hierarchies in view. So informed, she might issue this indexical Mentalese representation that also mentions, by demonstrating, a representation that realizes a crowning reflexive power preference. To wit:

*AH, HERE'S MY PREFERENCE HIERARCHY! AND THERE, AT*
*THE TOP, IS THIS REFLEXIVE EMPOWERING PREFERENCE:*
*I PREFER BOTH MYSELF OVER OTHER PREFERENCES AND*
*ALSO THIS, MY PREFERENCE HIERARCHY, OVER ANY SIMILARLY*
*CROWNED ALTERNATIVE PREFERENCE HIERARCHY IN MY*
*PROFILE OF JUST SO CROWNED PREFERENCE HIERARCHIES*

Assume that the above correctly depicts Lehrer's introspecting agent as she elects her prevailing preference hierarchy from her profile. Then—perhaps going beyond what Lehrer himself would say of her—we might pause to remark on the mental representation that serves to realize her power preference. It would seem to be a Mentalese performative (Austin 1975; Searle 1989; Bach and Harnish 1992). As such and also as suggested above, perhaps by its normal performative deployment it would suffice as the agent's implementation and authorization of the preferences, choices, and actions it serves to control. Furthermore, being the performative it is, it might well constitute an agent's assumption of responsibility for those of her choices and actions born of her authorized preferences (Clarke, McKenna, and Smith 2015). If so, then if an agent's power preference should figure in her will's being free, then that might prompt the plausible hunch that free will and responsibility are hand in glove.[34]

Consider then our agent's particular choice and action that, as a matter of fact, are controlled—that is caused—by her preferential hierarchy topped by its own effective power preference. Indeed, she has adopted this preference structure by electing it in the light of her then current information from among a lingering profile of preference structures each of which includes a power preference. She is apt—more or less rationally—to amend her preferences coordinate with amendment in her available background information. So, whatever she can choose on this occasion is a function of whatever her elected hierarchy serves to prefer. She has the chance to choose between vanilla and chocolate. Should she choose, then her choice is to be determined by a preference within her prevailing preferential net in which her power preference presides. Assume that she chooses vanilla over chocolate. Her choice is not capricious but rather prompted by the fact that her prevailing self-preferring preferential hierarchy at its lowest level prefers vanilla over chocolate. What, then, if not fresh information, would it take for her to alter her preference from vanilla to chocolate? Certainly, her available information might be otherwise than it actually is. Should it be, then she could and would thereupon elect from her available profile of self-empowering preference hierarchies one that prefers chocolate over vanilla. And in that case, she would prefer and choose chocolate over vanilla. So, although she in fact prefers and chooses vanilla over chocolate, she could prefer, choose, and act otherwise. And regardless of whether the case be actual or counterfactual, her operant preference structure would be topped with a power preference. So, she would choose and act as she does because she prefers to prefer exactly as she does. As Lehrer might put it, on this occasion it is within her power to prefer either vanilla or chocolate by embedding her preference in a self-preferring preference hierarchy.

Perhaps the same thought might be approached as follows: By hypothesis, on this occasion whatever her choice (with its associated action) may be, that choice and its action are under the control of her prevailing but mutable self-empowered preferential hierarchy. By the same hypothesis, the current conditions happen to be such that, her preferential scheme causes whatever choice and action its first-level preference—realized by a mental representation—specifies. Thus, her controlling first-level preference actually is

(A)  *I PREFER VANILLA OVER CHOCOLATE.*

Hence, were she to choose otherwise, her first-level preference would not be (A) but rather

(B)  *I PREFER CHOCOLATE OVER VANILLA.*

Still by hypothesis, *(A)* controls a choice resulting in an action aimed at acquiring vanilla while *(B)* controls a choice resulting in an action aimed at chocolate. Thus, were Lehrer's agent to choose otherwise, she would act otherwise (Lehrer 2020, p. 605). For after all, were she to choose otherwise, that would need be because her cognitively penetrable prevailing preferential hierarchy—culled on the fly from her considered profile of self-empowering preference hierarchies—would have evolved in a way rationally geared to a change in information available to her. Given determinism, preference-controlled choice is not random, arbitrary, or capricious. No doubt, it is subject to genuine scientific explanation waiting in the wings of cognitive psychology. Under the assumption that an agent's choice upon the occasion is controlled by preference (rather than, for example, desire), change in choice depends upon change in preference. So, what would be the agent's psychological situation were she to choose otherwise than she actually does? It would be as if she were to have fresh information pertinent to her preferences, as if she were to say to herself:

> "Wait! What? Really? Vanilla is toxic! Good God! Lucky me to have learned that! I better elect a new option from my always in view profile of preference hierarchies with power preferences. Ah, there's the one I hereby demonstratively elect. Bingo! I now prefer and, so, choose chocolate over vanilla. And

I prefer that I prefer exactly this way since I have a power preference in play. Whew, that was a nail biter!"

If you have followed the story so far, you might permit an analogy suggestive of the way that, by their nature, an agent's preference structures are apt to evolve coincident with fresh information. Preferential structures would seem to be related to the choices they control as is the overall shape of a balloon related to local pressures on its surface. Poke the balloon with your finger in any specific spot, and the overall shape of the balloon immediately varies in a specific way tuned to the poke. Poke it elsewhere, and the balloon again accommodates accordingly. No change in poke without a change in shape. So too, no change in choice without a change in preference. If on an occasion of choice, preference controls choice, then an agent who chooses one way would certainly choose otherwise only were she so to prefer. And she would were she to acquire relevant fresh information. Let an agent's choice be determined by her preference and her preference rationally tuned to information. Then whatever she might choose, one way or the other, is bound to be as she plastically prefers that she just so prefer.[35]

## Lehrerian Ultimate Preference

Let's assume, with Lehrer, that the above correctly describes the history of our agent's actual choice. Then, by his lights the proper explanation of why her choice and action are as they are would cite her prevailing power preference-crowned hierarchy of preferences. Why does she choose as she does? She prefers to choose just so while preferring to prefer as she does. Mindful of the different ways in which her preferences could be arranged, knowing her prevailing profile of preferences, she opts to prefer exactly as she does prefer. Her power preference explains her choice according to Lehrer. And, crucially, he adds that it *alone* suffices to *explain* her choice. As such, her prevailing power preference is, for Lehrer, an *ultimate preference*.[36] With this in mind, he lays down the thesis definitive of his version of compatibilism: If an agent's ultimate preference controls her choice and action, her choice and action could be otherwise consistent with determinism.[37]

Thus, in Lehrer's view freedom of choice—free will—hinges on the long-contested concept of explanation (Kitcher and Salmon 1962; Woodward and Ross 2021). Let's then turn to Lehrer's account of how it is that a choice may be under the control of an ultimate preference, that a choice be fully explained only by its being a function of a power preference. We turn, then, to how Lehrer deflects arguments that would contest the dominance of ultimate preference in explanations of choice.

What sort of explanations of choice compete with ultimate preference? Evidently, there are only two generic forms of explanations possible. Either things are normal, or they are not. Following Lehrer, we divide to conquer.

Suppose all is normal. Assume that our agent's self-preferring preference and choice arise in full deterministic accord with psychology conjoined with history. Imagine that an omniscient cognitive scientist should offer an explanation of the agent's choice simply by presenting a sound deduction of her adoption of her power preference hierarchy. Let the deduction show in full detail the steps by which the laws of nature, featuring the principles of psychology, and various historical facts jointly imply our agent's adoption of her prevailing preferences and, hence, her subsequent choice. That would indeed be impressive, but would that deduction thereby suffice as a genuine explanation?

Not necessarily, according to Lehrer. For he calls upon Bromberger's argument to the effect that nomological deduction sometimes fails to meet explanatory muster (Bromberger 1965, 1993). Lehrer teams with Bromberger to offer convincing counterexamples to the claim that nomological deduction suffices for explanation. Although they do not offer this counterexample, here is a quick clean one. It is evidently a Humean law that *all philosophers are human.* For certainly, all philosophers are human, and whatever would be a philosopher would need be human. And it is a historical and current fact that *I am a philosopher.* That law and fact imply that *I am human.* But that implication surely does not explain my humanity. For it fails to reveal why it is that I am human. A genuine explanation, say Lehrer and Bromberger, must suffice as an answer to a *why question,* a question whose answer presupposes an (implicit) conceptual scheme commonly presumed by the parties engaged in explanation. It would seem that the nomic deduction of my humanity fails because it does not zero in on the right explanatory condition. Clearly, I owe my humanity not to my profession but rather to my parents. To wonder why one is human engages a conceptual scheme appropriate to the concepts in question. Presumably, a scheme fit for the concept of humanity defeasibly disbars the property of being a philosopher from an explanatory role in accounting for the property of being human.[38] This point applies in parallel regarding psychological explanation.[39] Wondering in the relevant sense as to why one chooses and acts invites inquiry regarding intentions, preferences, plans, and purposes as explanatorily sources. And thus—in its explanatory context—the chosen action of Lehrer's free agent need not finally owe its occurrence to its implicational descendance from the marriage of the laws of nature and history. Rather, in her particular case (in which, by hypothesis, her choice happens to arise normally), the deep, adequate, and indeed true explanation of her specific chosen action must cite her hierarchically structured preferences just as they happen to be. Why she prefers and chooses as she does need not necessarily be revealed by their nomic implicational pedigree. But in contrast, if Lehrer is right, that her situation recruits a power preference does make plain why she prefers and chooses exactly as she does. That recruit, according to Lehrer, is the complete explanation of her preference structure. Nothing else need, or should, be said. So, nomic implication can differ from explanation in the face of this "*why*" standard, with the result that nomic deduction of choice need not suffice for its explanation.[40]

No doubt, there is a compelling scientific explanation that answers the question as to why I am human. But arguably it is not merely nomic deduction. Rather, it appears in scattered bits and pieces of the corporate body of material that represents current biology. Some of the bits are sentences sprayed across various books and journals. Others include computational models chasing algorithms or clay compositions displayed on teachers' desks. And other pieces are diagrams, charts, tables, and the like (Giere 1988). One who understands such a distributed explanation is like the reader of the mystery novel who realizes *who done it* though the novelist nowhere included a statement saying who did it. No doubt much the same applies to the psychology of preference. Even if today's science still wants an adequate explanation of quirky incarnate human preference, we should nevertheless charitably allow that it will, or would, in the promised golden age of science. Let's suppose that in the fabled future there is *The Golden Book of Psychology* that includes, perhaps in scattered fashion, all the bits and pieces that collectively explain human preferences. Call this explanation *The Gold Standard*. Since it does explain preference adoption, *The Gold Standard* explains how and why our Lehrerian agent adopts her power preference-crowned preferential hierarchy. Recall that, by hypothesis, we with Lehrer assume that his account of an agent's ultimate preference does suffice to explain her choice. Let's dub Lehrer's account *Ultimate Preference* and the agent's choice *Choice*. Thus, we have

- *The Gold Standard* explains *Ultimate Preference*
- *Ultimate Preference* explains *Choice*

Plainly, if explanation should be generally transitive, *The Gold Standard* would explain *Choice*. That transitivity would refute Lehrer's claim that *Ultimate Preference* is the sole and complete explanation of *Choice*.

It will be no surprise that Lehrer denies the general transitivity of explanation by appeal to counterexamples. Lehrer again credits Bromberger for noticing the failure of explanatory transitivity. But Aristotle too was alert to it in his discussion of the intersection of chance, causation, and the varieties of explanation in the *Physics, II*. I owe you money, and because I am in the store to buy eggs, I bump into you while you are putting apples in your cart. You demand payment. So, I pay you with my meager egg money and quit shopping. My planning to buy eggs explains why I meet you in the store; my meeting you in the store explains why I paid my debt; but my planning to buy eggs does not explain why I paid my debt. So, explanation is not generally transitive. Hence, unless scientific explanation should have exceptional but unspecified properties that underwrite transitivity, explanation of ultimate preference by psychology does not entail psychological explanation of choice explained by ultimate preference.

Having dispensed with both nomological deduction of preference-controlled choices and scientific explanation of the same per the above, Lehrer proceeds to address explanations of choice and preference under the assumption that the prevailing conditions are abnormal. So, by hypothesis, the agent does prefer her choice and action. Moreover, her choice is directly controlled by a preference structure that is, or appears to be, crowned with a power preference. Lehrer considers the two types of classic abnormal cases: manipulation and compulsion.

Suppose that things are abnormal courtesy of manipulation. By his way of describing manipulation, Frankfurt debunks the apparent conceptual connection between leeway free will and responsibility (Frankfurt 1969 and 1971). But for Lehrer the issue that such manipulation raises does not pertain to responsibility. Rather the issue is whether it suffices for choice being free that it be controlled by an ultimate preference even if a manipulator should be at work.

The actual preferences and choices of an agent manipulated in the fashion of Frankfurt are to unfurl as they would were there no manipulator at work. Because she prefers vanilla over chocolate, our agent chooses vanilla over chocolate while a manipulator sits covert but idle in the background. By assumption, the agent's choice is actually controlled by the agent's power preference of the sort Lehrer describes. But the idle manipulator is able to, and would, control her choice-controlling preference should she be normally en route to amending her preferences in the manner Lehrer prescribes. Were she normally to change her preference for vanilla over chocolate, she would choose chocolate over vanilla. But since that would be contrary to the manipulator's plans, he would prevent her from altering her actual preference. So, should the situation be abnormal and the manipulator preside, then although our agent would prefer vanilla over chocolate by dint of her power preference, she could not choose or act otherwise. As portrayed, the agent chooses as she prefers but, supposedly, she can neither prefer nor choose differently. And that would contravene Lehrer's compatibilism.

Of course, an unmanipulated agent's situation might be abnormal because she is compulsive. But the compulsive and manipulated agents both wear a similar psychic straitjacket. For regardless of the jacket, by assumption the unfortunate agent happens actually to choose as a result of her power preference, and yet, she cannot choose or act otherwise.

Lehrer accepts the counterfactual scenes as set. He immediately concedes that under such abnormal psychological circumstances the conditions do preclude the agent's preference-controlled choice being leeway free. For given the prevailing abnormal conditions, the agent's crowned preferential hierarchy simply is not the sole and complete explanation of the agent's choice. Hence, it is not, as his conception of free will requires, an ultimate preference. The manipulated agent's preference-controlled choice is such that it cannot be otherwise because, though it is controlled by her preferences, her preferences cannot be otherwise. That feature of her preference-controlled choice requires an explanation that adverts to the manipulator empowered to manage her preferences. Analogously, the compulsive agent's preferred choice is also such that it cannot be otherwise, with that feature also requiring an explanation that goes beyond the agent's crowned preferential hierarchy.

Neither of these variants on abnormal choice-controlling preference production troubles Lehrer's account. For recall that his account amounts to a sufficient condition on free will. His view is that *if* an agent's choice should be completely and solely explained by reference to her prevailing power preference, *then* her choice is leeway free. The abnormal situations—manipulation and coercion—are simply situations in which the antecedent of his conditional is not satisfied. There is no ultimate preference in play. Thus, the counterfactual cases do not refute his conditional claim that represents his compatibilism. So, yes, certainly, a choice, if manipulated or compelled in the manner described, is not free. But that concession is consistent with there being (perhaps rare) choices that, compatible with determinism, are under the control of Lehrerian ultimate preferences.

Lehrer is right to wave off the abnormal cases and hold that his theory of free will is immune to such objections. However, by way of complementing his claim of immunity, it may prove rewarding to probe the resources he has within his reach when confronting manipulation and compulsion. For we shall see that the counterfactual cases are counterfeit. For brevity, I'll consider only the case of manipulation.

In manipulation cases we are invited to compare the preference structure of an agent as she actually is with what it would be were a poised manipulator to intervene. That is, we are to compare an actual agent, for example Actual-Ann, with her counterfactual self, Counterfactual-Ann. We further assume that Actual-Ann and Counterfactual-Ann prefer the same and, hence, choose the same. Further, we are to assume that Actual-Ann's choice is under the control of, and solely explained by, her crowning power preference within her actual hierarchy, AH, of preferences. According to Lehrer's account, AH includes Ann's reflexive power preference, a preference for both itself and also the array of preferences it prefers. Thus,

AH = <*I PREFER BOTH MYSELF OVER OTHER PREFERENCES AND ALSO ALL THESE FIRST-PERSON PREFERENCES:* <$P_N$, $P_{N-1}$, $P_{N2}$, . . . , *I PREFER vanilla over chocolate*>>

In supposed contrast, Counterfactual-Ann is to be Actual-Ann's preferential twin, with the only relevant difference between the twins being that the manipulator controls Counterfactual-Ann's preferences. So, we are to suppose that Counterfactual-Ann has a preferential hierarchy, CH, isomorphic to Ann's, AH. Thus,

CH = <*I PREFER BOTH MYSELF OVER OTHER PREFERENCES AND ALSO ALL THESE FIRST-PERSON PREFERENCES:* <$P_N$, $P_{N-1}$, $P_{N2}$, . . . , *I PREFER vanilla over chocolate*>>

However, reflection on both AH and CH reveals that, as Shakespeare wrote, something is rotten in the state of Denmark. For notice that both AH and CH include mental representations featuring first-person indexicals. In AH we find *I PREFER MYSELF OVER OTHER PREFERENCES.* And that first-person mental representation is in fact true. For by hypothesis that very indexical representation actually does refer to itself and it does prefer itself. It is realized within Actual-Anne's cognitive system normally. A representation featuring a first-person indexical normally refers to its author. But if the situation is abnormal, all bets on reference are off. Here's why. Should you normally inscribe "I prefer myself to others" in your diary, that inscription would refer to you. Were Professor Plagiarist to inscribe "I prefer myself to others" in his diary, that inscription would refer to him. In this case, the diaries would be isomorphic with respect to these inscriptions, with each indexically referring to its author. But if, with pen in hand, Plagiarist were to inscribe "I prefer myself" in your diary, that misleading inscription would not refer to you. If it refers at all, it refers to him, its author. For the abnormal way in which the suspect sentence was inscribed in your diary violates the requirements pertaining to indexical reference although it satisfies grammar's standards. It is syntactically pure but semantically corrupt. Of course, the very same point would remain were Plagiarist to abandon his pen in order remotely to manipulate a fancy device to inscribe "I prefer myself to others" in your diary. How he performs his misdeed is irrelevant, but that he plagiarizes is critical. Moreover, assume that he has indeed entered his inscription into your diary unbeknownst to you. Should you read it later, mistakenly believing that you had entered it and that it refers to itself, you would be wrong. It is, at best, a counterfeit indexical and, hence, not an indexical at all.

The psychological situation of Actual-Ann and Counterfactual-Ann is similar to the situation you and Plagiarist would share were he to have manipulated you and your diary. Although the mental representations in AH and CH are syntactically the same, they are semantically different. In AH *I PREFER MYSELF OVER OTHER PREFERENCES—qua* distinct psychic inscription—occurs normally. Thus, it is a genuine mental representation, an indexical preference; it does in fact refer to itself. However, In CH *I PREFER MYSELF OVER OTHER PREFERENCES, qua* distinct psychic inscription, occurs abnormally; it owes its occurrence to the manipulative inscription of a covert Frankfurtian manipulator. So, what looks like a power preference in *CH* is counterfeit psychological currency. It is not a first-person indexical mental representation and, thus, is not a power preference at all. It is impossible that one's power preference be manipulated for the same reason that it is impossible for Plagiarist to record in your diary a first person indexical that refers to you. The moral of the story is, that although Lehrer does allow for the possibility that one's power preference be manipulated, he need not, and perhaps ought not, allow it.

Another way to appreciate that a manipulated preference of the Frankfurtian sort is not a genuine preference is to resurrect and alter an example Clark and Chalmers advanced to illustrate their hypothesis of an extended mind (Clark and Chalmers 1998). They endorsed the possibility of a mind some of whose mental representations would be encoded outside of the brain but nevertheless retain their requisite conceptual roles. Their fictional character, Otto, suffers from selected mnemonic deficits. To compensate, he regularly records what is important to recall in his handy notebook. Modifying the original story of Otto, let us suppose that he typically records his ice cream preferences so that he might use that record to guide his weekly shopping. As it happens, this week he failed to do that. However, for reasons of your own, you aim to manipulate him by manipulating his preferences. To that end you have entered this into his notebook (Dennett 1978a):

- *THIS IS MY PREFERENCE FOR ITSELF AND MY PREFERENCES BELOW*
  - *I PREFER THAT I PREFER THAT I NOT PREFER CHOCOLATE TO VANILLA*
    - *I PREFER THAT I NOT PREFER CHOCOLATE TO VANILLA*
      - *I PREFER CHOCOLATE OVER VANILLA*

Since Otto relies on what he finds in his notebook to guide his shopping, he leaves the store with chocolate ice cream. Has he chosen the chocolate as a result of his preferential hierarchy? Certainly not. For what is actually in his notebook is not a hierarchy of his preferences. For that record was abnormally encoded. None of the recorded first-person indexicals actually refers to him. None is among his externally encoded mental representations. If any of them do refer to anyone, they refer to you, not him. So, none of those representations containing those indexicals needs be true of him. None needs to constitute his preference. Hence, none needs be his power preference. Otto's situation is, of course, parallel to that of the manipulated Lehrerian agent. If Otto's extended mental representations need not constitute his preferences, then neither need the presumably internal representations of the manipulated agent constitute hers.

I conclude my treatment of Lehrer with three comments: two questions and a bet.

First, why lay it down, as Lehrer does, that if a will is to be free on an occasion of preference-controlled choice, there be a unique adequate explanation of the choice? That is, why insist that the relevant power preference be an ultimate preference? Why not allow that the choice might be ecumenically explained, that it admit of more than one satisfactory explanation? Certainly, there are phenomena that do yield to complementary genuine explanations. Presumably, there is a level of income that marks the poverty line. For simplicity, assume that the level is $100. If a person's income is less than $100, then she is poor. But if her income is above $100, then she is at least minimally wealthy. I discover that, shockingly, ne'er do well you are at least minimally wealthy. So, I investigate. I learn that your uncle Keith gave you $200, and your Aunt Adrienne gave you $300. So, I have discovered two complementary explanations for your being above the poverty level. Might free will be like being above the poverty level? There are various ways to emerge from poverty and into wealth. Might there not also be various ways for a will to emerge from determinism and into freedom?

Second, scientific explanation is unrivaled when we hope to explain nature's ways. But even excellent scientific explanations are subject to replacement and revolution. Although it is true that the sun rises each day, the best explanation of that enduring fact differs today from what the best once was. The psychology of preference is in the business of producing explanations of preference. Might not psychology's best explanation of preference change over time? Lehrer's account of free choice trades on choice being explained by preferences of a certain sort arising from cognitive processes in a certain way. Suppose that on Monday psychology's best explanation of preference should actually square with Lehrer's account of preference fit for free will. Let a particular agent's preference-guided behavior on Monday be best explained on Monday by Lehrer's account as incorporated by Monday's psychology. She would then be free on Monday. But imagine that on Tuesday, Monday's best psychology of preference is replaced by a better one. With tomorrow's sunrise our agent thinks and behaves the same as she did the day before. Her thoughtful behavior, like the sun's regular rising, is constant while psychological explanation evolves. On Tuesday, the explanation of her behavior on

Monday no longer applies. Does the shift in explanation contradictorily imply that the agent is free on Monday and not free on Tuesday? If human freedom is a function of ephemeral explanation, is freedom as ephemeral?

Third, I do not know whether the laws of nature are Humean or Spinozan. And so far as I can tell, neither does anyone else. But were the clouds to part and a thunderous omniscient voice proclaim that the laws are Humean, then I'd wager my little loot on Lehrer's compatibilism. Look at the history of philosophy's free will debate. What endures is a conceptual trifecta. Free will, it is said, emerges within a deterministic world through agents who, by lawfully calling on their psychological sources, are the ultimate causes of their leeway-laden chosen actions. When Lehrer calls the race, a free agent's choice gallops out of psychology's gate with the reigns so firmly in her hands that her thoroughbred runs the track just as she prefers. That looks like a pony in the money. But the pony pays only if the laws of nature are Humean. Are they?

## Contraltos Cantando con Frankfurt

In contrast to the sopranos, contralto compatibilists typically deny that a free agent's path through time need be forked with merely possible foregone actions. Although they largely agree with Lehrerian sopranos about the significance of the cognitive source of a free and responsible action, they differ from sopranos generally by rejecting the notion that an agent's responsibility-enabling free will requires her leeway to act otherwise (Frankfurt 1969 and 1971; Wolf 1990; Fischer 1994, chaps. 7 and 8; Fischer and Ravizza 1998; McKenna 2001 and 2013; Mele 2006; Nelkin 2011; Sartorio 2016; Campbell and Lehrer 2018, sec. 6; Pereboom 2018; Kaiserman 2020). Instead, with their eyes on Frankfurt's score and generally in tune with cognitive neuroscience, they variously intone that a responsible agent's free action owes its responsible character and attendant liberty simply to the rational character of its law-abiding efficacious *psychological source*.

That psychic source, as variously characterized by various contraltos, is among the subjects of cognitive science. As remarked above, this science treats a normal human agent as a biologically evolved, complex system of mental representations that physically realize interacting packages or modules of dispositions to react in approximately rational ways to fluctuations in information. Most importantly from the contralto perspective, the normal system *rationally brokers*—inferentially or computationally—the complex commerce in which information-bearing mental representations and behavior are the stocks in cognitive trade. Cognitive science adopts the hypothesis that healthy human incarnations of such normally situated systems are renditions of both practical and theoretical reasoning. Thus, behavior in general and action in particular standardly result from the ways in which an agent's systematized mental representations are apt efficaciously to interact. Some representations result, in part, from sensation, as if they were premises in inferences inscribed by the senses. Other representations result as if they were conclusions spawned by the inferential interactions of representations already in play.

Granted all this, psychology legislates that, normally, human agents are nearly rational brokers. Their covert cognitive operations are abductively revealed by models of the ways in which representations engage. Idealized, these models explain actions by displaying the rational structure of the mental representations that enable agents to tune their attitudes, and thus their actions, to their information about themselves and their surroundings.[41] The representations typically featured in promising models of (roughly) rational action evidently subserve the functions or roles characteristic of not only contextually fitting folk-psychological attitudes—both propositional and practical—but also the whole range of well-adapted affective states conjectured by the folk. Thus and as already noted, functionalists of various stripes may be apt to identify an agent's attitudes with tokens, if not types, of her physical states that, in virtue of their causal connections, realize the model's inferential processes (Turing 1950; Putnam 1960; Harman 1973; Fodor 1975 and 1983; Block 1980a; Lewis 1983a; Pylyshyn 1984; Dennett 1987; Pollock 1995; Ismael 2016). It is, then, in virtue of this identifying hypothesis that an agent's actions can arise from—have their explanatory and causal source in— her practical reason. Thus, action normally arises from an agent's practical reason as far as it results from her capacity rationally to register and exploit her functionally realized beliefs, desires, preferences, plans and feelings.[42]

Long contralto song short: when it comes to intentional action rather than stimuli-instigated reaction, normal people normally do what, consciously or not, they decide to do by means of the inferential relations or conceptual schemes that their cognitive systems realize. Indeed, this is why it is nearly irresistible within cognitive science literally to identify the agent herself with her cognitive system or a proper part thereof. That system is the set of relations or patterns fixed by the distribution of her cooperating psychological states over that region of the Humean mosaic her life constitutes. Better that, says cognitive science, than identifying one's self with a metaphysically mysteriously efficacious agental substance of the sorts championed—historically —by Descartes, Locke and Kant or—modernly—by Chisholm (1976 and 1989), O'Connor (2002), and Clarke (2003).[43] If just so scientifically identified, then the agent herself—*qua* exquisitely tuned cognitive system of inferential or computational dispositions—would qualify as the genuine causal and explanatory source of her actions.[44] With something like this in mind, different contraltos can differently distinguish not only better from worse ways in which agents might acquire their representations but also superior from inferior ways in which agents might manage their representations once acquired. And this permits contraltos to propose, with a nod to the Lehrerians, that it suffices for an agent's responsibility and thus her freedom that she herself, *qua* computational system of information-laden representations, be, in some to-be-specified proper way, the rational source of her action. Contraltos, when engaged in parochial debate, variously characterize the privileging forms of practical reason said to suffice for free action. But they concur that some, but not all, ways of acting deliberately underwrite freedom and responsibility. Agents whose selected actions arise from just the right sort of cognitive sources achieve their freedom in so acting. Should an agent, *qua* cognitive system, be that sort of source of her particular action, then by so acting she is free and responsible. According to contraltos, then, an agent's freedom of action, and the responsibility it enables, depends upon how she accrues, manages, and deploys her reasons for acting (Mele 2006, 164ff.).

## DETERMINISM DETERMINED

All compatibilists concede the possibility of determinism. But what, exactly, is the thesis or hypothesis of determinism? Or, perhaps better, how should we represent it? Strawson, Lehrer, and Austin tell us that determinism is itself a wily thesis (P. Strawson 1962, 1; Lehrer 1980, 197; Austin, Urmson, and Warnock 1979b, 231). Still, Ismael, adopting the Humean conception of (global) laws, helpfully distills the essence of the doctrine, writing,

> Determinism does entail that if we go far enough back and cast our net widely enough, we capture a logically sufficient basis for determining not only the external circumstances, but [one's] own initial state at any encounter with the environment, and these two things together determine behavior. (Ismael 2016, 112)

But Holliday, who—in contrast with Ismael—evidently sympathizes with Spinoza rather than Hume regarding the modal character and implications of natural laws, alternatively advises:

> In a world with deterministic laws of nature, at any time there is only one future evolution of the world that is possible given the laws and the state of the world at that time. Determinism is the thesis that the laws of our world are deterministic. If determinism is true, then the laws of nature and the initial conditions of the Big Bang determined a unique future for our world; every movement you will ever make is part of that unique future, determined eons ago. (Holliday 2012, 179)[45]

I do not pretend to know which, if any, of the various subtle formulations of determinism among those competing in the rich literature deserves selection, much less how the winner ought best to be expressed consistent with the ultimate mores of polished science. Neither do I suppose that determinism, once formulated with full logical precision, is true. Nevertheless, I do aim to contend that given even Holliday's especially strong conception of determinism we may be as free both as the sopranos and contraltos might approve but not for the reasons they suppose. It is, then, with this aim that hereafter and without explicit defense I adopt a trio of contentious provisional assumptions variously but ably defended elsewhere by others already or subsequently cited. These three disputed and here *protem* assumptions are

(A.1) The sopranos are right to suppose that an agent's freedom implies that, at a minimum, she be able to act alternatively to, or otherwise than, the way she actually acts (Lehrer 1980; Lewis 1981; Moore and Shaw 2005).

(A.2) The laws of nature are naturally necessary governing principles that, by governing events, establish—rather than supervene upon—the patterns framed in the mosaic of space-time (Holliday 2012, 193 and 203-204).

(A.3) History is immutable.[46]


# NOTES

1. In his enduringly influential paper on compatibilism, Chisholm states, "Perhaps it is needless to remark that, in all likelihood, it is impossible to say anything significant about this ancient problem that hasn't already been said before" (1989, 5). Nevertheless, it is fair to say that Chisolm characteristically bucked the probability.

2. I know of no better discussion of how philosophers ought to investigate the concepts that rightly command philosophical inquiry than the discussion by Graham and Horan (1994).

3. Lehrer is among those who, like Kane, refer to the will (Lehrer, 1960 and 2020).

4. Mele, while acknowledging Kane's work on the will, influentially writes, "Early in this chapter, I offered some standard definitions of common terminology in the literature on free will and moral responsibility. I did not offer a definition of 'free will': that expression has no standard definition. A comment is in order about how I use 'free will' in this book. Whatever, exactly, free will is, it is, most fundamentally, the power or ability to act freely. So one can try to understand free will by ascertaining what it is to act freely. One can develop an account of free action and define *free will* as the power or ability to perform actions that satisfy the account. For a combination of reasons, including the following, I would like to think that this approach is viable. First, I often cannot tell what authors mean by 'will' in 'free will'; second, I am blameless for this ignorance, as far as I can tell; third, I seem to have been able on various occasions to write about acting freely without using the expression 'free

will'. In any case, if free will may be simply defined in terms of free action—as the power or ability to act freely—one can go about the business of trying to understand free action without worrying about what (the) will is supposed to be. I find the thought liberating" (Mele 2006, 17).

5. Reid also posits mental acts (Reid 1785, bk. II, chaps. 5 and 16; and bk. IV, chap. 1). Others who opt for mental acts include Geach (1957). For discussion of whether (early twentieth century) psychology can legitimately appeal to mental acts, see Gallie, Sprott, and Mace (1947).

6. Although I ignore the urgency of an adequate account of the content of mental states, I acknowledge that exactly how and why functionally arrayed states naturalistically accrue their supposed semantic properties remains an unsolved riddle for functionalism (Searle 1980; Dretske 1981b, 1988 and 1995; Stich 1983; Fodor 1987 and 2008; Horgan, Tienson, and Graham 2004).

7. Indeed, it is their representational or inferential character that distinguishes states just so systematically networked *as mental or psychological* in contrast to other, but not psychological or intentional, systems of causally coordinated states.

8. Dennett (1975 and 1978a) categorically rejects the language of thought hypothesis.

9. Locke wrote, "This, at least, I think evident—That we find in ourselves a power to begin or forbear, continue or end several actions of our minds, and motions of our bodies, barely by a thought or preference of the mind ordering, or as it were commanding, the doing or not doing such or such a particular action. This power which the mind has thus to order the consideration of any idea, or the forbearing to consider it; or to prefer the motion of any part of the body to its rest, and vice versa, in any particular instance, is that which we call the WILL. The actual exercise of that power, by directing any particular action, or its forbearance, is that which we call VOLITION or WILLING. The forbearance of that action, consequent to such order or command of the mind, is called VOLUNTARY. And whatsoever action is performed without such a thought of the mind, is called INVOLUNTARY" (1690, bk. II, chap. xxi, sec. 5).

10. McKenna and Pereboom (2016, 7) cite Ginet (1990, 90), quoting him: "By freedom of the will is meant freedom of action." And Chisholm writes of the will and its freedom, "For even if there is such a faculty as 'the will,' which somehow sets our acts agoing, the question of freedom, as John Locke said, is not the question '*whether the will be free*'; it is the question '*whether a man be free.*' For if there is a 'will,' as a moving faculty, the question is whether the man is free to will to do those things that he does will to do—and also whether he is free *not* to will any of those things that he does will to do, and, again, whether he is free to will any of those things that he does not will to do" (Chisholm 1989, 11).

11. Notice that, so characterized, the functionalist complaint is not against *quiddities* conceived as whatever in the deep nature of efficacious properties ultimately may account for their causal roles within a theory. Rather, the functionalist objects that once an individual object's properties are said to account for its causal relations, it would violate the principle of theoretical parsimony to call upon an individuating substance or substrate to account for any of the same. Put differently, the complaint

is not against the quiddity of an efficacious property but rather against the efficacious haecceity of a property's instantiator. See Cowling (2012).

12. Describing the thesis for which he argues, Holton writes, "Action is not determined just by the agent's beliefs, desires and intentions. In addition willpower plays an independent contributory role. Agents whose willpower is strong can stick by their resolutions even in the face of strong contrary desires; agents whose willpower is weak readily abandon their resolutions even when the contrary desires are relatively weak" (Holton, 2009a, 113).

13. "And God said, Let there be light: and there was light," Gen. 3:1, King James Version.

14. Of course, if a sequence consists simply of a single psychological state—perhaps a decisive desire—then soloists are chorists of the simplest sort.

15. Frankfurt influentially allows that the will may be realized solo or choral. He writes, "To identify an agent's will is either to identify the desire (or desires) by which he is motivated in some action he performs or to identify the desire (or desires) by which he will or would be motivated when or if he acts. An agent's will, then, is identical with one or more of his first-order desires. But the notion of the will, as I am employing it, is not coextensive with the notion of first-order desires. It is not the notion of something that merely inclines an agent in some degree to act in a certain way. Rather, it is the notion of an *effective* desire—one that moves (or will or would move) a person all the way to action. Thus the notion of the will is not coextensive with the notion of what an agent intends to do. For even though someone may have a settled intention to do *X*, he may nonetheless do something else instead of doing *X* because, despite his intention, his desire to do *X* proves to be weaker or less effective than some conflicting desire" (Frankfurt 1971, 8).

16. Although I would not wish to saddle Kane with my simple view of the will, mine is certainly and gratefully instructed by his more complex conception (Kane 1999-03-18, chaps. 1 and 2).

17. The literature bristles with formulations of determinism. See van Inwagen (1983, 3) and Mele (2006, 3–4).

18. Contrast Lehrer (1960 and 1980), Lewis (1981), Horgan (1985), Frankfurt (1969 and 1971), Fischer (1994), McKenna (2014), Sartorio (2016), and Mele (2019) with Ginet (1966), van Inwagen (1975, 1983 and 2008), Pereboom, (2001), and Holliday (2012). And for optimal instruction about all topics touched in this book, see McKenna and Pereboom (2016).

19. Some may demur with my use of 'akratic.' In correspondence, Al Mele kindly tutors me that akratic action is generally conceived of as uncompelled or otherwise contingent intentional action that is contrary to the agent's overall better judgment (Hare 1965; Davidson 1980; Mele 1987). As I use the term, an agent acts akratically if she acts intentionally, purposefully or with awareness while also being in a psychological state in which she wills to act otherwise than she actually does. By my lights an akratic agent's action is determined by her overall typically complex indecisive psychological state. One part of her overall state may be her weak will being trumped in competition among other antagonistic parts of her state. An akratic actor, I say, is an agent with a plan of the sort Bratman describes that is overridden on the occasion

by her sensitivity to her prevailing circumstances (Bratman 1999, 2ff. and chaps. 3 and 4). Such may be the situation of the teenager whose amygdala gets the better of his or her too weak disposition to refrain from the whiskey offered by peers at the curfew-breaking beach party. Readers steeped in the literature on *akrasia* realize that many writers on the topic follow Mele in eschewing reference to the will and, hence, a weak will. Rather, they attend to the manner, for better or worse, in which an agent's psychological processes control her actions. These observant readers will realize that my conception of akratic action does refer to a weak will—and hence, the will. But being astute they will appreciate that, for me, the will, though real, is just the ensemble of psychological states that constitutes the cause of deliberate action.

20. For simplicity, let us ignore the notion of probabilistic laws.

21. I quote Lewis by calling upon Loewer's illuminating development and defense of Lewis (Loewer, 2012, p. 176; and 2004).

22. Ismael also recommends a graceful and nuanced Humean portrait of the laws of nature, including both global (cosmological) laws and, perhaps, local laws—all friendly to her subtle rendition of compatibilism. According to Ismael, typical domain-specific sciences attend to local laws emergent from regularities character-istic of various natural or functional kinds of complex objects (subsystems) within the universe. Cosmology, in contrast to domain-specific sciences, aims at global laws descriptive of the behavior of the universe as a whole. Always writing better than everyone else, she offers:

> Philosophers often employ [an] image of science, one that [focuses] not on the local laws that describe the behavior of open subsystems of the universe . . . but on the emergent [global] laws that describe the universe as a whole. The focus on global laws . . . makes us [mistakenly] think of the global laws as basic, and any description of the behavior of open subsystems as an incomplete description of the whole . . . [That inverts] the order of determination and [reifies] the laws, so that now it looks like the laws are not simply descriptions of a pattern that is partly constituted by our actions but are instead iron rails built into the spatial and temporal landscape that won't let us act in any way not in accord with them.
>
> There is a much more benign way to think of laws that starts from a constructive account of how a world composed out of simple mechanisms with a limited range of motion will exhibit some deep regularities. . . . The resulting picture of the universe is one in which there are no iron rails that keep our behaviors narrowly in check. There is only emergent regularity and complex creatures who exploit the regularity for strategic purposes. Far from being a threat to human freedom, science will appear in this picture as a systematic, holistic handmaid to effective action. (Ismael 2016, 110–12)

Halpin (1999) too adopts, with minor modification, Lewis's conception of the laws of nature according to which those pertinent to the actual world are best represented as theorems of a set of axioms that, with a pragmatic eye on simplicity and explanatory power, best accounts for the world's states. To flavor such laws with the faint taste of artificial modality tolerable to Hume's pragmatist allies, Halpin adds a psychological dollop. He asserts that optimal scientific practice involves embracing the perspective from which we may apply these laws to infer or compute the history and future of possible events—i.e., events in possible worlds accessible from the actual one.

Let me summarize the PBSA's [i.e., Perspectival Best Systems Approach to natural laws] account of necessity. That the laws "must" be true comes to the fact that we tend to project them onto hypothetical situations. And this projection has important pragmatic value. From this, I claim to have provided not merely a definition of nomic necessity consistent with a best system account . . . but to have provided an account that is explanatory. Second, the simple explanation in terms of practicality is based in scientific practice: projecting our best system is necessary to illustrate its possibilities and to model subsystems of the actual world. Moreover, this account is consistent with Humean Supervenience; nomic necessity is understood without reference to non-occurrent fact. So, the PBSA meets the goal set above: to characterize laws of nature in a way that explains modal character, makes sense of science and yet does not require the metaphysical extravagance of non-occurrent fact. (Halpin 1999, 641–42)

23. Spinoza's commentators differ regarding whether his universally acknowledged determinism includes necessitarianism—i.e., for him the thesis that all existing things and events are necessary throughout time (Della Rocca 2008, 69–78; Garrett 2018, chap. 7). Arguing the case in his book about the Dutch philosopher, Garrett writes, "Spinoza is unquestionably a determinist, but it has often been disputed whether he is also a full-fledged necessitarian—that is, whether he consistently holds that everything is logically or metaphysically necessary, so that the world could not possibly have been different in any way from what it actually is. This chapter argues for three theses. First, nothing Spinoza says commits him to the denial of necessitarianism. Second, several things he says do commit him to necessitarianism. Third, a commitment to necessitarianism explains (a) how he can maintain that modes of different attributes are parallel to one another without any causal interaction between them and (b) how he can maintain that every intrinsically adequate idea corresponds to its object. Together, these theses constitute a very strong case that Spinoza is a necessitarian" (Garrett 2018, 99). Quoting Spinoza, Garrett finds him affirming necessitarianism thus: "I want to explain in what sense I maintain the fatalistic necessity of all things and of all actions. For in no way do I subject God to fate, but I conceive that everything follows with inevitable necessity from the nature of God, just as all conceive that it follows from the nature of God Himself that He should understand Himself" (Garrett 2018, from Oxford Scholarship Online (October 2018): p. 2 of 1–28. https://doi.org/10.1093/oso/9780195307771.001.0001).

24. While referring to Perry, Holliday adopts a *governing*—rather than Humean—conception of natural laws (Holliday 2012, 193; Perry 2004, 234ff.). Although Holliday is puzzlingly mum regarding whether governing laws are necessary, Perry is not. Perry's opposition to Hume evidently resonates with Dretske's. Both Perry and Dretske concede that governing laws of nature need not be necessary, but each would base such scientific laws in the natures, properties or relations of the governed. That, however, invites the question whether the connections among objects secured by their natures or properties or relations are necessary (Perry 2004, 240–41; Dretske 1977, 252–53 and 263–64). Dretske states:

Once a law is understood to have the form:

(6) F-ness → G-ness
the relation in question (the relation expressed by "→") is seen to be an extensional relation between properties with the terms "F-ness" and "G-ness" occupying transparent

positions in (6). Any term referring to the same quality or quantity as "F-ness" can be substituted for "F-ness" in (6) without affecting its truth or its law-likeness. Coextensive terms (terms referring to the same quantities and qualities) can be freely exchanged for "F-ness" and "G-ness" in (6) without jeopardizing its truth value. The tendency to treat laws as some kind of intensional relation between extensions, as something of the form

$(x)(Fx \rightarrow Gx)$

(where the connective is some kind of modal connective), is simply a mistaken rendition of the fact that laws are extensional relations between intensions.

Once we make the ontological ascent we can also understand the modal character of laws . . . Although true statements having the form of (6) are not themselves *necessary* truths, nor do they describe a modal relationship between the respective qualities, the contingent relationship between properties that is described imposes a modal quality on the particular events falling within its scope. This *F must* be *G*. Why? Because F-ness is linked to G-ness; the one property yields or generates the other in much the way a change in the thermal conductivity of a metal yields a change in its electrical conductivity. The pattern of inference is:

F-ness $\rightarrow$ G-ness
This is F

_____

This must be G.

This, I suggest, is a valid pattern of inference. (Dretske 1977, 263-264)

Like Dretske, Holliday also assigns an undefined modal character to governing laws. Holliday glosses his conception thus:

On a "governing" view of the laws of nature, the propositions expressed by statements of laws fall into Perry's category (iii): they be true, but they are not made true by events. A law of nature is something that governs events as they unfold, so events fall into the patterns they do because the laws are what they are. On a Humean view of the laws, the propositions expressed by statements of laws fall into Perry's category (ii): they are made true by events, only they are not made true until the cascade of events is complete, if it ever is. Here the relationship between laws and events is reversed; a law of nature is just a regularity that turns out to be exceptionless over all time, so the laws are what they are because events fall into the patterns they do. . . . I will not argue here against the Humean view of laws, typically favored by miracle compatibilists. The argument for (FP) [the Fixity of the Past—author's insertion] and the Simple Argument [for incompatibilism -author's insertion] are to be understood under the assumption of the governing view of laws, which is in line with the backtracking compatibilists' principle (BT). Something like the idea that laws have a modal force beyond that of mere regularities must be behind the idea of (BT), the idea that if history had gone differently, it would not have been because the past would have been different all the way back. Our conclusion is therefore qualified, but still strong: incompatibilism follows on the assumption of a governing view of laws. (Holliday 2012, 203–04).

25. The perspicuous reader will have immediately seen through this diaphanous verbiage first to Ginet's (1966), van Inwagen's (1975), Pereboom's (2001), and Holliday's (2012) various renditions of the Consequence Argument and then beyond to the assessments of that argument by Lehrer (1980 (reprint 1990)), Lewis (1981 (reprint

1987)), Slote (1982), Fischer (1994), Beebee and Mele (2002), Menzies (2017-06-15) and others.

Van Inwagen's much discussed argument relies on a modality transferring principle in order to blanket actions entailed by the conjunction of the laws of nature and history with the sort of freedom-precluding necessity presumed to apply to both the laws and the past. For lucid discussion of van Inwagen's reliance on what Fischer dubs the Transfer Principle, see Fischer (1994) and McKenna and Pereboom (2016, 85–101). While various authors reject such a transfer principle applied to the sort of modality—power necessity—featured in van Inwagen's argument, Fischer takes the validity of the principle to be an open question. However, he rightly remarks, "It must be stated at the outset that the Transfer Principle is extremely attractive. . . . I have been interpreting the necessity operator as expressing power necessity. If one interprets it more strongly as some sort of logical necessity (in the broad sense), the principle becomes clearly valid: logical necessity is obviously closed under entailment" (Fischer 1994, 23–24 and 45).

26. Are there laws of psychology (inclusive of cognitive science) in particular and laws of the special sciences generally? Distinguish between representations that aim to signify laws (i.e., exceptionless governing regulations or regularities) and the laws so signified, stated or represented. Certainly, confirmed linguistic representations of what may seem to be laws of human action generally rely upon typically implicit and contextually sensitive *ceteris paribus* clauses so as to qualify as representations of the exceptionless. However, since *ceteris paribus* clauses defy explicit full specification, it is controversial whether the entrenched representations that trade in these clauses succeed in representing exceptionless laws of nature (Cartwright 1980; Davidson 2001a, 2001b, and 2001c; Fodor 1974, 1991, and 1997; Schiffer 1991, 2; Ismael 2016, 90–99). However, that representations of laws may fail fully or precisely to represent their semantic targets does not imply that the targeted laws themselves fail to be universal regularities to which the relevant objects conform without exception. "Normally, everyone wants something" is likely among the representations of confirmed laws to appear in the ideal revision of *The Principles of Human Psychology* promised by the mature psychology (James 1890/1905). The golden tome admits inability fully to specify normality. But that innocent shortfall is echoed by the fact that "Normally, water flows downhill" is equally likely to appear in the idealized book for finished hydrology despite the fact that hydrology may admit inability precisely to specify normality for water on rutted boulder-strewn slopes.

27. Compare Holliday's conception of determinism according to which the determination of the nonoccurrence of an event or action implies the impossibility of its occurrence relative to the laws of nature and history. "Here 'determined not to do $y$ at $t^0$' means that it is not possible for the agent to do $y$ at $t^0$, holding fixed the laws of nature and the initial conditions of the world" (Holliday 2012, 184).

28. For Austin's objection to Moore, see Austin's "Ifs and Cans" in Austin, Urmson, and Warnock, (1979-03-06). Also see Chisholm (1976, pp. 56–57), and compare Sterba and Kourany (1981). See Lewis (1981) for his disagreement with Lehrer.

29. Although Lehrer allows that an agent might falsely believe of something that it is an open option for her, I shall follow the practice in literature on preference

according to which the elements in a profile are in fact all open to an agent (Kahneman and Tversky, 1982a and b; Hausman, 2011).

30. Whenever I label a preference structure with "hierarchical" or "crowned," I use those terms to ease exposition. With "hierarchical," I point to the general notion of unifying connectivity. So, a hierarchical structure might be modeled by ascending steps in a staircase or by the nodes in a spider's web. And with 'crowned' I refer to the way in which an element in a structure is so positioned as both to secure and certify structural unity. So, its crown is to a preference structure as is a monarchy to its kingdom, a pair of bookends to the array of which it is a part, a mathematical function to its domain and—following Lehrer—a keystone to its arch.

31. In his "Introduction" to his forthcoming book, Lehrer remarks that his version of compatibilism accommodates conceptions of free choice that the literature labels with "leeway," "source," and "agental causation."

32. Of course, the notion of rationality relevant here requires a big pinch, if not a bucket, of salt. While cognitive psychology may idealize humans as rational, it is well and widely known that incarnate human theoretical and practical reasoning is liable to a range of non-rational biases including disruptive effects from emotions (Simon, 1957; Wason, 1968; Tversky and Kahneman 1974, Kahneman, Slovic and Tversky 1982a; Cherniak 1986; Stich 1990; Gigerenzer, Gerd, and Selten 2001).

33. As Fodor and Dennett independently made plain, the problem of formulating a theory of cognitive processes that explains how the mind recruits in real time representations that are relevant to producing contextually appropriate behavior then was—and remains—unsolved by cognitive science (Dennett 1978b; Fodor 1983; Pylyshyn 1984).

34. Lehrer rejects a logical connection between free choice and responsibility (Lehrer, forthcoming, "Introduction").

35. Same point in Lehrer's words, "I think of a power preference as an expression of an active power to form preferences. . . . Here I note a power preference over a preference to choose $A$ includes minimally preference over some alternative to $A$, call it $B$, that logically excludes $A$ and may consist simply of refraining from doing $A$. So, the power preference is not just a preference for choosing to do $A$, if that is preferred by the agent, but also for, contrary to fact, a preference for choosing to do $B$, if that were preferred instead. In short, the power preference is a preference for whatever the agent chooses in a profile of alternatives targeting $A$ (Lehrer, forthcoming, ch. 2).

36. Lehrer says, "The power preference of a person for a choice is the *primary* explanation of the choice, an *ultimate preference*, if and only if it is minimally adequate to explain the choice without appeal to any supplementation of it" (Lehrer, forthcoming, ch. 4).

37. See Lehrer's "Introduction" to his forthcoming book for his conception of the connections among free choice, ultimate preferences, power preferences and power generally.

38. See Carnap (1950) and Thomasson (2014, ch. 1) for accounts of conceptual schemes or frameworks.

39. The enormous literature on reasons for actions and reasons for propositional and practical attitudes is beyond our consideration here. But the interested reader

would do well to start with Velleman 2000; Davidson 2001a; and Mele 1992, 2017 and follow the branching trails.

40. Describing his current compatibilism, Lehrer writes:

> Ultimate explanation in terms of a power preference is now the central feature of my defense. My defense is based on the premise that scientific determinism may fail to explain our choices. Sylvain Bromberger . . . proved many years ago that nomological deduction is not sufficient for explanation. Bromberger (1965, 1993) argued convincingly, and I follow him, that an explanation is an answer to a why-question that such deduction may fail to answer. An explanation of a person's choice to do A must answer the question "Why did the person choose to do A? There may be many conditions (some remote, like having been born, and some present, like a supply of oxygen) that are necessary for the person's choosing as she does, or even sufficient, but that do not answer the question of why she chose as she did. It is something about our mental life, something about our preferences, that I propose as an ultimate explanation of free choice. This provides a sufficient condition of free will compatible with scientific determinism. (Lehrer 2020, p. 601)

Several pages later and where referring to ultimately empowering preference Lehrer adds,

> the power preference's being the ultimate preference for what the agent chooses from a preference profile entails that, whatever the agent chooses, he or she could have chosen otherwise. That is the power of the ultimate preference over a profile of preferences including alternatives other than what he or she chooses. The power preference as an ultimate preference of choice explains why the choice is of free will, up to the agent as he or she believes. (Lehrer 2020, p. 605)

41. Slote (1980) argues that contralto compatibilism fails because it does not correctly account for the autonomy, freedom and responsibility required of persons.

42. Accordingly, if Lehrer's soprano-song meets the conditions on practical reasoning contraltos postulate, his voice comfortably fits within both the soprano and contralto compatibilist ranges (Campbell and Lehrer, 2018).

43. See Dennett (1984 and 2003); Pollock and Ismael (2006); Ismael (2007, 182); Nelkin (2011-07-01); and Ismael (2016).

44. Aristotle's *Categories* and *Metaphysics Z* invite the thought that an Aristotelian substance is a subject of predication. A contralto source of an action is a subject to which the predicates of cognitive science apply. Accordingly, and perhaps in a way to be welcomed by libertarians who posit efficacious agents or substances, a contralto source of action (and hence a person) as studied by cognitive science may qualify as an Aristotelian agental substance (Chisholm, 1966 and 1967).

45. Not only is but one future possible according to Holliday. The past too is modally unique if determinism prevails. He writes, "For if determinism is true, there is only one history that is possible given the laws of nature and the initial conditions of the universe" (Holliday 2012, 183).

46. The immutability of history entails Fischer's formulation of what he calls the Principle of the Fixity of the Past, namely

for any action Y, agent S, and time t, if it is true that if S were to do Y at t, some fact about the past relative to t would not have been a fact, then S cannot at t do Y at t. (Fischer 1994, 78)

In his argument for incompatibilism, Holliday defends Fischer's principle, reformulated thus:

For any action y, agent s, and times t and t' (t ≤ t'), if it is true that if s were to do y at t', the past relative to t would (have to) be different, then s cannot at t do y at t'.

Holliday ingeniously argues that the past is immutably fixed under the assumption that the laws of nature govern, rather than merely supervene upon actual regularities. For granted that miracles are impossible and that the laws govern, every actual event is of the type such that its omission or alternation in any possible world is inconsistent with the history of that world (Holliday 2012, pp. 182–84, 191–94, and 201–03).

# Chapter 2

# The Logic of "Almost"

## AKRATIC COMPATIBILISM CONFESSED
## BUT DEFENSE DEFERRED

Recall that the previous chapter concludes with three assumptions, admittedly contestable, that I adopt going forward. For ease of reference, I repeat them here:

(A.1) The sopranos are right to suppose that an agent's freedom implies that, at a minimum, she be able to act alternatively to, or otherwise than, the way she actually acts (Lehrer 1980; Lewis 1981; Moore and Shaw 2005).

(A.2) The laws of nature are naturally necessary governing principles that, by governing events, establish—rather than supervene upon—the patterns framed in the mosaic of space-time (Holliday 2012, 193 and 203-204).

(A.3) History is immutable.[1]

I aim to exploit this trio of assumptions when, in chapter 3, I proceed fully to explain and defend in detail akratic compatibilism. It is the version of compatibilism scouted in the Introduction that I hope here further to advertise. But as a preliminary to the argument of chapter 3, in the present chapter I seek to lay the conceptual foundation for akratic compatibilism by considering a peculiar, but promising, property of our conception of approximation. Under some conditions, approximating a goal is, I contend, sufficient for achieving it. Appreciation of this fact, if it should be a fact, underwrites the claim crucial to akratic compatibilism. For the critical contestable thesis is that almost being able to act otherwise may, in special circumstances, suffice for being able to act otherwise—even granted (A.1)–(A.3). The idea that animates akratic compatibilism is that approximating an impossible goal under certain constraints can, should, and indeed does count as reaching the elusive goal. I will labor to lay the required foundation for akratic compatibilism in sections 3 through 8 below, where I discuss the logic of "almost." But as a run up to that, in what immediately follows I remark on the thoughts that animate, but do not incontrovertibly prove, compatibilism of the akratic kind.

Although in virtue of (A.1), I unreservedly side with the sopranos, I shall also urge in concurrence with the contraltos that a free agent is, in a certain sense, a virtuously functioning cognitive source of her liberated action. For her ability to choose and act otherwise in a world ruled by Spinozan necessity requires, I say, that her chosen action springs from the way her psychology moves her to act. If, consistent with determinism, she should act upon, and because of, those of her practical attitudes that induce defiance of the incarcerating destiny that life in the grip of necessity demands, then—I shall argue—she would be leeway free (Campbell and Lehrer 2018, 230–33). I shall urge that a free agent may inherit her ability to act otherwise by recognizing and consequently resisting, albeit unsuccessfully, the necessity by which manipulative nature would govern some of her actions. My argument does not pretend to be a sound deduction from steadfast premises. No, rather it is at best a defeasible abductive exercise under the provisional contestable assumptions set by (A.2) and (A.3). The conception of human freedom I advance comports with both what seems characteristic of human practical reasoning and also the troubling hunch that the laws of nature inescapably govern us. Mine is an account of a sufficient, rather than necessary, condition for freedom of the will. It looks to our laudable failures naturally and willfully—but inevitably too weakly—to resist the laws of cognition—the psychology—that govern us. My proposal would find in such peculiarly akratic episodes the germ that generates free will and flowers as moral responsibility. I ecumenically welcome the thought that various other conditions may suffice for the same freedom. Better that a thousand flowers bloom than only one! And I would be untroubled should freedom of the will prove to be a multiply realizable attribute of multiply realizable cognitive agents (Putnam 1967; Fodor 1974; Kim 1992). But the idea I do aim to defend is that—in cognizing creatures of our complex, fallible, and often conflicted sort—the frustrated willful effort to act otherwise, even when we simply cannot, surprisingly suffices within certain contexts for freedom fit for morality.

By adopting (A.2) and (A.3), I depart from soprano compatibilists who, in Hume's tradition, follow Lewis and Lehrer in supposing the comfortable contingency of natural laws and the possibility of variation among the events that colonize space-time. Rather, while acknowledging that it may be out of ephemeral philosophical style, I now don for the subsequent duration of this book the starched fashion of Spinoza. I cheer the plausible—though disputed—arguments of his too few *necessitarian* allies led once by Tooley, Dretske, and Armstrong, but more recently by Holliday.[2] From where I stand it looks as if Spinoza's persuasive confrères might be right. They plausibly point not only to the distinctive necessity of the laws of nature but also, and thereby, to rigid history's complementary immutability in its implicative coordination with the inviolable laws. Accordingly, my here unargued—but by others ably defended—tentative hypothesis going forward is that determinism ensures the necessity of all events and actions via their modal entailment from the union of nature's necessary laws and history's immutable tale.[3] Generously granted that necessitarian hunch, I argue—in a sense that skirts, but does not topple over, the edge of sound semantics—that our leeway freedom to act otherwise is compatible with Spinozan determinism. We may be leeway free in particular circumstances even if whatever we do is necessary. For we are leeway free if, as we must, we try but fail to seize the very plasticity in chosen action that eludes us. If, on some oddly akratic occasions, we unsuccessfully attempt to do what we will to do, we may then act freely and responsibly. For on such occasions and relative to our circumstances, we may achieve the ability to act otherwise although the laws should be Spinozan. Free will in a necessitarian world is a child of *akrasia* if I should be right about its genetics (Davidson 1970; Mele 1987 and 2012).

So, let us provisionally assume, although it is admittedly controversial, that determinism—real, ruthless, diamond-hard Spinozan determinism—is true. In order to set the bar appropriately high for compatibilism to clear, let's agree with—but perhaps go a step beyond—the way in which some leading incompatibilists plausibly cast determinism. Let's concur with the thread common to the Consequence Argument—as variously spun by Ginet, van Inwagen, and Pereboom—that freedom requires the ability to act otherwise than we do. En route to arguing for their individually distinctive conceptions of incompatibilism, they proceed insightfully to agree that we are *powerless* so to act otherwise. They say we are powerless to contravene the conjunctive governance of nature's laws and the past. If so, we are impotent too against the consequences of that circumscribing governance. But *why* would we be just so powerless? Here we answer in temporary sympathy with these incompatibilists that if they are correct regarding our impotence, that is because the laws of nature and history may both obtain and jointly apply with natural necessity.

Situated as I am here in locally Euclidean space, I am powerless miraculously to render any triangle a triangular quadrilateral. For the prevailing Euclidean laws ensure the geometric necessity of all their theorems, including that all triangles have exactly three, not four, internal angles and precisely three, not four, sides. I lack the magical power to compose water from elements other than hydrogen and oxygen. For among the necessary, even if *a posteriori* implications of the chemistry, is that necessarily, water is $H_2O$. Why am I powerless to make my suffered pain pleasant rather than awful? In virtue of its necessity, psychology implies that human pain is awful in every naturally possible world where humans endure it.

If, as Fischer considers and Holliday concludes, the past should be *fixed*, why is it so frozen that altering it is absolutely beyond our individual or collective abilities?[4] Why, in the face of history, am I powerless so to act that Caesar's having crossed the Rubicon would need be fiction rather than fact?

Well, every version of determinism insists that Caesar's having traversed the river is implied by the initial state of the cosmos conjoined to the laws of nature. Spinozan determinism lays it down that the laws are all necessary. But are the initial conditions also necessary? Yes, I'm afraid so. That initial state is to the laws of nature as is the null set axiom to the other axioms of Zermelo-Fraenkel set theory. The null set axiom, if true, settles the existence of the one and only empty set with the same modality as the other axioms settle various properties of sets generally. By jointly sufficing for the downstream theorems of set theory, including virtually all of arithmetic, the collaborating axioms of set theory bestow upon all their implicated progeny the same sort of mathematical necessity the axioms commonly enjoy. So too, each ontic bit in the mundane mosaic if Spinozan determinism should be true. For in that case the initial state of the universe conspires with the laws of nature to imply the occurrence of all events and actions within the mosaic. These materially realized theorems of the set consisting of the laws plus the one and only set of initial conditions are, Spinozans contend, all inevitable. For the materialized theorems, all the facts formed from the bits and pieces composing the mundane mosaic, implicatively inherit their common necessity from the same modality that inoculates the initialized laws against the possibility of difference. Thus, whatever we do, we do necessarily. Hence and as the Consequence Argument asserts, we do stand powerless before the laws, their initiation, and history thereafter. Thus, it is beyond the ability of any single person or thing or set of such, to secure Caesar's not having crossed the Rubicon. Since he crossed necessarily, his having crossed cannot be undone. That is, nature's full set of necessary axioms fixes with necessity each of the theorems implied and, hence, whatever one does as a theorem so implied. We are impotent over history because the modality of history's initiation is to the modality of Spinozan laws as is the modality of the null set axiom to the modality of the other axioms of set theory. In each case, the modality at work is a kind of necessity—natural or mathematical, as the case may be. If we reside in a Spinozan world, we are powerless so to act that history would need be different. Although we may gullibly conceive of Caesar as not having crossed the Rubicon, that conceptual proclivity is our sad susceptibility to a cognitive illusion misrepresenting how history might have been. Conceivability is no window on possibility.[5] That Caesar crossed the Rubicon was, and remains, necessary under Spinozan determinism though we may be apt wrongly to represent it as possibly otherwise.

Aspirants to compatibilism who would grant Spinoza his day in philosophical court, permit his testimony that reference to the laws of nature is crucial to scientific explanation of why mundane things and events are as they are. These would-be compatibilists may also concede to Humeans that, as Lewis says, "all there is to the world is a vast mosaic of local matters of particular fact, just one little thing and then another" (Lewis 1986, ix–x). But Spinozans add that there is more to the tale than Lewisian talk of the mosaic tells. For Spinozans append that nature's laws are more robust than suspiciously supervenient Humean generalities expressed by polished published science. Rather, Spinozans assert that all the patterns and regularities framed within the mosaic somehow depend—*yes, in a manner that begs for explanation*—upon the laws. They suppose that, despite the exclusion of their evidently abstract and presumably objective laws from the mosaic, the laws nevertheless coherently constrain, restrict, and dictate the placement and properties of each mosaic-making piece. Spinozan laws, conceived as the descendants of Platonic forms and abstract properties, imperiously govern the concrete mosaic from which they are distinguished. Somehow—who knows how—Spinozan laws are to settle, and are not to be settled by, the distribution of tesserae within the mosaic. I am here—as I am, and you are where you are—as you are, because the laws so dictate. Though alienated from the physical objects and events they relentlessly rule, Spinozan laws nonetheless ensure whatever patterns or regularities the governed instantiate. This Spinozan perplexity certainly wants explanation. I lack it. But the Spinozan puzzle is on all fours with the general (and hence, Humean) quandary about supervenience. Exactly how and why does supervenience ever prevail? That the mosaic is to supervene on Spinozan laws baffles. But that baffle is no more baffling than is the supervenience of Humean laws on the same mosaic (Kim 1990 and 1992; Horgan 1993). Conversely echoing Lewis's remarks about Humean laws, Spinozans ought to admit that no difference is possible within the set-in-stone mosaic without an impossible difference in the governing laws (Lewis 1986; Loewer 2012). Thus, each Spinozan event occurs only as it can; whatever happens, happens exactly as it must in a Spinozan world. So, our actions are all inevitable under Spinozan determinism. If we should be so determined, then, in at least one clear sense, we would indeed be powerless to act otherwise. For somehow—but how—the abstract laws of nature conjoined with history do govern the world of the flesh by necessitation. Yes, governance of material things by abstract Spinozan law pleads for explanation. But so too does governance of abstract Humean laws by material things. Supervenience, regardless of its direction, puzzles both Spinozans and Humeans.

Granted our provisional alliance with Spinoza and naturalistic psychology's token or type identification of the mental with the material, all our mental states and cognitive processes arise within us of necessity. Thus, we are ultimately powerless over the psychic processes that the laws dragoon to ensure our actions (G. Strawson 1994). However, the very fact that we cannot escape our own psychology remarkably enables us to take the first stumbling step to be free to act otherwise.

## AUTHORIZATION AND THE LAWS OF COGNITION

Folk psychology teaches, and cognitive science allows, that contraltos correctly assert that normally we are—at the intentional level—the explanatory source of our actions. On those occasions mental health is intact while wild hormones and cruel addiction slumber. In that case, folk psychological or intentional level explanations of our actions advert only, or primarily, to those cascades of our various mental states that constitute episodes of practical reasoning (Fodor 1978; Dennett 1987). Sometimes the explanations rightly credit us with practical wisdom, reasoning well from what we justifiedly believe and what, all things considered, we properly and coherently prefer and desire (Frankfurt 1971; Lehrer 2004, 2016, 2020, and forthcoming). Other times, accurate explanations admit to our rational failures by pointing to encapsulated "quick and dirty" psychological processes that ignore relevant information antecedently stored. Then too, such explanations might acknowledge that we are prey to various fallacious ways of thinking that succumb to misleading biases or otherwise sin against ideal judgment, hallowed logic, or simple good sense (Wason 1968; Tversky and Kahneman 1974; Kahneman and Tversky 1979; Kahneman, Slovic, and Tversky 1982a; Fodor 1983 and 2001; Carruthers 2005 and 2006). Evidently, the complex psychological processes that guide our actions sometimes include weirdly inconsistent and antagonistic contentful states. Such states can conflict with our well-founded beliefs, coherent preferences, and normal desires by including various affective states, with adversarial valences and vectors, that can trump the will. Here are five examples in which a witness of your behavior might justifiably explain your action by attributing to you psychological states some of which override what would then seem to be your will:

(a) Nervous during your doctoral defense of your *The American Civil War*, you mean to answer a hostile examiner's question by saying "Kentucky failed successfully to secede." But instead, you nonsensically blurt "Kentucky successfully failed to succeed."

(b) Watching *Jaws* for the first time on the big screen in the crowded theatre, you know that no shark can harm you where you safely sit. But still, you leap in screaming terror to your feet when the image of the open-jawed star of the movie suddenly appears on the large screen from the dark depths below.

(c) You swore to yourself that you'd stick to your diet, but since your glucose level has suddenly plummeted far below normal range, the blueberry pie that was on your plate is now in your stomach.

(d) To win our high-stakes bet, you've determined not to blink when my ominous finger approaches your eye. But although you accept my solemn oath not to poke your eye, you still blink when you detect my harmless digit encroach upon your eye's no-fly zone.

(e) Afflicted with blindsight, you deny seeing the stimulus presented to you in the prevailing experimental context. Yet, when asked by the experimenter to ostend it and describe its shape, you correctly respond at rates well beyond chance (Weiskrantz 2009).

In the first case, your usually reliable mentally encoded lexicon failed under pressure to deliver the right output on cue. In the second, your well-educated memory erred by not deploying your knowledge of scenes and seas so as to thwart your misplaced terror. This though your stored education would certainly have delivered the right answer had you been queried about any present peril of shark attack. In the third, while suffusing you with silent shame with each savored swallow, your precipitous drop in blood sugar induced a sudden primitive urge that defeated your too-defeasible dietary pledge. In the fourth, your evolved visual pathways carried incoming information that ran roughshod over your firm plans and intentions. In the fifth, due to the lesions in your visual cortex you deny possessing information that your behavior betrays. These familiar cases illustrate the all too common and often introspectively manifest fact that our biologically realized psychology, whether necessitarian or not, sometimes enables our actions while simultaneously priming competing routes to alternative ways of behaving. For better or worse on such occasions, the prevailing conditions evidently—and presumably of necessity—elect the winning actions and reject the losers, with the vanquished sometimes including actions willed but defeated. After all, aren't we merely natural selection's current guess as how to build an ecologically tuned device so cued by affordances and invariances as to satisfy the canons of reason well enough to forward its genes (Gibson 1966 and 2015; Dennett 1983 and 1996; Fodor 1983 and 2001; Stich 1983; Smolensky 1988; Maloney 1987; Pollock 1995; Tooby and Cosmides 2015)?[6] For presumably our physically realized mental states—like all other kinds of tesserae in matter's mosaic—are in their lawful places and relations. *If* so, then each step in our typically complex (and only sometimes conscious) action-inducing deliberations is antecedently legislated. Granted that Spinoza supersedes Hume, all the complex sequences of action-launching cognitive moves we make, normal or not, are necessary. This, of course, applies to privileged cognitive processes that qualify as the complete explanatory psychological sources of actions contraltos claim to suffice for an agent's free or responsible action. It is only to be expected, then, that on some occasions our arrays of action-activating mental states include our defeated too-weak willings that run contrary to our ultimately activated actions. Folk psychological or intentional level explanations of our actions typically feature citations of our practical reasons, preferences, wants, willings, and decisions, while allowing that the cited sources need not be conscious or plain to introspection. And from its early days onward cognitive psychology has always taught that the psychic springs of our thoughts and actions typically include subconscious information bearing states of various sorts. Such hidden contributing causes evidently range over moods, biases, emotions, covert attendings to ambient information, and memories—all normally unavailable to public expression. Then too, concealed urges, aversions, and appetites might be swept into the overall deliberative process.[7]

Be that as it may, it clearly remains that on some introspective occasions and upon adopting the first-person perspective, one successfully explains one's own action by correctly, albeit fallibly, identifying it *as one's own* and citing as its source *one's own* psychological states. And such explanations sometimes do acknowledge the imperfect coherence of the states and attitudes said to be at work. So, for example, should you be an especially perspicuous introspecting rational agent unafflicted on the occasion by psychic incoherence or volitional conflict, you might correctly explain why you attended college thus:

> I attended the university because of my carefully developed detailed plan to achieve my well-considered interlocking desires, preferences, and goals. I will spare you the tedious details of my plan. I know that my planning process and plan itself are imposed upon me by psychology. But it is my plan—and indeed my psychology—nonetheless. Biology imposes my body on me. But I may yet identify with parts of my changing body. And so too, though psychology imposes my mind—the way I think and feel—on me, I may yet identify with parts of my changing mind and some ways in which I think and feel. That I so self-identify is unthreatened by any necessity with which biology and psychology conspire to incorporate me. I am both what is psychological and corporeal regardless that each array is, if you like, imposed upon me by the laws of nature, whether psychological or biological.[8] The laws of arithmetic impose upon 4 that necessarily it is identical with 2+2. And so too, just as it is the case that I properly identify 4 with, and as, 2+2, that I identify myself with who and what I am, as I am, is undisturbed by any necessity that may make me so.

Typical first-person intentional level explanations of one's actions need not profess to much detail while confessing to recondite elements and abduced covert components. Nevertheless, such explanations might thereby cite an action's contraltos-source as one's own well adopted and properly deployed sequence of propositional and practical attitudes (Evans 1982; Davidson 2001a; Dennett 1987). But in any case, these autobiographical accounts may testify to not only the contralto-source of the author's actions but to that author's *authorization* of both the source and its action. Those who—by so citing their contralto approved cognition—correctly explain and coinciden-tally prefer their own actions are the self-professed *authorizing authors* of their actions (Frankfurt 1982; Watson 2003; David Shoemaker 2003 and 2015; Lehrer 1990, 2004, 2016, 2020, and forthcoming). This extends to first-person accounts of one's infelicitous behavior of the sorts illustrated by the examples (a)–(e) above. One might truthfully admit, "Yes, I own those goofy and maybe shameful psychological episodes. I was their source. So, though it is embarrassing, I authored and authorized them in the same way in which I author and authorize those of my actions that show me in a better light. I am what I am. And thus, for better and for worse, I am the authorizing author of my specified, even if regretted, actions."

We can usefully extend this notion of authorization. Agents are authors of the *autobiographies* composed in the form of their first-person citations of the various efficacious propositional and practical attitudes to which they testify. Granted that cognitive science is mostly on target, the propositional and prac-tical attitudes to which such correct explanations of actions refer are realized by computationally connected contentful mental representations. As chapter 1, section 1 notes, contesting models of such representations might cast them as would connectionists, as homogeneous networked nodes with many vari-ably and fluidly weighted connections (Smolensky 1988). Alternatively and as—for heuristic purpose—we previously supposed, mental representations might be viewed as Mentalese sentences in the Fodorian fashion urged by the language of thought hypothesis. If we may be permitted the continuing luxury of Mentalese to portray an agent, then imagine your dancing partner who adopts the first-person perspective toward herself and the second-person perspective toward you. She believes herself to be dancing with you. She would do so by doxastically tokening *I AM DANCING WITH YOU* within her cognitive system. Now consider the sequence of Mentalese representations realizing all of one's relevant attitudes fit for citation in one's first-person explanation of one's lifetime actions. That would amount to one's psycho-logically rendered autobiography encoded in Mentalese. It is, as it were, a version of one's own life story, a tale of how and why one sometimes acted as one did. Selected passages in such a covert Mentalese narrative encoded in an agent are available to contraltos to count as authorizing sources of some of her actions that are free and laden with responsibility (Frankfurt 1969; Fischer and Ravizza 1998; Velleman 2006; Fischer 2009, chap. 10; Lehrer 2011, p. 14; Lehrer, 1990, pp. 85–86; Lehrer, forthcoming; Campbell and Lehrer 2018, 230; McKenna 2013; Sartorio 2016).

Necessitarians too can welcome the notion that we may be autobiographers of the nearly, but not quite, sort described above. For they may be apt to question the implication from autobiographer to authorizer. Necessitarians roughly say that psychology is the sum of governing laws that necessitate all agential attitudes and their realizing mental representations.[9] Granted necessitarianism, the very Mentalese encoding of each mental representation is inevitable. Hence, Mentalese narrations cannot be other than they are. If psychology is as necessitarians suppose, it would seem that an encoding agent is no genuine author at all but merely a pen in the palm of psychology. The agent's system of representation would be simply a blank page awaiting the laws' dictation. Thus, generous necessitarians may grant that the source of an agent's action on an occasion may be her computationally arrayed practical attitudes correctly cited in her Mentalese autobiography. Nonetheless, all necessitarians add that since those attitudes, as inscribed, owe their inscription to the laws of thought, their citation in explanations of behavior is explanatorily shallow. Hence, psychic inscriptions neither fully explain nor genuinely authorize the actions they induce.[10] One's Mentalese autobiography, if governed by nature's laws, would no more authorize or liberate an action it produces than does the software that explains the printing of a text that, once printed, effectively mandates an action. My computer's software might cause my printer to display "Dance!" And that inscription might incite me to dance. But nonetheless, that controlling printed imperative does not authorize my dancing. The deontically disinterested laws of nature—including psychology—do not enable an agent's authorization of those of her actions lawfully explained. So, necessitarians may reason that if software-driven printings do not authorize the actions they trigger, neither do law-governed Mentalese autobiographies authorize the actions they induce. Rather, given necessitarianism, such psychic flotsam in the shallows of intentional psychology is doomed to be swept away by the rising tide of matured psychology's idiom unadulterated by reference to fictitious propositional attitudes and their fishy representations (Paul Churchland 1979 and 1992; Patricia Churchland 1989). Although that purified language is yet to be developed, it promises to be cast in the language and terminology destined to be common to the basic sciences when they supplant intentional psychology. If so, the agent would seem not to authorize her action by way of any of her first-person attitudes regarding her practical reasons. In that case, a rightly sourced action would be neither one for which the agent is contralto-responsible nor one she undertakes freely. One's authorization of one's action seems to require more than autobiography if the biographer is merely a humanly realized printer the output of which is dictated by the algorithm of Spinozan psychology (Kane 1999).

But surely this necessitarian complaint is short of compelling. It controversially depends upon the reasonably contested and certainly controversial elimination of intentional level psychology from the structure of the sciences (Fodor 1974 and 1987; Horgan and Woodward 1985; Baker 1987; Rosenberg 1994; Lehrer, forthcoming). Recall too from chapter 1 that among our provisional assumptions already noted is the working hypothesis that radical eliminativism is false. And so, with the arguments of the defenders of folk psychology in mind, we ought here to rehearse our admittedly contestable claim that intentional level psychological explanations have a place in science even if only as situated in the special sciences immune to classical reduction. Granted that, we can set aside the necessitarian concern about authorization.

But beyond the above plea for the preservation of folk-psychological explanation, we might secure an agent's authorization of her Mentalese autobiography by reflecting on the semantics of the concepts in play. For consider the logic of the concepts expressed by "author" and "authorization" in their literal contexts as applied to published authors and their copywritten texts. Even if the laws of nature should have necessitated Mark Twain's composing *The Adventures of Huckleberry Finn*, Twain certainly *authored* the book and *authorized* its publication. It is important to notice here that to say that Twain authored the book is really to say that the writing of the book was the effect of a complex array of Twain's mental states constituting the practical reasoning he realized over time and with which he is to be identified. No matter how we should cast determinism, it is simply a bald literary fact—and no legitimate intellectual property court would rule against it— that Twain not only authored the book but also, by dint of authoring and publishing it, authorized it. That is why, legally, Twain is both entitled to claim the copyright and liable to answer complaints against his book. The same would seem to apply to a person and her plan regardless of whether we portray determinism as Humean or Spinozan. If so, she would be the authorizing author of her autobiography though her psychic authoring be naturally necessary owing to Spinozan determinism. To see that this must be right, imagine an agent who, by publishing it in her native language, expresses the content of her mental autobiography. If, under necessitarianism, Twain authors and authorizes his story, then our imagined agent is the authorizing author of her public story. But that public memoir is the same tale (translated into natural language) as the psychologically encoded story (represented in Mentalese) from which it originated. Hence, the agent is the authorizing author of the original psychic rendition of her mental autobiography. Therefore, in what follows I shall suppose that though the laws of nature and their implicants should be necessary, by authoring her psychic autobiography, an agent does indeed authorize it. I shall proceed to contend that authorization of the sort implicated in freedom of the will under the provisional assumptions in hand requires a certain kind of autobiography, one that honestly recounts one's resistance to nature's dictation.

Some may complain that my above dismissal of the necessitarian complaint about authorization is too hasty. Complainants might object thus: Imagine an ideally rational agent in a necessitarian world who knows that psychology so governs her that all her thoughts occur necessarily. Assume too that she understands herself well. She introspectively and correctly attributes to herself those of her practical attitudes coherently adopted and warranted in the light of her optimal reasoning. She knows the psychological source of her actions. Grant too, that her introspective self-attributions are physically realized in the form of first-person Mentalese representations of the kind appropriate to autobiography. Such a true Mentalese autobiography would, *if complete*, include the author's admission or confession of impotence pertaining to how she reasons or thinks whether in theoretical or practical mode. It is as if *I AM NOT RESPONSIBLE FOR WHAT I WRITE* were part of her autobiography. And that would seem to undermine the hypothesis that she authorizes what she mentally authors in a way compatibilism might hope. Much the same point evidently emerges under Spinozan psychology if, as individual persons, we are properly identical on occasions with representations within our cognitive systems. For from the necessitarian perspective we are like the range of a mathematical function. The range is nothing but a sequence of numbers each element of which is entirely and necessarily determined by the function's domain. The range has no power over its constituting members; as a set it owes its identity to the function's domain. And we too, as systems or sequences of representationally realized propositional and practical attitudes, would be merely the passive repositories of representations encoded in us in accordance with the Spinozan laws of cognition. If so, we are powerless over the sequenced representationally realized attitudes that identify the persons we are. For the mental states with which we may be identified are selected for us by psychology just as the members of a function's range are selected by the function's application to its domain. Thus, if determinism should be necessitarian, we are ultimately powerless over what we think, who we are, and the characters we take ourselves to be.[11] Since our identifying mental states all arise necessarily, with none of our practical attitudes admitting of omission or tolerating alternatives, necessitarianism might deny that any such alternative attitudes flicker with possibility (Fischer 1994, 134–47). Where in that rigid arrangement is there room for genuine authorization? Would not, then, an agent who doxastically tokens in her Mentalese autobiography *I AUTHORIZE WHAT I WRITE* encode what is false? So, must not a committed necessitarian despair of authorization and the chance for freedom it would promise? Must the disappointed necessitarian admit, with a nod to Luther's dictum, "Hier stehe Ich. Ich kann nicht anders. Denn kann Ich nicht anders denken."

I think that the case for authorization and compatibilism is not as dire as the above cornered source compatibilist might fear. For though Spinozan psychology may utterly enslave us by necessitating the conformance of our attitudes and actions—and hence our psychic autobiography—with its prescriptions, we may yet be free and responsible thanks, surprisingly, to the peculiar logic of predicate modifiers adapted and applied to agents who would resist the laws that govern them. But to see why, we must turn to the logic of "almost."

## THE LOGIC OF "ALMOST"

Generally, but not always, almost enough is—by implication—simply not enough. Should I have only ninety-nine pennies, I almost have—and, thus, do not have—one dollar's worth of coin. As a rough rule of thumb, *"almost"* almost always functions logically as a negating predicate modifier (Clark 1970). However, the rule is curiously pliant and bends as the mischievous modifier's variable contexts may require. For in some contexts to which we are remarkably sensitive, this semantically plastic modifier's valence flips from negative to positive so as to signal the satisfaction of the predicate *sans* modifier. In such atypical—often broadly normative—contexts almost enough is indeed enough—maybe only barely enough—for what really counts then and there in the moment. This semantic fact figures centrally in the way in which, by my lights, compatibilism comports with necessitarianism. For, as I shall argue, in the special case of freedom of the will in a necessitarian world, our contextually sensitive freedom to act otherwise depends upon what is at stake and the decisive actions we individually and collectively take. I contend that by being the authorizing cognitive source of some such actions we rebel—unsuccessfully yet significantly—against the necessitating laws that determine our thoughts, characters, and actions so as to make us who we are. A rebel's doomed nomic rebellion, if authoritatively sourced in something like the way *contraltos* may prescribe and included in the insurgent's psychic autobiography, suffices for the rebel to be almost as free as *sopranos* require. And that, I contend, is enough to be as free as both sopranos and contraltos, once converted to necessitarianism, should sing that we are. By being so defiant as almost to shed her nomic shackles, an agent almost liberates herself from nature's supposed Spinozan governance and—I say—thereby becomes free in a fashion fit for responsibility. Almost free is free enough to be free. That, anyway, is the core of the edition of compatibilism the foundation of which I now proceed to lay.

## CONTEXT OF OCCURRENCE

Those unintimidated by the contextually colored logic of predicate modifiers may immediately scoff. For if unpersuaded by Quine's critique of
analyticity, they might popularly insist that, *analytically*, for any predicate,
*F*, whatever is almost *F* is, simply and absolutely not *F* (Quine 1951; Grice
and Strawson 1956). Surely, they say, the meaning of "almost" implies that
the adverb must negate. Once applied to its hosting predicate, doesn't the
sheer logic of *almost* ensure the host's negation? Isn't that an *a priori* or
conceptual truth denied only at the cost of ridicule? After all, consider a
naïve child who is ignorant of currency but adept in English semantics. The
child is able correctly to infer that Mother doesn't yet have a dollar—whatever that is—upon knowing that the parent has only almost a dollar. And if
a child without a penny in her pocket is that smart, wouldn't she be right to
conclude—and might not a philosopher insist—that whoever is only almost
free is not yet free?

But the scoffer's scorn is far too facile. For the skeptic ignores the importance of information that may be pragmatically carried by a true declarative
statement in the particular context of its occurrence as various examples
demonstrate (Lewis 1983c).

Consider a vast plain extending forward from the base of the alluvial
fan of a ragged mountain range set off on the north by the range's sheer
dog-tooth cliffs. The plain, in stark contrast to the abrupt mountains and in
gentle comparison to the unhurried fan, is flat (Unger 1971 and 1975, 65–66;
Dretske 1981a). On that we—and accurate maps—may all prudently concur.
Yes, of course, should we be overly cautious, we might want to qualify our
concurrence, admitting—after tedious measurements—that the plain does
roll a tiny but insignificant bit. The plain's patient topology varies less than
negligibly to the seasoned hiker's eye. The actual mean, median and mode
difference above sea level between any pair of points on the plain converge
near zero. That Lilliputian measure of central tendency contrasts starkly with
the large and obvious difference between the highest and lowest peaks in the
serrated range. Really and precisely—nit now cautiously, but consistently,
picked—the plain is *almost flat*. And yet so different is the almost flat plain
from the contrasting mountains that in most communicative contexts and
without explicit hedging qualification, we may correctly and informatively
say—and our trusty maps may also represent—that the plain is flat. Period.
We can have it both ways: almost flat, as well as flat. That's how things are
correctly represented in the casual parlance of geography and the more formal representations of cartography, though that need not be how the same
things are, or ought to be, represented within fussy geology relying on its
finely calibrated instruments.[12] If our circumstances are not ordinary and

our geologically tuned interests on the occasion worry about the slimmest deviations in elevation across the plain, then we may truthfully whisper to our colleagues in that science that the plain is merely almost flat and, hence, not flat. So long as the joint cost of representation and computation remains cheap, we might match every deviation our persnickety devices detect with a matching mark on a map, a point on a graph, or a sentence in a geological tome. In principle, but not in practice, we might mar our topological maps with increasingly inscrutable—because ever too densely packed—contour lines. And we might waste ink and pages in our books with tedious bits of uselessly dense and utterly idle information. But if our interests are normal and the costs of augmenting representation and computation escalate ineffi-ciently, then we may acknowledge—but ignore—that the plain is only almost flat. Normally, practical wisdom prevails. If wise, then upon acknowledging that the plain is almost flat, we should be apt truthfully to add—and prudently to trade upon the fact—that being almost flat is flat enough for *this plain* to be flat in *our prevailing communicative context*. That's enough to be flat for a token of its geographic kind under typical representational constraints. Situ-ated as it is and as measured in the manner that both good sense and practical science commend, this particular almost-flat plain is simply flat. The plain, in its place, satisfies the truth conditions that a realistic semantics for the context demands (Austin, Urmson, and Warnock 1979-03-06a; Barwise and Perry 1983; Maloney, 2013).

None of this is to say that our interests or preferences determine in a nasty relativistic fashion whether the plain is flat. We cannot make the plain be flat merely by believing or asserting so. Rather, my claim is that the prevailing circumstances may determine it is in our interest to act upon the fact that the plain is flat. That the plain is a token of its geographic kind *permits* this almost flat plain (in contrast to the toothy mountain range with which it dif-fers in kind) to be flat, flat full stop. Indeed, that the plain is just such a token of its kind in its particular situation pragmatically implies or otherwise car-ries the information that it is flat. *In situ*, this particular plain is almost flat. As such, it is so similar to flat things of its kind that, in the reigning context, good judgment and practical reason recognize the fact that it is flat enough to be flat. Indeed, given the context, a sound system of representation would be entitled to represent the plain as flat without fear of falsification. That's why an accurate map of the terrain made by a good cartographer for standard purposes may rightly represent the plain as flat. And that is why this particular plain—being the kind of thing that it is and situated as it is in the mundane mosaic—is flat.

Logicians and poets differ in kind from geographic sorts of things such as plains. A logician, such as Abelard, or poet, such as Eloise, who is almost the best of his or her kind is just not the best. Someone else is better. A plain, however, may be almost flat without there being any plain flatter or flatter in ways that matter. For the logic of predicate modifiers is sensitive to the properties predicated by the predicates modified in their contexts of occurrence. That logic resonates to the kind, character and, yes, the context-constituting relations of the subjects of such modified predication. The plain under discussion exists in partnership with, and so is differentiated from, the rugged mountains and the intervening fan. The recognition that the plain is just so situated sanctions in part the contextually sensitive sound inference from its being almost flat to the conclusion of its being flat. Thus, may a qualified cartographer rightly represent the plain as flat while depicting the fan as rutted and the mountain as ragged, all on the same coherent map or in her correct published survey report.

So, "almost" only almost always negates. Whether it does depends in some contextually or pragmatically determined ways that refuse comprehensive specification in any useful text offering instruction about English predicates and their modifiers. But while no good manual for English can enumerate the contexts to which English statements resonate, native speakers of the language are amazingly—but in ways we poorly understand—adept at understanding in real time statements relative to the uncountably many possible contexts in which they occur. Were it not for that uncanny ability, we would be unable to appreciate jokes or metaphors. Plausibly, the context in which "almost" occurs as a predicate modifier in a tokened declarative sentence of simple subject/predicate form contributes to the determination of that token's truth conditions. However, despite the barges of ink bled on the subject since Austin, Grice, and Searle filled their pens, no one yet knows how generally to characterize either what counts as the relevant context of a contextually sensitive declaration or its range of pragmatic implications (Searle 1969; Austin 1975; Bach and Harnish 1979; Barwise and Perry 1983; Grice 1989; Kaplan 1989). Certainly, no one knows how we predicators are able remarkably to find on the fly the needle—what's relevant to interpreting a tokened sentence—in the infinite haystack of possibilities. Nonetheless, it remains that some predications do rely on their contexts for the determination of what the worldly conditions must be in order that the predications be true. And that, anyway, is the hunch I am chasing.[13]

## SOCIAL CONTEXT

The case of the almost flat plain illustrates that in some contexts some things that almost meet a mark thereby suffice to meet the mark. Once we appreciate this example of the sufficiency of "almost," other examples come to mind.

Consider social artifacts: According to traffic laws, a stop sign is a red octagon of specified dimensions and signed with "STOP" in solid white lettering in designated font. But measure any randomly selected sign planted by the authorities at an intersection that not only looks as if it fits the bill but also reliably causes motorists to stop. Cops normally ticket those they catch not stopping there, and fair judges deny appeals of the properly cited. By hypothesis, the weary sentinel is in fact a functioning stop sign. But is the aged and dented sign at which you too may have stopped exactly octagonal? Was it ever? Likely not, though it once probably approximated an octagon about as well as any that the certified factory ever produced. The actual dented and slightly bent sign *in situ* is almost octagonal. Though the sign's dominant sun-bleached two colors are no longer—if ever—quite the shades of red and white the State mandates, they almost once met the chromatic standard away from which they have since drifted over the years. The lettering when applied in the factory may have been solid, but the word on the sign has long been pocked and scarred by gravel tossed by spinning tires. So, the somewhat deformed sign is almost octagonal, almost red, almost "STOP"-signed. It is almost a stop sign. Yet, by approximating—but not meeting—the standard for such signs, it actually is one. So, it is both almost octagonal and octagonal, both almost red and red, both almost "STOP"-signed and "STOP"-signed. Otherwise, it would not be what we all know it to be, namely a stop sign. Thus, being only almost *F* does not imply—analytically or otherwise—being not *F*. Sometimes being almost *F* is enough to be *F*. The logic of predicate modifiers is tricky.

## PHENOMENAL CONTEXT

What about the phenomenal character of mental states? Functionalism rules the psychological sciences and type identifies mental states—always physically realized—by their holistically characterized causal or computational relations to stimuli, other mental states, and behaviors including actions (Putnam 1960 and 1967; Fodor 1975; Block 1980a; Lewis 1983a). Functionalists recognize that so identifying mental types risks naïve psychological chauvinism. Lewis, for one, wonders about the possibility of the "madman" who, because he is your internal physical twin, occasionally feels just as you do when you suffer searing pain of the sort caused in you by application of a scorching flame to your hand (Lewis, 1983b). However, the madman's physically duplicative internal state oddly differs relationally from yours in virtue of its peculiar causal connections to stimuli, other mental states, and behaviors. Your internal state, but not his, plays the causal role typical of such states in creatures of your common humankind. However, while your normally flame-triggered state causes you and most other humans to wince, retreat, complain, and adopt avoidance plans, his otherwise caused abnormal state prompts him to giggle, scratch his leg, recite Eliot's "The Wasteland," and consider how to improvise at the piano. Your edition, but not his, of your common physical state actually plays the causal role typical in humans. If, as a naïve functionalist would propose, mental states should be identified by their actual dispositions to relate to stimuli, other mental states, and behaviors, then—but contrary to the hypothesis—you and your mad twin would not both be in the same kind of agonizingly painful conscious mental state.

To correct naïve functionalism, Lewis notes that the madman's duplicative physical state is actually an instance or token of the kind of state tokens of which in humans normally play the role that *your state* actually plays. Your mad twin's token of your common kind of physical state is indeed fit or apt to play—but in fact fails to play—the very same role that your state plays. His causal circuitry, but not yours, is abnormal. That is why a sophisticated functionalist may say that you and the madman are in the same mental state. Both you and your physical twin are in tokens of the same sort of psychological state in the sense that you both are in a state tokens of which are apt normally to play a certain psychological role. Your tokens of the state, but not his, actually play that role. Although various of your twin's tokened mental states are fit to play the same roles as do yours, his happen to play a different role in him. Perhaps an intuitive way of framing Lewis's correction to naïve functionalism would be to say that the madman feels pain exactly as you do because his materially duplicative state almost plays the same role that your state actually plays. You and he are, as Lewis says, both members of the same population (or natural kind). Contingently, you are normal, while he is not. That is to say, were his tokened physical state yours rather than his, it would play in you the role such states normally play. Your mad twin is almost in pain because he is almost like you. And that he is almost psychologically like you, if Lewis is right, is just enough to make him psychologically like suffering you. Thus, since you feel pain, so too does he. Once again, almost enough is enough.

## COGNITIVE CONTEXT

Consider the cognitive, as opposed to the phenomenal, side of psychology, still functionally characterized. Functionalists typically maintain that propositional and practical attitudes are representational states, states consisting of physically realized contentful mental representations, maybe language-like but maybe not. Above we adopted the hypothesis of the language of thought according to which the content and type identity of a Mentalese representation—that is *ELECTRON*—is to be determined by the way in which it functions—that is its conceptual role within its cognitive system. Thus, if *ELECTRON* is a mental representation in your cognitive system, that it then means the same as "electron" is settled by the way in which you are inclined to employ it. Being a renowned physicist, you are apt to token *NEGATIVELY CHARGED* after deploying *ELECTRON*. However, since I am your unfledged acolyte, I am not yet disposed to exploit my *ELECTRON* in the same sophisticated ways as are you. Like you, I am inclined to issue *PARTICLE* in reaction to tokening *ELECTRON*. But unlike you, I am not yet—and maybe will never be—inclined to go as far and wide with our shared premise as are you. The role that *ELECTRON* plays in me isn't quite the role it plays in you. Nevertheless, since the representation's role in me approximates its role in you, it means the same in me as it does in you. Otherwise, but contrary to fact, what you and I think would be incommensurable (Kuhn 1962; Davidson 1973; Stich 1983). If I almost use *ELECTRON* as do you, then in me it means the same as it means in you. But, per functionalist hypothesis, sameness in such meaning or content requires sameness in conceptual role. Hence that my *ELECTRON* is content-similar to yours—that mine almost has the same role as yours—suffices for mine having the same role as yours. You think about electrons when you issue *ELECTRON*, and so do I when I issue the same. Almost enough, once again, is enough.

## MATHEMATICAL CONTEXT

Going beyond our previous examples of the contextually sensitive logic of "almost," and perhaps crucially for our case, we turn to a corner of mathematics: Suppose $\Phi$ is a perfect Euclidean circle with area $\alpha$ and radius $r$. Assume *r = 2 inches. Thus, $\alpha = \pi 2^2$.* Of course, $\pi$ is irrational. Suppose the final examination you've set for your students requires them to compute $\alpha$. Good student Zelda takes $\pi$ to be 3.14, puts her pencil to paper, and identifies $\alpha$ as 12.56. But apple-polisher Zach, armed with his permitted calculator, takes $\pi$ to be 3.1415926535 and identifies $\alpha$ as 12.56637061.

Who's right? 12.56 is almost $\alpha$. And so is 12.56637061. Surely, you should and rightly would give each student full credit, even if Zach complains that his answer is better than Zelda's. Each of the values to which their respective answers refer is almost the area of the circle, and each answer results from unerring application of the same certified procedure. Those two facts should induce you, charitable but fair teacher that you are, to recognize that each student is correct, that *in the prevailing context each of the values designated by the students is* equal to $\alpha$. Surely, relative to the students' situation, each answer correctly identifies $\alpha$.

Same point differently put: Arguably, possession of a property can be contextually sensitive. The current boiling point of a pot of water depends upon the atmospheric pressure at the pot's place. At sea level, water's boiling point is 212 degrees Fahrenheit but only 198 degrees at 8,000 feet higher. So, two samples of boiling water can both have the property, *B*, of boiling, though in one sample *B* may be identical with *being 212 degrees* while in the other *B* may be identical with *being 198 degrees*. From this and the symmetry and transitivity of identity, it impossibly follows that *being at 212 degrees* is identical with *being at 198 degrees*. Of course, we can easily deflect the contradiction by making explicit the too casually suppressed reference to the samples' different elevations while also remarking on the overall context that tempers our statement. So, we amend, soberly saying that—*in the context of boiling water—being at 212 degrees at sea level* is identical with *being at 198 degrees at 8,000 feet*.

Mathematical identity is a property. So, it too might be contextually sensitive. Consequently, with Geach's (1967) notion of relative identity in mind and with deference to Lewis on the importance of contextual plasticity (Lewis 1983c), we may allow *in the implicit context* of the students' examination that both[14]

(i)   $\alpha = 12.56$

and

(ii)   $\alpha = 12.56637061$.

So, *in that same silent context*, if identity should be symmetric and transitive, then

(iii)   $12.56 = 12.56637061$!

But you won't be dissuaded from grading your students each as correct. For you know that (iii)'s implicit prevailing buffering context is their important examination. It imposes on you, the teacher, the duty to assess your students in a manner sensitive to their abilities under the pressures and constraint of the tough test. In that context the fact *that 12.56 = 12.5663706* is just the fact *that 12.56 and 12.56637061 each so closely approximate α that any difference between them makes no difference—no relevant or practical difference—at all*. That each is almost α is enough that each be α relative to the reigning context. In other words, *12.56 is the same correct solution to α's identity as is 12.56637061*.[15]

We can reinforce the lesson of Zelda and Zach by noticing that, in a clear sense, they each are idealists. For each asymptotically pursues the elusive, because impossible, ideal of exactly identifying $a$, $\Phi$'s fugitive area. They do this by faithfully applying, though to different lengths, their common trusty algorithm. Like Sisyphus, they are on an impossible trek. They too may know that what they aspire to do is beyond accomplishment. Certainly, Zach's overly zealous answer, excessively running to eight decimal places, more closely approximates the ideal than Zelda's temperate solution. Clearly, however, it is not mere proximity to the goal that matters most. For consider fanatical Waldo who overshoots, but not by much, the mark. Like Zelda but unlike Zach, Waldo relies on his pencil to compute the circle's area. Yet like Zach, Waldo takes $\pi$ to be 3.1415926535. However, Waldo mistakenly scribbles his way through the multiplication. He exceeds the mark a wee bit and, to his discredit, submits 12.56637062. Zach, Zelda, and Waldo deliver their answers to you, still the teacher. Zach's and Waldo's answers are closer to the exact area of the circle than is Zelda's. But whereas both Zelda and Zach correctly chugged through the arithmetic, Waldo fell off the rails at the end. Recognizing this, you will prefer Zelda's answer to Waldo's. If you are charitable but fair, you'll score Zelda and Zach the same but ding Waldo. So, whereas each student is almost right, only Zelda and Zach manage thereby to be right.[16] Zelda and Zach kept to the asymptotic curve to be ridden in pursuit of their common goal. Though Zach rode the curve further than Zelda, each rode far enough and within its bound. Waldo did not. By doing what they did, Zelda and Zach achieved what Waldo failed to accomplish. That Zelda and Zach computed as prescribed by geometry figures crucially in whether they achieved their common goal, whether they did in fact complete their assignment. Luck is not enough for achievement. Consider their classmates, Lucky Lucey and Cheater Charley. Lucey simply guesses that $a = 12.56$ without computing at all. Her guess is the same as Zelda's correctly completed computation. And Charley surreptitiously copied Zach's submission. Knowing the histories of Lucey's and Charlie's submission, you would be obliged to deny them any credit. For the assignment was to compute the circle's area. Zelda and Zach each did that, but neither Lucey nor Charlie did. Achievement demands more than luck, and it refuses cheating. It requires getting the goal in the right way. Context somehow determines when almost enough is success enough and achievement enough. Sometimes, how you try to do what you can't gets you so close that you almost do the impossible. And if you almost do the impossible in just the right way, what you almost do might, in your context, suffice for doing the impossible. This, as we shall see, is why we can act freely even if we act necessarily. Freedom of the will is an achievement by those who manage to free themselves from nature's shackles. But it may not be an achievement by all.

# NOTES

1. The immutability of history entails Fischer's formulation of what he calls the Principle of the Fixity of the Past, namely

> for any action Y, agent S, and time t, if it is true that if S were to do Y at t, some fact about the past relative to t would not have been a fact, then S cannot at t do Y at t. (Fischer 1994, 78)

In his argument for incompatibilism, Holliday defends Fischer's principle, reformulated thus:

> For any action y, agent s, and times t and t' (t ≤ t'), if it is true that if s were to do y at t', the past relative to t would (have to) be different, then s cannot at t do y at t'.

Holliday ingeniously argues that the past is immutably fixed under the assumption that the laws of nature govern, rather than merely supervene upon, actual regularities. For granted that miracles are impossible and that the laws govern, every actual event is of the type such that its omission or alternation in any possible world is inconsistent with the history of that world (Holliday 2012, pp.182–84, 191–94, and 201–03).

2. As previously noted, for necessitarianism see Kneale 1950; Dretske 1977; Tooley 1977; Kripke 1980; Armstrong 1983; Fales 1990 and 1993; Carroll 1987 and 1994; Swoyer 1982; Sydney Shoemaker 1998; Fine 2002; Bigelow, Ellis and Lieres 2004; and Holliday 2012. Consider Schaffer (2005) and Wilson (2013) for their contrary assessments of selected editions of necessitarianism.

3. Slote (1982, pp. 10 and 22–25) doubts that the necessity of Spinozan laws, even if attached to the past, is both agglomerative and closed under implication. He writes on page 10,

> Anyone who assumes the validity of arguing from 'Np' and 'N(p ⊃ q)' to 'Nq' would seem to be tacitly assuming that the necessity expressed in the operator 'N' is both agglomerative (closed with respect to conjunction introduction) and closed under logical implication, so that one can, e.g., validly move from 'Np' and 'N(p ⊃ q)' to 'N(p·p ⊃ q)' and from the latter to 'Nq'. If we do not think about these subinferences, when we move from 'Np' and 'N(p ⊃ q )' to 'Nq' or assert the main modal principle that corresponds to that larger inference, that is only because it is so natural to assume that any necessity operator will have the properties of agglomerativity and closure under logical implication or entailment.

While I recognize the basis of Slote's doubt, I am working under the assumption that the modality featured in various versions of the Consequence Argument sustains the validity of the inference.

4. Suspend the question whether the laws are time symmetric or time-reversal invariant (Ismael 2016, 153–61).

5. Here, by way of reductio ad absurdum, is why conceivability does not imply possibility, where $\Diamond$ and $\Box$ are respectively the familiar S5 modal operators for possibility and necessity as applied to (nominalized) sentences or propositions.

(a)  You conceive that p (Assumption)

(b) Therefore, ◇p (from (a) and the thesis for reductio: conceivability implies possibility)

(c) I conceive that □~p (Assumption)

(d) Therefore, ◇□~p (From (c) and the thesis for reductio: conceivability implies possibility)

(e) Therefore, □~p (From (d) and S5)

(f) Therefore, ~◇~~p (From (e) and S5)

(g) Therefore, ~◇p (From (f) and S5)

(h) Therefore, ◇p and ~◇p (From (b) and (g))

(i) Therefore, the thesis for reductio is false (From (h) and reductio ad absurdum)

6. See Carruthers's discussion of his dual aspect theory (inspired by the work of Milner and Goodale) of how perception contributes to the rational formation of propositional and practical attitudes that control action in real time (Milner and Goodale 1995; Carruthers 2005, chap. 6; Maloney 2018, 152–59; Goodale and Milner 2013).

7. For a glimpse of the compelling relevant literature on the complexity of pervasive cryptic mental processes, see Sperling 1960; Neisser 1967; Lackner and Garrett 1972; Shepard and Cooper 1982; Marr 1982; Coltheart 1980; Pylyshyn 1984; Libet 1985; Dennett and Kinsbourne 1992; Clark 1993; Milner and Goodale 1995; Schacter 2001; Peacocke 2001; Carruthers 2005; Block 2007; Siegel 2010; Phillips 2011; Nadel and Sinnott-Armstrong 2012; Goodale and Milner 2013; and Maloney 2018, chaps. 4 and 8.

8. Compare Frankfurt's remarks on the conditions under which a person may identify with some subset of those of her psychological states that she does, or is apt to, endorse (Frankfurt 1988, 60ff.).

9. This is only approximately correct. For presumably psychology is the residual sum of the laws governing thought and action from which the principles of the more basic natural and complementing social sciences have been redacted.

10. In a characteristically insightful passage, Chisholm remarked that if a person should be distinct from—not identified with—her action-causing beliefs and desires (i.e., what here we consider to be her will or action-inducing practical reasoning), then she would not be responsible for (and not free to do) what she does. However, in contrast to Chisholm's distinction between a person and her operant reasoning, it is my thought that a person is to be identified with selected bits of her practical reasoning. Here is a bit of what Chisholm instructively wrote about an agent under the supposition that responsibility enabling freedom requires the power to act otherwise than one actually does:

> But now if the act which he [the agent] did perform was also an act that it was also in his power not to perform, then it could not have been caused or determined by any event that was not itself within his power either to bring about or not to bring about. . . . If a flood caused the poorly constructed dam to break, then, given the flood and the constitution of the dam, the break, we may say, had to occur and nothing could have happened in its place. And if the flood of desire caused the weak-willed man to give in, then he, too, had to do just what it was that he did do and he was no more responsible than was the dam

for the results that followed. (It is true, of course, that if the man is responsible for the beliefs and desires that he happens to have, then he may also be responsible for the things they lead him to do. But the question now becomes: is he responsible for the beliefs and desires he happens to have? If he is, then there was a time when they were within his power either to acquire nor not to acquire, and we are left, therefore, with our general point). (Chisholm 1989, 6)

11. This, if humans do in fact have characters (Harman 1999 and 2000; Doris 2002; Annas 2011; Kamtekar 2004; Russell 2009).

12. Recall Carnap's (1950) notion of objective, scientific frameworks according to which the propositions they embed admit of truth values and truth conditions only in the context of the theoretical frameworks or conceptual schemes to which they are assigned.

13. The mystifying ability of competent speakers to detect a sentence's context of occurrence would seem to be tantamount to their ability to solve the notorious frame problem described by Dennett (1978a and 2006), Fodor (1983), and Pylyshyn (1987). Those with at least one lifetime to spare and curious about our sensitivity to context will want to consider the literature in the joint domain of pragmatics and epistemic contextualism exemplified, among others, by Recanati (2010), Cohen (1986 and 2013), DeRose (1992 and 1999), Sosa (2000), Rysiew (2002), Maloney (2013), and Conee (2013).

14. Also see Griffin (1977).

15. Perhaps Geach would put (iii) this way: 12.56 is the same properly computed area of $\Phi$ as 12.56637061. For he begins his influential but contested essay thus:

I am arguing for the thesis that identity is relative. When one says "x is identical with y," this, I hold, is an incomplete expression; it is short for "x is the same A as y," where "A" represents some count noun understood from the context of utterance—or else, it is just a vague expression of a half-formed thought. Frege emphasized that "x is one" is an incomplete way of saying "x is one A, a single A," or else has no clear sense; since the connection of the concepts one and identity comes out just as much in the German "ein und dasselbe" as in the English "one and the same," it has always surprised me that Frege did not similarly maintain the parallel doctrine of relativized identity, which I have just briefly stated. (Geach 1967, 3)

In the third edition of his Reference and Generality (originally published in 1962) regarding his notion of relative identity, Geach states, "On my view of identity I could not object in principle to different A's being one and the same B, conceivably . . . as different heralds may be one and the same man (Norroy is historically a different herald from Ulster, but at the present time they are the same man)" (Geach 1980, 181).

16. Suppose that, qua teacher, you know that were Zelda to calculate the area of the circle beyond two decimal places, she, like Waldo, would calculate incorrectly. If Zelda's computation stops at two decimal places because that is the limit of her ability to stay on the right track, then there is a sense in which her performance was her best possible performance. She did as well as she could under the prevailing circumstances—all things considered. Waldo did not. He could have done better by stopping at the seventh decimal place—his limit—rather than going for the eight.

*Chapter 3*

# Lessons, Charity, and Freedom's Proliferation

## LESSONS FROM STRAWSON AND NEWMAN

Understanding the situations of the students Zelda and Zach we met in the previous chapter requires us to acknowledge the kinds of things they are relative to their individual situations. Thus, we think of them as students and apply what we know of that social kind when we reflect on how to judge their efforts. These students can teach us how we ought correctly to judge ourselves and others when we ask whether any of us are free—free to act otherwise than we do—even if it would seem that we cannot act contrariwise. But to appreciate the lesson the students offer, it helps first to recall Peter Strawson's influential discussion of how social psychology bears upon freedom of the will (P. Strawson 1962; McKenna 2012-03-28). As socially situated humans, we are like teachers assessing their students, mindful of who and what they are. For if Strawson is right, human psychology evidently induces us to assess the wills of agents—including ourselves—whose actions, when known to us, bear upon ourselves and various others. As Strawson would have it, our assessments are prompted by our human tendency to adopt various sophisticated reactive practical attitudes directed at the assessed agents. Strawson tells us that these attitudes are exemplified, but not exhausted, by those on the dense scale that ranges from resentment to gratitude.

Still with Strawson in mind but going beyond his remarks, it seems introspectively plain that we naturally and reactively resent and resist certain sorts of manipulation (Kapitan 2000; Pereboom 2001 and 2014; Mele 2019). Aren't you often apt to react to the appearance of another's efforts to manipulate you with resistance prompted by resentment? Why? Well, sometimes manipulation aims so to control us as to benefit others—perhaps only the manipulator—at unwelcome cost to ourselves. But this initially plausible cost-benefit analysis fails to generalize in the face of our tendency in some contexts resentfully to resist control that is patently paternalistic. Our proclivity to resist incontrovertibly benevolent alien rule is introspectively revealed when we merely feel the pull of caution and recognize the taste of hesitation upon considering the prospect of some sorts of beneficial dictation. Suppose honorable you are playing small pot poker with friends while devious I, without your approval, wander around the table to peek at their hands. Would you welcome or resist my unsolicited covert kibitzing that you know would, if followed, win you the few coins in the pot? I bet you'd rightly resent my interference, refuse my advice, and consider recommending me for the shame of the stockade.

Raise the stakes. What would you prefer were you the subject of the familiar thought experiment annually conducted in Introduction to Philosophy 101. You are assured always of what you most and wisely prefer in exchange for resigning your autonomy to the goodwill and omniscience of your trustworthy and reliable would-be benefactor, whether human or not. To ensure that you be happier than you otherwise would be, would you forego being a psychic autobiographer, the authorizing contralto-source of your actions? Would you prefer that the narrative of your life be a biography ghost-authored by your benefactor rather than your own *apologia pro vita*, an apology of the sort Newman once penned (Newman 1864; Dennett 1986; Velleman 2006; Fischer 2009, chap. 10; Baker 2016)? Would you opt to retain the volitional wheel to steer your own way through the risks of life? Or would you choose instead to be a satiated passenger throughout a lifelong road trip without any dip, disappointment, or displeasure due to your autonomous will?

Upon reflection, the beckoning answer is muffled. The loot is tempting, the candy sweet. Sometimes we do seek to offload the burden of deciding what to do, perhaps by trusting to a financial advisor to decide upon confusing investment options. Other times with other concerns and problems, we willingly rely upon various other kinds of reliable experts. Shall it be the surgeon's knife or the oncologist's cocktail? However, if teaching philosophy for almost fifty years provides a roughly representative sample of humanity, then I may have some evidence that, *ceteris paribus*, we do tend to prefer autonomy to its enriching thought-experiment alternative. Each of the many times I've presented the thought experiment to large classes, undergraduates by an overwhelming majority elect risky autonomy over dictation's trumpeted guaranteed rewards. If that suggestive *Gedankenexperiment*, though short on experimental design, shows anything, it indicates that when the road ahead looks long—as it does to sampled young—we are apt to prefer autonomy for what else we might value. If so, that may be a deep fact about our psychology. It suggests that, of the necessity with which Spinozan psychology would govern us, we are prone to resent and resist control by *whatever* would either rob us of the sort of autonomy we naturally cherish or cut against—what Fischer and Ravizza call—the guidance control we have over our own actions (Fischer and Ravizza 1998). That in turn perhaps implies that normal psychology so regulates all our thoughts and efforts as to necessitate not only our compliance with its dictates but also and thereby our occasional contextually sensitive resentment of, and resistance to, psychology's manipulative dictation.[1] It is as if in certain contexts psychology at once manipulatively necessitates both what we thoughtfully do and also our willful efforts to omit so thinking and acting (Fischer and Ravizza 1998; Bernstein 2015; Clarke 2014; Sartorio 2016 and 2021).[2] Evidently, the psychology that governs us ensures that we are subject to a certain kind of cognitive conflict. If so, then in such contexts we act with the impossible aim of omitting some of our actions, all of which occur necessarily. In any such case it would seem that although it is hopelessly beyond our reach, our objective is that of having personal control over our own actions, actions that are ultimately inevitable if psychology is Spinozan. If so, then it would appear that we are sometimes doomed to a peculiar kind of *akrasia*. For in such situations we find ourselves to be in a doubtlessly complex psychological state that not only suffices for our deliberate action but also includes our willful, but too weak, opposition to that very action (Mele 1987). That resisted action, since intended and deliberate, is in one sense under our control due to its cognitive origin. But it is also action that is necessary since ensured by psychology. And yet when we resent and unsuccessfully resist the workings of the laws of thought, we necessarily will—though inevitably too weakly—to be able to act otherwise than we necessarily act. If the laws of psychology hold with necessity and thereby compel us to act as we do while we resistantly will possibly to act otherwise, then we are oddly akratic actors fated sometimes to will—inexorably without success—to be able to act otherwise than we willingly do.

We can recast in positive terminology the above negatively put point about our occasional efforts to resist doing what we necessarily do. I primarily characterized the experience of resistance as the effort aimed at the ability to omit doing what nature necessitates, the effort to be able not to do what one is unavoidably about to do. But the same experience admits of a complementary—and, I think, equivalent—positive description. For such resistance is not merely the effort to obstruct. It is also at once typically the effort to be the source of action that is both inevitably foregone but yet somehow possible. When we resist nature's irresistible tide toward upcoming action, we undertake the effort to be the source—the full explanatory and authorial font—of an impossible action willed but trumped. In the hallowed traditional conception of the will he follows, Kane insightfully calls the doomed effort that I would describe as resistance as the effort to be *ultimately responsible* for—or the sole author of—what we do (Kane 1999-03-18, 33ff. and chap. 6, 196ff.).[3]

And although he does not address psychological resistance akin to that now before us, Lehrer's notion of an agent's ultimate preference is in its neighborhood. Such cognitive effort or resistance in a Spinozan world is the ill-fated attempt to be the ultimate source of an action that cannot occur. The effort aims at not merely one's not being the sole referent of the full and correct explanation of the action one actually intentionally performs. Rather, the effort is dedicated to being the source of an action foreseen and willed but nevertheless necessarily precluded by prevailing psychology. So, the resisting agent instantiates a psychological process aimed at rendering possible an action, $\Sigma$, (say, donating to a worthy local charity), that she cannot perform because it is precluded by an action, $\Psi$ (betting her whole wad on a horse with her local bookie). Given her psychology and financial resources, it is necessary that her necessarily performing $\Psi$ entails her necessarily not performing $\Sigma$. Therefore, her willful resistance to $\Psi$ has as its objective rendering the possibility of $\Sigma$ despite the fact that $\Sigma$'s failure is necessary. The aim of her effort is to make it be the case that it be possible that it not be necessary that she not perform $\Sigma$. She so strives that possibly, not necessarily not $\Sigma$. With a dash of modal logic, her modal objective amounts to so striving that it be possible that $\Sigma$ is possible, or—iteration dispensed—simply that $\Sigma$ be possible. And that uniterated possibility is what would be the case were $\Sigma$ to be an alternative to $\Psi$. To be clear, then, our agent's relevant aim in resisting $\Psi$ is not her doing $\Sigma$, though she might also aim to do $\Sigma$. Rather, her more modest aim is that it be possible that she do $\Sigma$, that she be able to act otherwise than she necessarily does. To his credit, Kane offers his readers a richly nuanced account of his conception of ultimate responsibility that for present purposes we may respectfully set aside. But regardless of the adequacy of his description or mine of an agent resisting a cognitive process that shall result in her actual action, our compatible descriptions coincide in their referent, the (complex) psychological state of one whose frustrated will would, if fulfilled, meet the requirement of leeway freedom.

Paradoxically then, while Spinozan psychology's manipulative rule would so govern us that we must submit to its manipulation, its very rule arguably would mandate our ill-fated resentful resistance to its manipulation. Perhaps, then, Milton was spot on in *Paradise Lost*. There we read that God (representing the laws of nature) so made Lucifer (representing us) to be who he was that the defiant archangel simply had hopelessly to rebel against his omnipotent creator's manipulative prescriptions. For if Spinoza supersedes Hume, then by necessity we are creatures occasionally apt to resent and resist detected manipulation or governance regardless of whatever, if any, benefit the supervision may promise. We are, it would seem, related to the laws that dominate our lives as is the slave to the insidious omnipotent master. That unrelenting master mandates the slave's resentment of, and certain-to-fail resistance to, the master's very mastery. "Do whatever I order!" the manipulative master demands, "But do it while, with resentful resistance, trying not to do it!" And yet, it might be this akratic conundrum that permits us to be free. *Akrasia* of this odd ilk—one of one's willing pitted against another willing of one's own—may liberate us from nomic servitude. For it may suffice for our remarkable ability—even in a Spinozan world— to be able to act otherwise than we necessarily do.

By resentfully resisting psychology's governance, we may almost break free of its manacle. Our resentful resistance has as its objective the possibility of not doing—omitting from our lives—some of our actions and their launching deliberations, both of which we may recognize and experience as necessary. Thus guided, we aim so to act that what is necessary not be necessary—that an omitted alternative be possible. If the psychology that regulates our practical reason and attitudes dictates our occasional inclination to resist the enforcement of that same cognitive *logos*, it ensures that we are disposed to aspire to a life sprinkled in selective contexts with possible alternatives to what we actually do. Just as Zelda and Zach in their different ways each unproblematically aspire to what is impossible, so too may we. By acting on their geometrical aspirations these two students so asymptotically approach their common objective that they each independently and differently almost achieve the impossible. We are like that duo when we attempt so to act as to omit the necessity of our actions. If we should be modal kin to the computing kids, then we too, when charitably but fairly judged in the light of our prevailing context, may almost hit our impossible mark. We would so act that, in the context that counts, we almost shed the necessity we resist by almost omitting to do what we must in favor of doing what we can't. We would then act in such a way that there would almost be contextually tuned leeway in our lives of the sort that freedom to act otherwise wants. We would thus be almost free. And, for creatures like us in the context of our conflictive predicament, almost being free just might be free enough to be free.

## LESSONS FROM SPARTACUS AND AUGUSTINE

We can see our way to this uncertain abductive conclusion if—by way of suggestive models—we first look afresh at Spartacus and then apply what we find to akratic Augustine and finally to ourselves.

The centuries since his rebellion cloud the details of the nearly successful slave revolt Spartacus led in 73 B.C. against his Roman masters (Strauss 2009). The rebellion was destined ultimately to fail. Rome's awesome power, once finally mustered, was massively more than sufficient to ensure the defeat of the rag-tag many who gathered in resistance under the lead of the heroic gladiator. Initially the rebels managed to defeat in various battles the too small and ill-led forces overconfident Rome sent against them. Thereafter worried but relentlessly resolute, the imperial authorities continuously improved their efforts until sufficient to crush the rebellion, with Spartacus slain in futile final battle.

Although Spartacus could not have succeeded, he almost did. Had the indecisive and imprudent Senate not sent against him a force as strong as that which Crassus finally led, Spartacus would have liberated himself along with his confederates. We can think, then, of Spartacus, in particular, and his comrades, in general, as engaged in a *quasi-asymptotic* struggle for emancipation. Each of the rebels' successes took them one constantly diminishing step closer to the freedom they could never reach. But each of the early rebel victories naturally prodded Rome ever more effectively to augment and direct its power against them. We can conceive of the rebels as being in a situation tellingly like that of Zelda and Zach. Each actor—whether slave or student—does what she or he best can do under the prevailing limitations that preclude her or his perfect success. With each decimal extension of their computations, the on-track students' solutions better approximate, but finally fail to fix upon, the answer that continues to elude them. So too, with each additional arrow the rebels fling against their masters, those overlords mass ever more effective power against the rebellion. Before he was enslaved as a gladiator, Spartacus fought as an effective auxiliary under Rome's *aquila*. So, he would have known how Rome would respond to rebellion of the sort he might lead. He knew his defeat to be inevitable. Nevertheless, resenting enslavement's manipulation, he resisted. Like Zelda and Zach, once aware of the asymptotic character of their computational efforts, Spartacus did what he could to do what he knew he could not do.

We know that Spartacus knew the futility of his effort and the certainty of his defeat. So, why do we consider Spartacus heroic rather than foolish? Supposing that we should, why should we judge defeated Spartacus to surpass in human dignity victorious Crassus?

If Strawson is close to the mark about human nature, then as Spartacus's fellow humans who know his story, we are bound to assess his will and character by the attitudes with which we react to willful actions that matter to us. Perhaps we who assess Spartacus's effort to free himself from dehumanizing slavery should, and do, evaluate him with the practical wisdom exhibited by Zelda's and Zach's charitable but fair teacher. The teacher recognizes the equal success of Zelda and Zach in their different solutions to their assigned circle's area. The wise teacher understands that a student who successfully solves the circle's area does so by computing in accordance with a procedure that defies successful completion. A sharp student who embarks on the right procedure knows in advance, or discovers along the way, the impossibility of concluding the process. At the personal point of futility that reasonably varies across students, a savvy student resists by terminating the proper computation with the result then in hand. It is as if the student were to append the following autobiographical note addressed to the teacher explaining the student's submission.

> *Enough is enough. I have done enough—all in the way the governing algorithm commands—to compute the solution I set out to compute. But I resent that the algorithm defies my successful completion. So, with good reason I resist by refusing, by means of this my submission, to go beyond what I've done so far. By following the algorithm, my answer is almost right. And that is enough for it to be right.*

Spartacus in rebellion, like a successful student engaged in computation, follows a procedure he must if he is to march toward emancipation. The student's procedure is set by mathematics in the context of her individual situation and the expectation of her teacher's charitable but fair assessment. Analogously, Spartacus's path is set by the laws of nature in the context of Crassus's legions. That Spartacus followed the only procedure open to him is revealed by his Mentalese autobiography that, by putting ourselves in his sandals—that is by *reading* or *simulating* his mind—we might abduce (Gallese and Goldman 1998; Goldman 2006 and 2013). His psychic autobiography— as imaginatively read by us—recounts the sequence of attitudes he adopted that, at the intentional level, serve as the explanatory source of his rebellion. If his cognitively encoded autobiography should be both true and complete, it would conclude with a Mentalese representation, not unlike the student's note, perhaps ending as follows:

> *ENOUGH IS ENOUGH. I HAVE DONE ENOUGH—ALL IN THE WAY THE LAWS OF NATURE COMMAND—TO ACHIEVE THE FREEDOM I SET OUT TO ACHIEVE. BUT I RESENT THAT THE LAWS DEFY MY SUCCESSFUL COMPLETION. SO, WITH GOOD REASON I RESIST BY REFUSING, WITH MY DEATH, TO GO BEYOND WHAT I HAVE DONE SO FAR. BY FOLLOWING THE LAWS OF NATURE, MY EMANCIPATION IS ALMOST SECURE. BY DIEING AS I DO, I ALMOST HAVE THE LEEWAY TO ACT OTHER THAN AS A SLAVE MUST. AND THAT IS ENOUGH FOR ME TO DIE WITH THAT LEEWAY IN HAND, TO DIE A FREE MAN.*

If we assess Spartacus in accord with Strawson's account of human nature, our evaluation turns on our assessment of his will. Charitably but fairly to assess his will, we must abduce the content of his psychic autobiography. If you think his autobiography includes a representation of the sort conjectured above, then won't you—being charitable but fair—conclude that Spartacus in defeat secured dignity not less than that of his masters? If so, then you'll reason that since theirs is the dignity of free Romans, so too is his. Spartacus achieved the dignity with which he died because although his rebellion failed of necessity, it almost succeeded. He was almost free as he died. Was he then—in that final moment and relative to the specific context in which he fell—a free man? You be the judge! Do you, if their teacher, assign a high passing grade to Zelda and Zach? I bet you do. And if you do, then you should give full credit too to Spartacus there at his end. You ought to recognize that although human psychology necessitated Spartacus's decision to revolt, he authorized his decision because its source was his autobiographically recounted resentful resistance against the irresistible power of Rome. That is why, as you ought, you do recognize him as heroic rather than foolish. Mindful of that, won't you conclude that since, *in the context* in which he fell, Spartacus was almost free, *that in his final fleeting context* he was free enough to be free at last?

We can now apply our account of Spartacus to guide the charitable but fair Strawsonian way one ought to assess the will of a person—whether oneself or another—whose situation is analogous to that of the heroic slave who liberated himself in defeat. We proceed under the assumption of necessitarian determinism and the presumption that psychology ensures that we are apt in some contexts to resent and resist recognized manipulation regardless of its origin.

To facilitate the discussion, let's consider an example in which we assess the will of someone whose psychic *apologia pro vita sua* we know full well, someone whose mind we have reliably read. Consider, then, assessing Augustine's will in the light of our knowledge of that autobiographer's *Confessions* (1991, chap. 8).

Of special interest to us is Augustine's apparent acknowledgement of *akrasia* (Mele 2012-06-01). Let us set aside the difficulties of both exegesis and also the logical puzzles posed by weakness of the will. We may, then, attribute to Augustine belief that some of his deliberate actions were contrary to his will because they were inimical to his overall better judgments—that is counter to his rationally considered overall preferences. We take Augustine's first-person narrative, in both covert Mentalese and published Latin, to recount that if he suffers intense temptation to act akratically, he greatly resists whatever within his cognitive system seems manipulatively to compel him to act as tempted. Augustine's akratic situation is analogous to that of a sophisticated perceiver presented with an irresistible illusion such as the familiar Müller-Lyer. The veteran cognitive psychologist certainly knows the parallel lines in the stimulus to be equal in length. Nevertheless and inevitably, it erroneously seems to her that the lengths of the lines differ. Her visual phenomenal experience is as if the lines differ even though she knows they do not. Her perceptual and doxastic systems both competitively contribute to her overall psychological state, but her perceptual system inevitably wins the contest and determines the phenomenal character and content of her terminal experiential state. She wills to see the lines as equal but succumbs to seeing them as different. Augustine's plight is similar. His admittedly sinful action is akin to the culmination of the psychologist's admittedly erroneous visual experience. He wills to act other than he sinfully does. She wills to experience other than she erroneously does. Each resists his or her respective psychological fate. But neither succeeds because, psychologically, neither could. Psychology launches in each of them a competitive process. It establishes in him contrary willings—one for virtue, the other for vice. In her it establishes contrary representations—one for truth, the other for appearance. In him, psychology determines that vice trumps virtue; in her, that fiction defeats fact. Psychology necessitates both his wayward action and her wayward experience.[4]

Given our mind-reading of Augustine's mental autobiography, we attribute to him resentful resistance of psychology's manipulation against which he contends. For in his published pleas, laced with complaints against his manipulation, he occasionally beseeches evidently deaf God—personifying all Spinozan laws—to intervene on his behalf against the manipulative seductive power over which he himself has no control. With his plea ignored, Augustine confesses to those of us who would understand and assess his regretted weak-willed conduct that the manipulation he resisted was, in the end, irresistible. It is our hypothesis that his mentally encoded autobiography includes

*I HAVE ACTED AS IRRESISTIBLY MANIPULATED BY WHAT I KNOW NOT. HOWEVER, I RESENTFULLY RESISTED THIS MANIPULATION AS BEST I COULD. I WILLED—IN THE LIGHT OF MY OVERALL BEST PRACTICAL REASONS AND HIGHEST VALUES—TO ACT OTHERWISE THAN I DID. BUT I NEVERTHELESS ACTED DELIBERATELY AND CONTRARY TO MY FRUSTRATED TOO WEAK WILL. I UNSUCCESSFULLY RESISTED DOING WHAT WAS IN THE END IRRESTIBLE. I ALMOST SUCCEEDED, BUT I FINALLY FAILED. MEA CULPA.*

## CHARITABLE ASSESSMENT

How, under the assumption of necessitarianism, should we assess Augustine's will? We should recognize that Augustine's claim to have been manipulated by his governing psychology is correct. As necessitarians *pro tempore*, we know, even if he did not, that the ultimate manipulative source of the practical attitudes that explain his actions is Spinozan psychology. By hypothesis, that natural *logos* of the *psyche* determines with natural necessity the ebb and flow of all his mental states implicated in his actions. We do not doubt that he resentfully resisted manipulation in the manner he reports. For we already know that human psychology necessitates that a person who detects manipulation is prone to react with practical attitudes that spawn resentful resistance. Thus, we realize that psychology necessitates Augustine's detecting on the occasion of his sin both that he is being manipulated and also that he is reactively resisting that manipulation. By including psychology, the laws of nature necessitate Augustine's employment of his Mentalese representations to compute, in accordance with psychology's prescribed algorithm. So, his reckoning consists of a sequence of representations that realize the practical reasoning that causes him to resist in exactly the manner he does. Unfolding according to the laws of cognition, his resistant attitudes and behavior sum to his asymptotic approach to acting otherwise than he actually does. But being so akratic by natural necessity, Augustine sins—simply fails—in the end, succumbing as he must to psychology's enslavement. But his sinful action is, *qua* resentful resistance, also at once his almost possibly acting otherwise than he does.

Our assessment of Augustine's will ought to mirror not only a good teacher's assessment of Zelda and Zach but also our own assessment of Spartacus. We must give the Sisyphean saint full credit in accomplishing his impossible modally tempered goal. Like Zelda, Zach, and Spartacus, Augustine almost does what, though impossible, he set out to do. He does this by conforming to the procedure specific to the impossible task of avoiding the sinful fate to which psychology assigns him. Zelda's final computational and authorized action is her computing the area $\alpha$ of circle $\Phi$ to equal 12.56. That action almost identifies $\alpha$. And her wise, charitable, and always fair and objective teacher credits Zelda, in the prevailing context, with identifying $\Phi$'s area. For her teacher realizes that Zelda did as well as she could do while doing what the laws of geometry prescribe to identify the area. The teacher's contextually sensitive assessment of Zelda is that since, in the prevailing context, Zelda almost identified $\alpha$, in that context she did identify $\alpha$. Ditto for Zach. And Spartacus? The fatal act that finalizes his drama is realized by his autobiographically authorized, terminal, but futile effort against Crassus. That very authorized action is more than his mere mortal failure. It is also his asymptotic approximation of possible success. It is his almost being able to act otherwise than his master's mandate. Hence, his authorized dying effort is his almost being leeway free. And in the circumstances surrounding his death, that Spartacus was almost free sufficed, I contend, for his being free in, if only in, that moment.

Our assessment of Augustine should follow suit by acknowledging the context in which he wrestled with irresistible temptation. Akratic Augustine's final cognitive computation and his resulting sinful action is his resentful resistance of psychology's manipulation. But it is at once also his autobiographically authorized solution to the problem of what to do in the context of his prevailing and determinative temptation.[5] His concluding cognitive state guides his behavior (Fischer and Ravizza 1998). He is thus like Zelda and Zach. Their individual last thoughts when doing their assignment result in each submitting to the teacher her or his different—but nevertheless full-credit—contextually suffused solution to their vexing common assignment. Augustine's akratic action is what he submits to his witnesses, including himself, for evaluation. His weak-willed peccant act, like Spartacus's authorized dying effort and the students' authorized solutions, is more than the failure it may seem. Augustine's behavior is akin to the students' submissions and Spartacus's finale. Those submissions and that finale are more than may meet the harsh glancing eye blind to the contexts that prevail. Though they may look like errors to an unsympathetic or underinformed critic, the students' submissions are so nearly on point as to count as full-credit correct relative to their contexts. Yes, of course, the fair teacher's assessment of the students is not sanctioned by any universally recognized standard. Nowhere is it written that a solution to computing the area of their assigned circle must run just so many places past the decimal point. There is no principle that specifies how close along the asymptote to the circle's area a student's answer must be in order to qualify as correct. Yet, the teacher's wise judgment is rendered although the critical concept in play is vague, essentially so. Competent use of the concept of asymptotic approximation to a goal requires sensitivity to the context in which the judgment is rendered, how the approach to the goal was realized, and the inescapable fuzziness of the very concept of approximation. A fair and sympathetic assessment of Spartacus recruits just this sort of sapient sensitivity. It enables the assessor to recognize that, despite falling before Crassus, by falling in the fashion that he did Spartacus was so near to his liberation from his enslavement that, in the end, one must count him, in that context, momentarily free then and there. His dying as he did was more than his failure to defeat Crassus. In, but only in, that fleeting predicament how he died was the way in which Spartacus ephemerally achieved the ability—denied to a slave—to be and act otherwise than Rome's governance would determine.

The same applies both to Augustine's reluctant sinning and also to the sensitivity to his plight that is required of anyone who, in the fashion of Strawson, would fairly assess him. Augustine's sin is the product of his confessed resentful resistance to nature's manipulation. The cognitive process he engages by way of resistance asymptotically approaches his possibly acting otherwise than he necessarily does. His process in the impossible ideal closely approaches the innocent omission realizing its asymptote. Appreciating his plight and progress toward his impossible goal, we—if perceptive and just—should judge the regretted product of his cognitive process as Augustine's contextually penetrated full-credit solution to his vexing problem. What Augustine submits as his response to irresistible temptation is, he confesses, his authorized sin. By authorizing it, he instantiates responsibility—an indicator of free will—for it. And his wise witness should assess his submission for what it is. It is the best that could be done to do what cannot be done. By means of his asymptotic process of resentfully resisting nature's manipulation—a futile cognitive algorithm imposed by nature's necessitarian ways—Augustine approaches the possibility of the elusive virtuous behavior to which he aspires, but which psychology precludes. Let, Augustine's evaluator be as wise, charitable, fair, and objective as the students' teacher and as understanding as Spartacus's appreciative assessor. That just so tempered evaluator would score Augustine's actual sinful action as his asymptotic approximation to virtue and, as such, his almost being able to act otherwise than is nomically necessary. The right Strawsonian assessment of Augustine's specific action affirms that, as a particular contextually embedded token of human endeavor, it is as asymptotically near to unmanipulated—nomically unnecessary—as a human action could be if governed by Spinozan laws of cognition. How, then, should a wise, charitable, fair, and objectively minded Strawsonian judge who is alert to Augustine's peculiar context ultimately evaluate the confessed defendant? Appreciative of all that prevails, the judge ought to tune her assessment to the prevailing relevant context (Graham and Horgan 1994, 444–45; Lewis 1983c). So tuned, her verdict should be something like this:

> *In the prevailing context, Augustine almost acted unmanipulated by natural necessitarian law. Hence, on that specific occasion and in that context, he did act unmanipulated. His action, properly portrayed and contextually considered, was not nomically necessary. Augustine's token of his action's type demands assessment tuned to the specific context of its occurrence. And because the source of his deed, as correctly represented in his apologia pro vita sua, was his resentful resistance of the laws of nature, he authorized it. Contextually embedded as it was, his authorized performance—what he did—was not necessary by dint of nature's governing laws. Relative to the context of his personal struggle and by his resentful resistance, Augustine rendered contingent an action that would be necessary were it not for his situated resistance. Hence, he could have acted otherwise. And so, in his prevailing context Augustine acted freely and responsibly when he sinned.[6] In the moment and context of executing his action, Augustine was in fact leeway free.*

Zelda's sub-ideal computation of 12.56 was enough for her to have identified the area of circle $\Phi$. And Zach's imperfectly calculated 12.5663706 was enough for him to have done the same. By the spectacular way Spartacus fatally fell short, he fell free and thereby made his ephemeral freedom possible. So too Augustine's akratic action sufficed to emancipate himself in that morally errant moment from the presumed necessitation of nature's enslaving laws. By undergoing the conflictive cognitive process that eventuated in his sinful action, Augustine almost acted otherwise in the context of what he actually did. Thus, he was almost able to act otherwise relative to his prevailing circumstances. His case is like those of the students and Spartacus. What each of them did suffice for them to be able to do what a fair Strawsonian judge would have been asked to determine. Were Zelda and Zach, in their situations, objectively able correctly to compute the area of the circle? Yes. Was Spartacus, in his desperate plight, objectively able to liberate himself? Yes. And, yes, Augustine, in his psychological turmoil, was almost able to act otherwise than he did. So, too, on the occasion of his sin—since Strawsonian assessment discerns, but does not subjectively make, the ways in which we fit in the mundane mosaic—Augustine was free, *free in that context*.[7] Hence, just as Spinozan sopranos may sing, Augustine's freedom to act otherwise is compatible with our provisional assumption that Spinoza may have been right where Hume may have been wrong. So, let nature's laws be necessary! Concede history to be immutably fixed! Grant that the conjunction of the laws with history entails human actions are of types that occur of necessity! Assume even that we are accordingly powerless over the conspiracy of nature's inviolable laws and immutable history. Nevertheless, we may seize a little contextually colored leeway in what we sometimes do. Augustine did. If, like that moral miscreant, we resist the plague of irresistible biases and compelling addictions by which governing nature manipulates us, we might also wrest leeway freedom from determinism. Augustine wrestled in a certain psychological way when he fought psychology's overpowering manipulation. Should we follow his suit by resentfully resisting nature's dictation, then we too might achieve freedom to act otherwise.

Let me be clear. My thesis is not the willowy claim that Augustine came close to being free but fell short. I am not tepidly proposing that Augustine achieved a faux freedom. Neither am I promoting a condition that is only a shadow of the ability to act otherwise but that is, gosh, "as good as it gets" if the laws prove to be necessary. No. My position, akratic compatibilism, is that, in his particular circumstances and as he cognitively resists doing what he ultimately and inevitably does, Augustine acts freely. Then and there, on that occasion and relative to his cognitive context, he is almost able to omit doing what he actually does. That is why, being just so steeped in his situation, he is able to act otherwise. For a free will is an achievement won by resisting nature's necessity almost to the point of success. Sometimes—relative to a cognitive context of the sort illustrated by Augustine—almost free is free enough to be free.

## FREEDOM'S PROLIFERATION: LESSONS FROM
## ROSA PARKS AND BILL MAZEROSKI

By offering a sufficient condition for leeway freedom, I have argued that freedom, so conceived, is compatible with determinism under the provisional assumption that the laws of nature are necessary and history is immutably fixed. The account of freedom I've proposed implies that it is an accomplishment, perhaps a rare accomplishment if ever accomplished. I would credit an agent with free will upon a specific occasion should she deliberate in the conflicted akratic way I portrayed Augustine on his agonizingly difficult deliberative road to his regretted action. He is, I say, of two competing wills: one triumphantly willing that he sin, the other heroically, but unsuccessfully, willing that he be able to act otherwise. However, if he acts freely, his defeated will is asymptotically to approach the possibility of acting otherwise than he does. I say that by conflictedly willing in this asymptotic way, he achieves leeway freedom in acting as he regretfully does. Evidently, his autobiographically cited psychological struggle is not typical of every occasion of his regretful action. No doubt, like the rest of us, sometimes he simply unconflictedly yields to temptation without a hint of contrary willing. Perhaps, then, he rarely achieves leeway freedom in a Spinozan world. And perhaps few, if any, of us ever deliberate in an adequately Augustinian way should the laws of nature be necessary. How rare is the sort of leeway freedom I've described? Even if my abductive account of free will's compatibility with Spinozan determinism should be correct, that leaves open the disturbing possibility that none, or lamentably few, of us ever are, or would be, leeway free in a world where all is necessary. For who among us actually defiantly resists nature's manipulating governance in an adequately Augustinian way? Indeed, did Augustine himself actually reach that hard-to-hit asymptotic mark? Or is his *Confessions* more fiction than fact?

While I do think, based on his *Confessions*, that Augustine probably so resisted psychology's manipulation as to achieve freedom of his will, I concede that my reading is fallible and that, as evidence, his testimony is defeasible. Maybe, despite what he wrote of his struggles with temptation, Augustine's resistance simply fell too short on the asymptote to omission. Maybe he simply did not resist enough so as, thereby, to have been almost able to act otherwise. Perhaps, though I doubt it, neither Augustine nor anyone else ever hits—or could hit—*that* fugitive mark.

Nevertheless, I think it reasonable to take Augustine at his word. I do assume that, where relevant to our inquiry, his autobiography rings true. Although I acknowledge that you might consider this, my assumption, false, I ask that, over the next pages, you suspend your doubt if only for the sake of the argument to come. Join me, if you would, in tentatively assuming that, as a matter of historical fact, Augustine did enough, by dint of his desperate effort against human psychology on an occasion, then to secure freedom of his will as my account would have it. For, after all, just as a fair teacher's assessment of Zelda and Zach ought charitably to acknowledge their intractable computational challenge, so too our assessment of Augustine ought to be tempered by empathetic appreciation of his dire plight. Thus, going forward, I suppose that, if not Augustine himself, then at least once in the history of human society, some conflicted individual or individuals do achieve freedom of the will in the fashion I've described. For simplicity, let's take Augustine to be our proxy for someone, if not himself, who hits the mark on the asymptote to freedom of the will. But what about the rest of us poor souls? It would be an ashen victory for a version of compatibilism in a Spinozan world were it to entail that so terribly few of us are free that persons generally fail to be morally responsible for want of freedom's proliferation.

To see our way to freedom's proliferation, going forward let us select and unreservedly adopt some of the concepts central to social psychology and its affiliated ontology as found in the primary literature[8]. These notions will be critical to the argument ahead. Crushed, the argument compresses to this:

- Norm-governed social groups do exist; they are among the entities an adequate ontology must recognize.
- Social groups are capable of collective actions sufficient to ensure that each member of a collectively acting group participates in the action.
- There exists a particular social group—the Augustinians—that includes Augustine.
- Augustine's assumed occasion of leeway freedom is an occasion of the Augustinians collectively acting so as to achieve leeway freedom for each Augustinian.
- Thus, leeway freedom proliferates among Augustinians.

Like the free will literature, the literature within both social psychology and social ontology about our social lives is not without internal controversies. Nonetheless, it is sufficiently settled to permit its recruitment to explain how Augustine's presumed achievement of free will might actually redound to many, if not all. The blend of philosophy and psychology I here recruit countenances within its allowed ontology socially constituted structures and their complementary properties suited for explanations of collective practical attitudes and agency. This alliance of philosophy and social psychology marshals and regiments its joint proprietary theoretical vocabulary (which I cast in italic) to refer to the various categories, kinds, and kind-constituting properties cognitive and social psychology jointly abduct to explain socialized human behavior. Primary among the kinds countenanced by psychological

social science and its affiliated ontology are *social groups.* Even a glance
at the literature characteristic of the intersection of social psychology and
social ontology reveals the jointly accepted practice of liberally positing the
existence of quite specific groups. Both the science and its sibling ontology
tend without hesitation expansively to quantify over groups cited in plausible
explanations of our social lives. Of course, although social groups are heterogenous, they are composed of, and constituted by, their *members,* individual
persons all of whom abide by the laws of nature including cognitive psychology. Given that groups vary by kind, they variously supervene upon various
relations among their members. Groups can be formal or informal, officially
chartered or not. Although membership in some groups requires ceremonial
induction, membership typically comes without pledge-taking or dues-pay-
ing. In any case, group members are to be sensitive to selected *norms*—either
implicit or public— to which they are apt to be variously *committed.* Groups
can be more or less *cohesive,* depending in part on the aptitudes of their members individually to conform to such norms. Members of cohesive groups
may be prone to *empathize* with other members. In some groups members
manage to *coordinate* their practical and propositional *attitudes* as well as
their actions pertinent to matters of *interest* to the group. Members of a group
may be apt, even if only implicitly, to *self-identify* as members of the group
by their attitudes, words, or actions. And others may be apt—again perhaps
implicitly—to identify members of a group as such. So, members of a group
may have a common *social identity.* And individuals who are a member of
various groups may have corresponding social identities that are, pairwise,
more or less cohesive.

Some, but not all, groups are hierarchical in the sense that influence
among members is asymmetric. Importantly, groups—regardless of hierarchy—admit of *trendsetters.* They are influential members whose known
conformance with, or violation of, the group's norms affect both the stability
and evolution of the norms as well as how other members conform. Membership itself can be more or less exclusive and contingent upon various factors.
Groups are typically irreducible to their members since a group might endure
over entry and exit of members, while those who migrate in or out may be apt
to amend their self-identities accordingly. Although it is certainly composed
of individual persons, a social group is typically more than the sum of its
present parts. For, by way of what some of its individual members willingly
do, a group might be able to do what no proper subset of members willfully
can. Thus, an explanation of a *group's collective action* might posit a *plural
self,* a *we,* with its own *pool of wills* somehow filled by the willings of some
of its members (Gilbert 1989, pp. 2–18 and chap. 4; Velleman, 1997).[9]

Like literature arising from other continuing research programs, the relevant work in social psychology that exploits the italicized concepts we have

just dragooned into service bristles with differences and disputes on myriad matters of detail. Nonetheless, when viewed from the stratosphere, the turbulent local squabbles seem to meld into concurrence. Squabblers concur on the general structure of models of how situated cognitive agents naturally fit together—like moving jigsaw puzzle pieces—to form social groups of coordinating, if not cooperating, individuals. And though they squabble about their competing theories of this or that group, the squabblers generally agree that, within cooperative groups, members are remarkably adept at coordinately evolving their personal practical attitudes so as to enable cooperation. Thus, it certainly seems that some such social groups somehow supervene upon the way their members commonly tune some of their action enabling individual attitudes.

It is my hunch that attention to the conceptual scheme just scouted above indicates that Augustine's empathic fellow travelers form a social group—the Augustinians—inclusive of Augustine. I contend that Augustinians so collectively act that each is, thereby, leeway free. For we shall see that, plausibly, freedom of the will propagates within communities characterized by cooperation and populated by persons of the empathetic kind Peter Strawson once described and contemporary social psychology continues to study. Let us take on board, then, a bit of the psychology of social groups that act collectively. If we do, then we shall see that individual agents may achieve freedom of their own wills simply by participating in some select social groups. For by the individual achievements of selected members, these special groups collectively achieve freedom of will for all members. Your being free to act otherwise might, I say, suffice for my being similarly free. This, I say, applies if we should be committed members of a group in which you are a trendsetter like akratic Augustine.

Consider, then, familiar social groups: small and large, ephemeral and enduring, informal and chartered. Social psychology welcomes some of these aggregations of interacting agents into its models, and hence its ontology, of our social lives. Among the human flocks nested in social psychology's ontology are more or less cohesive collections of persons typified by those groups we may be pretheoretically apt to recognize as such by common sense in partnership with folk psychology. As already noted, real social groups are often distinguished by the remarkable aptitudes of their norm-sensitive members for coordinated interaction.[10] Fred and Ginger, elegantly waltzing, form and exemplify the smallest of informal groups gathered from the fewest of interacting participants. The elegance of what, as a spontaneous duet, they synchronously do owes its grace to the fact that each dancer intentionally, though perhaps unconsciously, moves in mutual conformity with unwritten norms applicable to those who would waltz in response to an orchestra's cue. Fred and Ginger need only coordinately move as they virtuously do, each sensitive to the other's streaming intentions, in order that their duet exist as a social group for the duration of their dance. By each dancer doing what she or he purposefully does, the waltz that is done is collectively done in accord with the norms for waltzing as opposed to, say, tangoing. Their waltz is a collective action done by their duet. Alone, neither can waltz. Yet their duet waltzes as well as can be done. In contrast to the cohesive unchoreographed duet, the United States Congress is a much larger and formally constituted social group situated in a cacophonous environment more plastic and expansive than the duet's modest melodic niche. Unlike the graceful dancers, the members of Congress frequently interact disgracefully. Some unwittingly and sporadically fail to comply with the codified norms to which they are explicitly pledged, while hostile others aim strategically to violate the principles undetected. Our correct recognition of both the gracious duet and the ungracious institution signals that, as we ought to conceive it, a social group, though distinguished by norms applicable to its participants, does not depend for its existence on its participants—all or always—actually abiding by the norms to which they are—as Tuomela argues—committed and normally apt to follow (Tuomela 2013, chap. 2). Each of our two exemplary groups—the one small, temporary, and balletic, the other large, enduring, and brawling—may arise quite naturally within the environments of their occurrence: the couple, by their individually sensitive waltzing reactions to the orchestra's sudden seductive summons; the Congress, by its members' responses to the certifying summons of votes cast in accord with the Constitution of the United States. These two examples of different kinds of ordinary social groups obviously differ dramatically in their apparent structure and evolutionary paths without cost to their admissibility into the ontology of social psychology. Nevertheless, that tolerant science need not, and does not, import into its easygoing ontology of social groups and their defining properties merely mereological sums or hodgepodge sets of people who satisfy concocted "grue-ish" predicates (Goodman 1983; Armstrong 1978; Lewis 1983d; Sider 2011). The unentrenched phony predicate "born on March 1 in a leap year of protracted drought with one blue moon" fails to designate a concept of a social group or a property definitive of a genuine group. And that remains so even if the set of such uncoordinated folks should not be empty.[11] However, lest we be distracted here while we focus on what is familiar in our ordinary social experience of this or that social group, we shall ignore the gnarly and philosophically disputed issues about how and whether to characterize or analyze the *most general notion or concept* of social grouping. Instead, as Thomasson wisely recommends and current social psychology productively presupposes, we adopt the working hypothesis that particular social groups of various kinds fit for recognition within flourishing empirical research programs do indeed exist (Thomasson 2003, 2014, chaps. 3, 6 and

9, and 2019; Ellemers, Spears, and Doosje 2002; Hornsey 2008; Ellemers and Haslam 2011; Turner and Reynolds 2003 and 2011).[12]

Evidently, when our pragmatic interests turn away from social psychology and toward sociology and public policy, we may catch ourselves speaking too casually of various *default* collections of people (e.g., by census tract residence or generational cohort) as if they were social groups in the sights of social psychology. But unlike families, friends, and linguistic communities such default conglomerations do not tax their members with common norms, cognitive involvement, interpersonal engagement, and coordinated intentional action. So, social psychology shoos such ersatz groups from its flexible ontology (Mathiesen 2003 and 2006). And so do we. Thus, Fred and Ginger's bona fide duet presupposes that each is apt cyclically to adapt to the other's actions by empathetically appreciating what the other is also apt adaptively to do when the music plays. They coordinate, and that they do presupposes that each manages implicitly to know the other's practical attitudes pertinent to waltzing. Each must represent—probably unconsciously—what the other aims to do before it is done if they are to reciprocate the movements of the other. So, Fred must move through representational mental states that reflect Ginger's while she progresses through mental states that answer his. Their mental states could be just as long-arm functionalism would have it. Recall from chapter 1 that functionalism, whether short-arm or long-arm, describes mental states as physically realized representational states within a relational system. The short-arm version of the doctrine supposes that states so related must be internal to a particular cognitive agent. But the long-arm edition is not so parochial. It allows that one's mind be extended. It permits that among one's mental representations—or as constituents thereof— may be some that are physically realized outside of one's body. Functionalism, if long-arm, recognizes that Fred's mental states, since relational, may include relata external to his body, even such as Ginger's internal mental states. That the two dancers form their small social group may be thus enabled by the fact that Fred, as it were, reads Ginger's mind while she, in like manner, reads his. Alternatively, each partner might internally simulate the streaming psychological states of the other in order that, together, they dance. Thus, no matter that the psychological states each partner reads or mimics are the other's. Hence, granted the long-arm functionalist hypothesis, some of Fred's mental states would be parts of Ginger's and some of hers would be parts of his. Or again alternatively, by way of simulation, each partner would replicate for a while the psychology of the other. Their duet is, in a sense, single-minded. The cooperative, cohesive social group they form supervenes upon its two members owing to their psychological coordination. They pool their practical attitudes so as to form what Gilbert calls a pool of wills in the service of their small group. It is an open and contested question as to how, as individuals, we human perceivers of other human agents are able to see others *as partners* in coordinate actions or how we manage to "read or simulate other minds" (Goldman 2006 and 2013; Stich and Nichols 1992; Goldman 2006 and 2013; Gopnik 2009a and 2009b; Siegel 2010 and 2017; Zeimbekis and Raftopoulos 2015; Mole 2015). But although how we empathetically read or simulate other minds awaits consensus, that we do excel in fallibly knowing and reacting to the thoughts and sentiments of those with whom we interact remains indisputable. No doubt, this is partly why teenage years are so tough. For as any survivor of the high school social scene knows, teens are, by nature, hypersensitive to what their peers think of them as well as what cliques rule the social scene. Like so many other kinds of animals, we are deeply social creatures (Henrich et al. 2012; Sussman et al. 2007; Bloom 2010; Wynn and Bloom 2013; Tomé et al. 2012; Wynn et al. 2018).[13] By nature, birds flock, bees hive, and, in our many—better and worse—ways, we do too.

By seeding us with dispositions to adopt socially tuned normative practical attitudes of various kinds, our psychology ensures our common and doubtlessly complex cognitive abilities naturally to form groups. Evidently, our socially sensitive adaptive psychological abilities, if not innately rooted, are exhibited in surprisingly early childhood as the wonderful work on developmental psychology over the last fifty years indicates. From infancy forward, children progressively behave empathetically and in ways indicative of both their germinal moral attitudes and their concomitant budding abilities to recognize—and differentiate among—social groups (Hamlin, Wynn, and Bloom 2007; Gopnik 2009a, chap. 4; Rhodes 2012; Powell and Spelke 2013; Wynn and Bloom 2013; Bloom 2013; Hamlin 2015; Wynn et al. 2018; Marshall, Wynn, and Bloom 2020). Enrolled in the telltale experiment, the very young child looks long and twice when the nasty puppet shockingly mistreats the nice one. And the child reacts much the same should she see a gaggle of puppets shun another. The child's perceptual responses evidently reveal moral and social—even if immature—sentiments that trade on the child's empathy-salted mindreading abilities.

Certainly, such nascent norm-sensitive social attitudes and complementing skills are apt to evolve with maturity and learning. As a result, without conscious cognitive effort, we are prone to find ourselves—automatically as it were—both recognizing and participating in various social groups. And that implies our capacities, first to detect, and then to conform to unpublished cooperation-enabling norms peculiar to specific groups. Indeed, one's unwitting conformance to the norms of a particular group may betray one's unaware membership. Thus, being both well-trained and much practiced dancers, Fred and Ginger might, without a word or written contract, immediately turn to each other and waltz when the music begins. The couple can, without explicit prior agreement, spontaneously form their minimal group because their respective psychological systems of practical attitudes echo each other. He thinks of her in his way; she thinks of him in her way. That they form a waltzing couple—a kind of social group—supervenes on the fact that they think of each other as they do and act accordingly. Fred and Ginger each would likely be fully aware of being a duet. However, you, I, and others in their captivated audience—since we all keep their beat and clap in final applause—would be members of their temporary fan group although we each may be unaware of our common membership. No doubt, such supervenience of a group upon its members admits of multiple realization. For two other dancers might also make a waltzing couple by each appropriately thinking of the other while not exactly replicating the cognitive patterns of Fred and Ginger. The familiar topiary trope helpfully exemplifies the ways in which an instance of a higher-level common kind may supervene on different clusters of lower-level things: A particular shrub's elephantine supervening shape arises from, and depends upon, the way that shrub's many individual branches align. But, the trope continues, the very same shape might be shared by different shrubs with different numbers of differently distributed dendrites. So too may a supervening social group arise from, and depend upon, how the cognitive systems of would-be participants align. Thus, different instances of the same type of group can supervene upon different arrays of different cognitive systems of different agents in different milieus. By instantiating one, rather than another, of such ecologically calibrated systems of cooperation-controlling practical attitudes, an individual thereby contributes her share to the creation of an instance of one, rather than another, kind of social group. Once sufficient contributions have been made, the contributors thereby become participants in the group thus coalesced. No contract need be signed in order that a group be bound by its particular social contract. A shrub comes to realize its elephantine shape coincident with its individual branches all playing their different roles on schedule. And so too does a set of persons come to realize its group identity coincident with its individual members all playing their different cognitive roles as the clock requires.

By individually realizing and coordinating their contributing systems of practical attitudes, agents share in forming a group and join all other contributors in enabling the group's collective actions. For example, both the septet that Miles Davis led in recording *Kind of Blue* and Dave Brubeck's quartet for *Time Out* were both social groups of the cool-jazz sort. Yet the members of the one group likely did not replicate the practical attitudes of the other. So, different groups of the same kind can differ on the psychological demands they impose on their members. And consider two teams: one women's soccer, the other men's doubles tennis. The one fields eleven women, the other, two men. Still, each is a sports team; each team presupposes that the mates it gathers coordinate on their practical attitudes. But that each group is a sports team does not require that the members of the one team be much like members of the other team in terms of physique or practical attitudes. With this in mind, it is natural to repeat, in agreement with Gilbert, that a group's participants may in their own way so marshal their individual cognitive capacities as literally to establish a *plural self*—a *we*. And again, it would then be this irreducible *we* that does what the group collectively and willfully does by exercising its previously mentioned pool of wills. That effective volitional resource is filled by—supervenes upon—selected coordinately instantiated practical attitudes of sufficiently many of the group's members. Thus, it was the septet he led, not Miles himself nor any member of his group, that performed "So What" on *Kind of Blue*. The *we* that the seven briefly were played that tune when recorded. Six of the seven members of the group contributed musically to "So What," but no one of them performed it. None could truthfully say, "I played it." However, each was entitled rightly to say, "*We played it.*"[14] Indeed, group participation such as this suffices for one's being a group member. And it at once amounts to establishing what social psychology construes as one of one's social identities. By performing and recording together, Miles, Cannonball Adderley, and the others in the septet, each may be apt, either implicitly or explicitly, to self-classify as a member of their ensemble. Of course, jazz musicians, like Cannonball, who regularly play with various groups within a given period may at once self-identify with each. And so too might we at once participate in multiple social groups while self-identifying with each. For though it is not necessary, it suffices for such social identifications to stick that one simply be inclined upon appropriate occasions to coordinate one's practical attitudes with others similarly inclined.

Of course, multiple memberships can also come with crippling cost to the coherence of one's multiplied social identities. The professed devout Catholic who voluntarily sits on the Planned Parenthood board and identifies with both her religious and reproductive rights groups may be courting a crisis of her social identities that ultimately necessitates resolution. For in this case her group memberships supervene upon different antagonistic subsets of her practical attitude aptitudes. Her crisis might be solved by expulsion or resignation from one of her groups. Each such resolution could simply consist of a modification of individual practical attitudes: expulsion if other group members amend their attitudes toward her, resignation if she amends her attitudes toward them.[15]

I urge that we adopt the bit of social psychology and its ontology described above. If you concur, then that is roughly equivalent to granting that our everyday—folk-psychological—practice of recognizing various particular social groups and their characteristic activities is generally epistemically reliable though certainly fallible. Accordingly, with your permission presumed, our references to social groups typically designate existing groups of the sort social psychology is prepared defeasibly to affirm and study. We take to heart, then, the idea that the social groups we are apt to cite in categorizing human interaction are, as categories or kinds, plausible candidates for ontological election by social psychology. As this developing science would have it, among the facts to be explicated are those that arise from human psychology's reliance on categorizing or conceiving oneself—and others—as being a member—or members—of social groups of various sorts. Let's now begin to exploit social psychology and its ontology to consider the chance that leeway freedom proliferates.

Consider, as an *explanandum*, the arrest of Rosa Parks on December 1, 1955, in Montgomery, Alabama, for refusing to vacate her seat on a segregated bus. Why was she arrested as she was? We know that the explanation, if complete, must refer to the fact that Parks was committed to the civil rights movement. The explanation must cite her membership in a particular social group, that she, through the NAACP, was a member of the civil rights movement with which she courageously identified. She was determined to abide by the norms she considered to be most appropriate to her group. Were it not for the existence of that group, and her so self-identifying, she would not have done what she bravely did that induced her arrest and incarceration. Our warranted acceptance of this certainly correct explanation of the famous incident trades on recognition of the existence of the social group to which the heroine belonged. The *explanans* presupposes that her membership resulted in her actually instantiating some of the properties—that is being arrested—that figure in the *explanandum*. Now what makes the case of Parks relevant to our inquiry into human free will is that it illustrates that some of the properties we individually instantiate may result from the ways in which we individually identify with particular groups. That Parks was a committed member of the civil rights movement contributed essentially to her being arrested in the politically charged context surrounding her bus ride. Her group membership altered her personal liberty: upon boarding the bus she was neither under arrest nor incarcerated, but thereafter she was arrested and incarcerated. Moreover, soon after her incarceration she was released on bail provided by the president of the local chapter of the NAACP. So, both her incarceration and release as well as the president's provision of bail are in large part explained by her membership in a group with which she strongly identified. Because of her membership in the movement, not only was she changed but so too was the bail-providing president. However, and crucially, Parks's membership in the civil rights movement transformed not only herself and the chapter president in the way described. For her activities as a member also ultimately contributed to the explanation of the transformation in civil liberties for many others then and long thereafter. Rosa alone boarded the bus, but by her doing that, the group to which she belonged acted collectively so that each in the civil rights movement could truthfully say, "We are achieving our civil rights."

That Parks was a dedicated member of the civil rights movement certainly is part of the explanation of why and how others who suffered from the then prevailing oppression managed to achieve the freedom they rightly did. What she did, *qua* trendsetting group member, changed the political status and rights of others as well as herself. Her decisive individual action was due in large part to her group membership in virtue of which she coordinated her practical reason with that of many others in the civil rights movement. Civil disobedience of the sort that her personal action realized resulted from the pool of wills filled by the wills of those in her social group. In the context of the civil rights movement, her action brought to fruition a collective action—the achievement of liberty—attributable to the civil rights movement of which she was a critical member.

Although her individual act of resistance was crucial to the group's collective action, Parks could not, and did not, claim it as uniquely hers. It was, and remains, a collective action properly attributable only to the plural-self that the civil rights movement then was and still remains. It was that specific, ever evolving *we* who commonly achieved civil rights upon the heels of Rosa's action. Acting as a member of her group, Parks's individual act of resisting oppression sufficed for changes in the civil standing of herself and others, including the many who—until she resisted—would not dare to do the likes of what she bravely did. By her action, Parks effected a change in the civil rights of others who were safe in their homes while she was unsafe in jail. The take home point is this: If you and I should be members of the same group, then although I don't lift a finger to change myself, by your action, you, being a trendsetter, might change me along with others in our group. Thus, by hopeful analogy and depending on the circumstances and group, might not one's group membership enable changes in one's and others' freedom of the will? Might one who is unable to act otherwise become able so to act with that alteration finding its explanation in one's membership in an empowering group? And if so, might not that also eventuate in the same sort of change in the status of others in the group? I think that this analogy might apply, that the answer might be yes. If that uncertain answer should be correct, then—as we shall see—the proliferation of freedom of the will is possible even in a Spinozan world. Parks, by belonging to a social group, was able to change the political freedom of both herself and others in her group. Might then Augustine, by belonging to a social group, be able to induce a collective action that achieves leeway freedom for both himself and his allies all at once? Might the akratic man in Hippo be like the brave woman in Montgomery? Might Augustine be like Parks?

Hold this question since it will soon be important. And add this thought to it: As the following example indicates, our psychological ability to recognize social groups that exist and which play their parts in altering the lives of their members is evidently cognitively penetrable and contextually sensitive (Pylyshyn 1999; Siegel 2010 and 2017; Maloney 2018). With your disheveled lecture notes falling from your hands and scattering in the hall, you race to your first class on the opening day of the fall semester. Breathless, you stumble into your classroom a moment after the bell. Once there, you are nonplussed oddly to find the students self-segregated by gender. All the women stand together on your left. All the men sit together on your right. An empty row of seats divides the two groups. You've recognized all the women *as women* and all the men *as men*. Hence, you are alert to the fact that some of your students belong to one social group, while the rest belong to another. Yet, it is curious that you perceptually categorize your students as you do. You think of all the women *as* women, so grouped, and all the men *as* men, also so grouped. This is how you then think of them despite the perceptually manifest differences that, on the one side, distinguish each of the women from all others and, on the other side, differentiate the men from one another too. This woman is tall and holding a briefcase, but that one short and clasping a big heavy book. This man is clean-shaven and hatted, but that one is bearded and bald. Some women as well as some men hold briefcases, but you fail to classify them as in the group of briefcase-carriers. More peculiar and, as you certainly know, comprehensively they all are students. But you've not identified them as such, though you would have had they not self-segregated.

Because of the way in which your visual system functions upon entry you were blind at first glance both to the cited perceptible differences and also to the universally comprehending student category. Instead, and because your visually instigated judgments are tempered by your biased but innocent cognitive history, you cannot help but categorizing your just so segregated students by gender. On that ephemeral occasion you represent the world of your classroom as including two social kinds or categories of individual persons—women here, men there. You notice neither the differentiating diversity of the individual students nor their unifying student status. And what would you then say of yourself—if pressed in a clever experimentally controlled way—to say on the spot what sort of person you are? Your prevailing recognition of the two gender groups would probably lexically prime your response.[16] For your social classification of your students by gender is apt cognitively to trigger and determine the specific psychological processes that prompt your own social self-categorization. Hence, you'd likely reply to the experimenter by identifying or categorizing yourself by your own gender. But your so self-identifying by gender is itself doubly peculiar. For only moments before—when scribbling your notes in your office and, thus, differently primed—you'd probably have categorized yourself, if asked, by your profession—professor—rather than by your gender. If so, then not only is one's inclination to recognize the social groups to which others belong contextually mediated, but so too is one's aptitude for social self-categorization and self-identification subject to cognitive penetration. Although those whom one socially categorizes may recognizably participate at once in various social groups, the groups one is apt to recognize on an occasion situationally vary. Moreover, depending upon the prevailing context, one may be permanently oblivious to some of the existing social groups to which oneself or others actually belong over long periods of time and with which the members—even oneself—strongly but implicitly identify.

Now, throughout we have supposed that scientific psychology's conceptual scheme is nestled—reductively or not—within the comprehending hierarchy of scientific schemes from physics on up. Thus, the social kinds psychology countenances, even if not reducible to more fundamental kinds, presumably conform to scientifically sanctioned kinds generally (Fodor 1974; Rosenberg 1994; Kitcher 2001; Massimi 2016; Woodward 2016). Thus, if we reify scientifically registered kinds at all, then we should not flinch at admitting social kinds into naturalized ontology when we think about free actions in a world ruled by Spinozan laws. The relationally defined properties of being a planet and being a predator admit of reification within astronomy and ecology, respectively. But neither of these physically realized properties admit of neat reduction by way of physics. Nonetheless, each of these supervening properties figure in confirmed theories pitched by astronomy on the one hand and ecology on the other. So too, then, for the kinds and properties proposed by social psychology's conception of how social groups figure in explanations of human affairs. This point shall pay dividends when we turn to social groups to which someone, such as Augustine, recognizably and perhaps prototypically belongs. For if social psychology tends to reify the kinds of social groups which we ourselves are apt to employ in categorizing ourselves and others, the group typified by Augustine in his resistance to Spinozan psychology should be as real as groups such as civil rights movements, dancing duets, houses of Congress, jazz ensembles, women, men, and professors. Got it? Good!

So, consider major league baseball, both as played by few and as attended by many. Just as each player and fan individually exists, so too the team and the fans, each *qua* social group arguably exists. Why Roberto Clemente, but not Mickey Mantle, wears a Pittsburgh Pirates uniform is explained by their different team memberships, Roberto being a Pirate, Mickey a Yankee. And we explain why some folks cheer for Pirates while others root for Yankees by citing their memberships in the different fan clubs of the different teams. Evidently, each group—the team and its fans—supervenes, at least in part, on various psychological norm-sensitive dispositions characteristically common to the players and fans respectively (Gilbert 1989, 2004, and 2010; Gaus and Nichols 2017; Bicchieri 2017, chap. 5; Thomasson 2019). Roberto is apt to play right field when Mickey is batting, and Mickey tends to play center field when Roberto is at the plate. Pirates fans are likely to applaud should Roberto, but not Mickey, hit one over the center fielder's head; Yankees fans most likely will stand and yell should Mickey, but not Roberto, drive the ball beyond the right fielder's reach.

Though a group's members may be reliably disposed to comply with their group's norms, it is often hard, if not impossible, formally to state the norms abided. For norms—as controllers of agents' behavioral dispositions—are often conditional upon wide open disjunctions. Being a team member, the norm-sensitive compliant catcher is apt, *ceteris paribus*, to toss a pitch, once caught, back to the pitcher unless, *non ceteris paribus*, the inning is over, or a runner is attempting to steal a base, or the umpire demands to examine the ball for scuffs, or the manager summons a reliver, or the game is called on account of rain, or whatever. The norms to which participants resonate might, in part, be publicly available and accessible by formal procedures, as in baseball's rulebook. Or, without promulgation or publication, sensitive group actors might modulate their activities in reliable concordance with norms never mentioned but effectively enforced. Thus, the fans naturally cheer when their team, not its opponent, scores although it is neither etched on stone tablets nor by Moses proclaimed that each individual fan should cheer just so. As Bicchieri convincingly argues and Thomasson allows, norms can subtly emerge *in the wild* without the formal or contractual conspiracy of the would-be rule followers. For a group's norms to take seed in an enduring social niche it roughly suffices that, over time and perhaps with reinforcement, individuals become stably apt to interact in certain predictable patterns because of the ways in which their individual practical attitudes, including mutual expectations, eventually align.

Whether cultivated or wild, a group's norms, once sprouted, can grow and evolve so as to fit the group's changing environment and the mutating attitudes of individual members, especially if *trendsetters* are active (Bicchieri 2017, chap. 5).[17] For trendsetters—like Parks—though few, are apt to risk the cost of violating prevailing norms and—by such noticed violations—nudge others to amend their own practical attitudes. Depending on the contexts in which a trendsetter nudges—intentionally or not—group norms might fluctuate as members, wise to the trendsetter, individually adjust their own attitudes to accommodate trends newly set. Before, but not after, Parks's refusal and arrest, most of her local co-members in the civil rights movement understandably were apt to abide by the prevailing unjust laws and customs regarding bus riding. As a trendsetter, Parks publicly stood against the prevailing injustice. As knowledge of her violation spread among members of her social group, the group's supervening norms bent to match the evolution in the practical attitudes of its members inspired by Parks's defiance. Thus, in a given social environment, the evolution of a group's prevailing norms can be a partial function of the witnessed risky and maybe costly actions of daring trendsetters. A typical individual group member is inclined minimally and adaptively to conform to her group's plastic norms. That implies that her practical attitudes are apt to co-evolve with those of others in her group. Thus, it would seem that the sheer inclination to conform to a group's norms may suffice for group membership. For consider the person who, prior to Parks's trendsetting, may have been disposed to join the movement but verbally refused an invitation for fear of his life. Suppose, because he was so disposed, that upon learning of Parks's stance, courage replaces his fear. And he immediately and publicly announces his support of her movement. It would seem that, although previously he had publicly declined to join her group, even then—despite his nay saying—unbeknownst to him his psychological disposition may have sufficed for his covert membership in, and identification with, the movement.

If you are apt to act as others do in ways that resonate to common norms, then you and the others are evidently members of the same group. If membership is a function of such aptitude rather than its activation, then one might be a group member simply in virtue of being apt practically to reason and act coordinately with others without ever actually reasoning or acting as other group members do. The baseball player who gets splinters from the bench and never runs onto the field is a team member not because he actually does what those on the field do. Rather, his place on the roster is secured, at least in part, by what is he apt to do should he ever get into the game. With this in mind, we might well conjecture that an agent's inclination minimally to conform to the norms characteristic of a group constitutes his implicitly identifying with that group whether or not he actually avows his own social identification. Thus, particular fans, if asked to identify themselves upon exiting the game, may individually actually say, "I'm a Pirates fan." And other enduring fans, if unquestioned but apt to answer the same, might never actually declare allegiance but yet remain always allegiant. Analogously, the catcher and pitcher might actually answer the same question in the context of a game by saying, "I am a Pittsburgh Pirate," while their uninterrogated benched teammates may be mute but on the same payroll.

Something like this, with a slight twist, applies to Parks and some who, unlike her, never violate the laws and customs of segregation. For someone who—when it counts—would do, but never does do, what Parks did may yet participate in the same civil rights group as does Parks. This, even if that surrogate is never due the credit Parks merits. Parks and her would-be surrogate both identify with their common group in virtue of their common aptitudes to adopt and act upon selected similar practical attitudes. Their psychological similarity need not be exact in every detail to suffice for membership in the same social group. Parks might be apt publicly to say, "I am dedicated to civil rights." However, her shy but equally courageous surrogate, might be disinclined to announce herself as would Parks. Yet the surrogate might, like Parks, refuse—or be disposed to refuse—to surrender her rightful bus seat. In some contexts it is what one is apt to do, not what one is apt to admit, that suffices for one's social self-identification and determines one's group membership. One might be inclined to be supportive of civil rights and, thus, be among the group of like-minded people while being disinclined verbally to announce it. But that should not surprise us when we recall you, the professor, late for your first class. Because of the way your students are seated, you may be apt verbally to classify your students and yourself by gender, while being disinclined on that occasion to testify that the students are all students and yourself a professor.

To announce one of one's social identities is linguistically to ostend or confess to a set of dispositional practical attitudes sufficient for group membership. The forthright fan's assertion that she is a Pirates fan is a bit of her overt behavior. It evidences that she is apt to encode and deploy a host of mental representations characteristic of Pirates fans. It is, then, as if her assertion should indicate not only that *I AM A PIRATES FAN* is among her Mentalese tokens jointly enabling her assertion but also that she harbors *I WILL CHEER WHENEVER A PIRATE SCORES*. Together, those mental representations contribute to the control of her behavior *qua* Pirates fan. If so, we can tie this diagnosis to what we have said far above about one's authorized autobiography. Some of one's social identities that are secured by entrenched practical attitudes figure crucially in the composition of one's authorized autobiography. For the Mentalese representations that encode these attitudes are among the very psychic inscriptions that constitute one's autobiography. If the Pirates fan deeply identifies as being a fan, then—by our lights—that amounts to the centrality of *I AM A PIRATES FAN* and *I WILL CHEER WHENEVER A PIRATE SCORES* in her autobiography.[18] They, along with other of their partnering representations would be near to practically ineliminable parts of her *apologia vita sua, her authorized autobiography*.

Much the same applies to Parks and, with another small twist, to her shy surrogate. Parks's assertion of "I am dedicated to civil rights" indicates that *I AM DEDICATED TO CIVIL RIGHTS* is part of her authorized autobiography. However, her surrogate is disinclined to say what Parks says but otherwise inclined to do what Parks does on the bus. That the shy surrogate is apt to mimic Parks's courageous refusal to surrender her bus seat is evidence that, like Parks, she too tokens *I AM DEDICATED TO CIVIL RIGHTS* in her own authorized autobiography. It accounts for the fact that she shares Parks's courage. However, since—unlike Parks—the surrogate is shy, that same encoded bit of her autobiography does not control her speech. Although she harbors it, its control over her speech is blocked by those of her psychological states that constitute her diffidence without blocking her courage.

With the above conception of social identity in hand, wind the clock back to the seventh game of the 1960 World Series. The underdog home team Pirates face the awesome visiting Yankees. Put yourself in Pirates manager Danny Murtaugh's shoes. Before the first pitch, your team's dugout and bullpen hold the league-allowed twenty-six rostered members in uniform, all ready to play. But when the climactic game starts at old Forbes Field only your best nine take to the grass. As the game progresses, you substitute some on the bench or in the bullpen for others on the field. When Bill Mazeroski steps up to the plate at the bottom of the ninth inning, the score is tied at 9. With the count 1–0, Maz hits his unforgettable walk-off homer over the ivy-covered red brick wall. Your team wins to the wild cheers of the local fans. By the time Maz crosses the plate to finish the triumph, only fifteen of your team's twenty-six players have been on the field. Of these fifteen, only eight have had hits. Some others may have touched neither the ball nor a base, though all have tried their best. The eleven who sat the bench throughout the game did less than the others toward the win. But when the game was over, all on the roster, every fan in the stadium, and indeed each Pirates fan far away could correctly say, "*We* did *it*! *We* won!"[19] For the winning was collectively done when the last hit cleared the ivy. The Pirates' win was a collective action collectively willed by a *we* that called upon its pool of wills. Each Pirates fan and player, in her way or his, was a winner thanks to being among that *we* who willed winning.

Each committed victor variously willed winning. And by that willing contributed to the pool of wills that eventuated in the collective actions over nine innings that finally won the game. A benched player contributed only to the pool of wills and added no individual action to the winning team's collective actions. A fan's contribution was much the same as a player on the pine. Nevertheless, all players with unwrinkled uniforms and all fans on their feet were among the winners because, by their contributions to the effective pool of wills, they shared in the collectively willed collective actions. Their different kinds of aptitudes for practical attitudes sufficed for their membership in the winning ensemble that included, but was not limited to, all uniformed players and fans. For the winners included those who contributed to the winning collective actions, if not by actually playing, then by otherwise chipping into the winning group's pool of wills. That the benched player was willing to play and that a fan was willing to cheer was what, at a minimum, they contributed to what was collectively done. Those entitled to say, "We won!"

varied in their individual contributions some merely contributed to the pool of wills, others contributed individual actions such as hits, pitches or catches. But all were apt to do what, even if little, they could toward the collective victory. Only Maz hit the walk-off home run; he alone contributed that particular crucial individual action to the winning collective actions. Still, what he did was willed by the pool of wills, and that made his hit a game winner for all.[20] Neither Mazeroski nor any single individual was *the* winner. For that winner was the social group to which indefinitely many belonged. That group—the winner—included those who, by way of their various aptitudes contributed to the group's effort. Hence all others, if any besides team members and fans, who in one way or another properly, even if silently, identified with the hard to enumerate victorious group, would be champions too. So, a dozing accountant in the team's finance department may well have qualified among the winners entitled to claim a share of the victory, even though that dutiful pencil pusher may not qualify as a player or fan. For what that accountant willfully or intentionally did or was apt to do as part of the job may have contributed both to the pool of wills and the collective winning action.

It is hard to know—and I certainly don't—how many and how far from the field the winners were when that last October hit cleared the outfield wall in Pittsburgh. It is the hard task of social psychology, not philosophy, to settle the particular parameters that define a specific social group the science might opt to cite in its account of our social lives. The sciences of the social are entitled to reify that over which they would existentially quantify. These existential arbiters assume the tough task of identifying real social groups and specifying the people and their attitudes upon which a particular posited social group is to supervene. The difficulty of the duty is characteristic of disciplines that recruit supervenience into their conceptual schemes. After all, it is hard to discern an individual branch and the exact configuration it contributes to the elephantine shape of its dense supervening shrub. And it is harder still to discern the pattern of practical attitudes that an individual member contributes to the character of her supervening group. The accountant who never cheers might by his or her work and practical attitudes be like you, the professor, entering your classroom on the semester's first day. Upon arriving, you implicitly identify with your profession, and in fact you are then a member of that group. But being biased by your current classification of your students by gender, you are primed explicitly to self-classify and self-identify by your gender rather than your profession. It may not cross your mind at the moment you linguistically self-identify by gender that you also then covertly self-identify as a professor. And so too, may the accountant only implicitly and even unwittingly identify with the Pirates' collectivity simply by being apt dutifully to balance the books, process the payroll, and submit the team's quarterly tax forms when due. For by willfully fulfilling the job's duties, the accountant might in a quiet way contribute to either the winning group's pool of wills or the indefinitely many individual actions that sum to the collective win. If the pitcher's pitch contributes to the team's collective action, then might not the accountant's signing the pitcher's paycheck contribute to the same collective action? Of course, though the winners be as many as there actually are, the rewards to the winners may be differentially and perhaps unfairly distributed. Maz got both lifelong glory and maybe a modest cash bonus, the accountant maybe a day off for the victory parade, and each fan, near or far, only a deserved gulp of gratification.

Much the same importantly applies to Parks and the civil rights movement for which she did so much. Her civil disobedience contributed critically to the passage of civil rights legislation. She did her part to enable some of the victories achieved by that hard to enumerate, ever changing, but still continuous important group. It was that evolving social group—the civil rights movement—that achieved what was achieved upon Parks's arrest. All members of that social group, including those in 1955 and all other participants thereafter, are entitled to claim achievement in the first-person plural. The admiring young person today whose practical attitudes complement the attitudes exemplified by Parks surely makes no mistake should she say, "In Montgomery long ago and before my birth, *we* achieved something worthwhile then and ever since."

Let us now apply, first to Spartacus and second to Augustine, what we've cadged from the ontology of psychology, both social and cognitive. Above I argued that because of the ways in which Spartacus and Augustine each resisted their different fates, the former achieved momentary freedom from Roman servitude while the latter secured freedom of the will. But the question that has since stalked us is whether their liberating achievements were necessarily restricted to themselves. Or might such achievements proliferate to others? The answer is uncertain.

Perhaps Spartacus is like Mazeroski while the rebels he led are like Mazeroski's teammates. Or better still, let Parks model Spartacus while those active with Parks in the civil rights movement serve as analogues for the rebels. And might those Roman slaves who only from afar cheered the rebels' initial victories over their Roman masters be akin to Pirates fans who deeply and publicly identify with Mazeroski's team? Or, again better, perhaps the remote slaves ought to be likened to late arriving civil rights sympathizers only recently sensitive to the problems Parks and others confronted many years past. And what of others in Roman shackles who dared not cheer the revolt but, hating their bondage, surreptitiously disregarded their masters' cruel whims whenever they could? Might these surreptitious insubordinates be analogous to the diligent accountant who covertly, implicitly and perhaps unwittingly participates in the Pirates' victory by being apt productively to adapt to the demands of the hard job? And would we be wrong to think of the silent but resistant slaves by likening them to those who quietly participate in the civil rights movement not by publicizing their approval but rather by how they are apt to live their daily lives with subtle dignity in defiance of racism? If so, then it may not be wildly wrong to conjecture that just as Maz's teammates and all their fans share his *we-won* status, so too did all of Spartacus's soldiers and supporters—both daring and surreptitious—share his ultimate status. And again, just as Parks's entire coalition, both then and thereafter, share her *we-achievement*, so too might have Spartacus's moment of liberty proliferated among all who were for him in one way or another. Ought not we who judge the various allies of Spartacus judge them as we judge him? For weren't they, all together, a cohesive social group of variously committed and variously involved individuals with complementary aptitudes for practical attitudes appropriate to their individual circumstances? Wasn't the occasion of Spartacus's valiant death an occasion of collective action collectively willed, a group achievement willed by many wills pooled? Isn't what the revolt achieved something that all achieved for all rather than something that only one achieved for only himself? Spartacus was uniquely heroic. But that did not entitle him to affirm, "*I did it!*" Rather, he was entitled to say exactly and only the same as all who, either with sword or in spirit, joined him. And what they all could rightly say was, "*We did it!*" Surely, wasn't what was done by the slave rebellion not done by any one person alone but rather by many collectively?

I uncertainly say *yes* to each of these admittedly rhetorical questions, knowing that my answer trades on tremulous analogies. I concede that you might answer contrariwise, demanding more certainty than my argument can sustain. How properly persuasive is my analogical derivation of the proliferation of momentary liberty among the allies of Spartacus? I teeter on the brink of persuasion but appreciate that you might rush away from the rim. Still, I will stay here at the edge. For isn't what passes for defeasible proof always grounded in analogy with the previously proven? Moreover, don't we indefeasibly approve a fresh instance of *modus ponens* because it is analogous to prior approved instances long since forgotten? Here you justifiably question my hunch on behalf of the proliferation of emancipation from Roman slavery. The embryonic idea is new and wanting confirmation. It is still a foal on wobbly legs. To answer your challenging opposition, can one do better than, like Frege, plead for a pinch of salt and ask that, for now at least, analogy suffice *demonstrare quid demonstrandum*?[21]

So much, then, for Spartacus and the attendant possibility that the revolt's presumed achievement of momentary freedom from bondage may have spread beyond Spartacus himself to those included within his rightly defined revolutionary group. However, what of Augustine, his freedom of the will, and the prospect of its proliferation? The answer to this question is our pressing primary concern. I have argued that, by his asymptotic approach to leeway freedom in the context of temptation to which he succumbs, Augustine manages almost to be just so free. And that, I say—though you may not—suffices for him to be leeway free in that context. But does his remarkable achievement, if genuine, propagate? Are others thereby ever free? Might we be free now because he was free then?

In order to see how leeway freedom of the sort I've attributed to Augustine might propagate, consider that we know of Augustine's experience of akrasia through his published—and hence publicly accessible—autobiography. His *Confessions*, as a confession, is a form of communication with others, his would-be secular confessors. That Augustine published his autobiography in the form of a confession is tantamount to his designating and recognizing some, if not all, of his genuinely interested cross-centuries readers, regardless of their theistic attitudes, as those to whom he asynchronously confesses. Whether penitently or not, secularly to confess is to submit a bit of one's authorized autobiography for assessment. Even if impenitent, a confessee may simply be uncertain as to the status of the acknowledged action on a given relevant spectrum of evaluation. Effectively, the confessee might be saying to the confessor, "Here's what I did. I'm doubtful as to what to make of it. What's your assessment?" An autobiography can, and in Augustine's case presumably does, amount to a true recounting of one's life suffused with an accurate explanation of why one lived just so. Viewed this way, Augustine's autobiography is a public representation of those of his practical attitudes that induced him to live as he did. It is as if through his *Confessions* he were to say to his confessors, "Here is what I akratically did and how and why I did it. Was I leeway free or not? How do you, my confessors, assess me?" Augustine's *Confessions* is, then, his testimony submitted to his audience over time—his qualified jurors—who, in a way sensitive to norms of the sort Strawson described, are positioned to assess the quality and, indeed, the freedom of Augustine's will. By publishing his autobiography Augustine initiated a continuing philosophical conversation about the way in which conflicted willing ought to be assessed under the assumption of determinism (McKenna, 2012). The question up for discussion is whether a will such as his, when akratic in the manner described, is leeway free. But who exactly are these would be jurors, his secular confessors? Do they include all who ever read his story? No, for the relevant readers are those who would function as genuine confessors—qualified jurors. They are then to be wise, fair minded, and most certainly empathetic readers of Augustine's *Confessions*. To qualify as a juror in Augustine's perennial trial, one must deeply understand his autobiography. That requires not merely studying his written words but also, thereby, so to read his mind as to simulate those of his practical reasons that he offers as his *apologia pro vita sua*. His empathetic jurors, by knowing his mind full well, are to put themselves in his shoes, to think as he thought and to feel as he felt. By simulating his psychology, they vicariously experience what—and as—akratic Augustine experienced. His jurors are to assess his akrasia by way of vicariously experiencing it. They are to assess Augustine in the fashion of an audience to a compelling performance of a drama. In attending to Augustine's *Confessions*, his confessors are to assess him in the manner in which Antigone's audience may evaluate her by thinking and feeling as she would. Or they are to evaluate Augustine in the manner in which Hamlet's audience would evaluate him, or as would Willy Loman's audience consider him. Call all who would be just so properly qualified to appear in Augustine's trial, either as juror or defendant, Augustinians. They include both Augustine—the defendant, testifying in his own behalf—and his fit secular confessors—the jury. I say that the Augustinians constitute a social group that persists across a continuing stretch of time. Should I be right, this group tolerates the immigration and emigration of individual members. But as they come and go, Augustinians are all apt empathetically to identify with akratic Augustine. Thus, Augustinians are disposed—perhaps implicitly, unconsciously, or even unwittingly—to self-identify as Augustinians. They are prone philosophically to wonder with him, under the assumption of determinism, whether the will, if akratic, might yet be free. Their social bond is their common, nondogmatic, open-minded compatibilist concern. Among the Augustinians, the jurors are those who are apt to understand and wisely assess what I have called Augustine's akratic asymptotic approach to the ability to act otherwise. These wise and just assessors are, as his peers, deeply to appreciate the circumstances particular to Augustine's confessed akrasia. For they simulate his akratic psychology and in that mimetic way cathartically suffer it in much the way he confesses it to have sustained it. They know the content of his conflicted deliberation and vicariously endure its phenomenal character. It is no easy matter to sit, as an Augustinian, on Augustine's jury. Together, I claim, Augustinians constitute a cohesive secular social group: defendant here, jurors there. Their common project is to discover whether Augustine's akratic psychology suffices for his being leeway free. Augustinians are poised to act collectively since, *qua* jurors, their project presupposes that, like any jury, they so pool their wills as to reach and report a verdict. Theirs is a task none of them singly can do. If it is to be done, it is to be collectively done by the *we* that Gilbert would have their social group be.

Pause to reflect upon a representative jury trial in a properly functioning criminal court of law. The jurors are presented with scrutinized evidence, including testimony. They are charged with rending a verdict: guilty or not guilty. That is, they are assigned the task of discovering whether, as a matter of objective fact, the defendant is guilty or not. Their duty is not merely to make it be the case, sheerly by virtue of their collective decision, that the defendant is either guilty or innocent. Rather, the jury's charge is to complete a sequential two-step process: first, discover the truth in light of the evidence; second, announce their finding—the objective truth—guilt or innocence. It is because their duty is correctly to assess the defendant that a retrial is permissible should it come to be known that the jury objectively erred in its discovery effort. In this sense, a jury's difficult task is much like that of a scientific community. A scientific community comes to possess scrutinized evidence. It is charged, on the basis of the evidence, with discovering the objectively best hypothesis, if not some hard permanent truth, sufficient to explain the phenomena of interest. The charge is not to substitute by proclamation some subjective post-modernist counterfeit explanation for the real coin. The common job of science and the court is discovery. Nothing else will do to do the job. It matters not whether the job falls to jurors with wrinkled brows seated in the box, to scientists sitting at the bench bent over microscopes, or to Augustinians with Augustine's autobiography opened (Goldman, 2014; Pettit, 2014).

So, then, how should the Augustinians proceed in assessing Augustine's will? Their proceedings virtually consist of many episodes over time in which individual Augustinians carefully consider and assess Augustine's akratic deliberation. Such episodes are formally like the proceeding pertaining to Zelda, Zach and their fair-minded teacher. The students undertake to determine the slippery area of their assigned circle. They each compute in accord with the governing formula, and each submits a solution, with the one differing from the other as the decimal expression expands. The teacher assesses each student, knowing—as the students may suspect—that their task is beyond Sisyphean. And yet, the circle's elusive area is exactly what it is. The teacher, since fair, gives each student full credit for answering correctly although their answers do differ. For the teacher recognizes that, given their particular problem, each student did as well as need be done to get the job done in the prevailing circumstances. Each almost got the area exactly right. And that, the teacher properly concludes, is enough for each student, relative to her or his particular situation, differently but correctly to have achieved the same evanescent goal.

In the virtual Augustinian court Augustine submits for assessment his confession of akrasia. It is his proposed solution to achieving leeway freedom should Spinozan determinism prevail. His jurors, fellow Augustinians, adopt the Spinozan presupposition. They consider whether, by dint of his akratic episode, he asymptotically approached the ability to act otherwise than he actually did. Augustine's psychological mimes are empathetically mindful of both the content and phenomenal character of the practical attitudes constitutive of his conflicted willing. By simulating his psychology, they aim to determine, in the glow of their scrutinized evidence, whether Augustine did as well as need be done in order to be leeway free. Relative to his circumstances in which Augustine's simulating jurors are steeped, they consider whether he almost achieved the elusive leeway at which he aimed. Did he do as well as one might so as to choose to act on his well-reasoned preferences while his psychology ultimately determined that he not so choose? Augustinian jurors are, I say, bound to conclude in Augustine's favor. They would approvingly assess Augustine in much the way her fair teacher assesses Zelda. Each of these two—sinner and student—is, and ought to be, judged to have done well enough almost to have achieved their different but commonly fugacious objectives. And, so, each assessor, whether teacher or Augustinian juror, is respectively committed to concluding that, relative to their individual prevailing circumstances, Zelda and Augustine each respectively achieved her or his goal. Zelda actually solved her problem. So did Augustine. That, in each case, ought to be the objective determination of every right-minded assessor.

Augustinians, empathetically illuminated by their compelling evidence, discover that Augustine was in fact leeway free within his prevailing circumstances. They could not have soundly abduced this conclusion were it not for his critical testimony. His contribution is crucial to their discerning his leeway freedom. Moreover, and perhaps surprisingly, their discovery is conversely critical to his being leeway free. For, the very fact that Augustine composes his autobiography in the form of a confession implies his own uncertainty as to the adequacy of his solution to the problem of leeway freedom under Spinozan determinism. His dubious situation is possibly like that of Zelda tasked with successfully completing her computational assignment. Notice that her completion of the assignment requires both that she do something and also that her teacher do something. Zelda must, first, compute in accordance with the governing algorithm and, second, her answer must be approved by her teacher. Otherwise, the project is incomplete. The successful completion of Zelda's assignment is a two-step process. If Zelda should take the first step correctly, the process is only half complete. For the teacher must then proceed to discover, by checking Zelda's calculation, that the student's submission is, in fact, correct. This is not in any way to say that the teacher's assessment makes Zelda's answer be correct. Rather, the teacher certifies, confirms, or otherwise signals her acknowledgment that, even if the student was dubious of her achievement, her doubt was unfounded. Zelda achieved her goal because both steps necessary for the two steps to achievement were taken, the first by Zelda, the second by the teacher. Zelda's project is, it turns out, a group project, with the group consisting of Zelda and her teacher. Each must contribute to the project if it is to be completed. If so completed, then neither Zelda nor her teacher can rightly claim, in the first-person singular, its completion, though each might rightly register the claim in the first-person plural. It is the *we*—who together they are—is who gets the project done.

Augustine's achievement of leeway freedom of the will is analogous. Successful achievement in his case is again a two-step process: the first, his, the second, his jurors'. First, he must endure and confess his akratic computation of his regretted action. Augustine's endurance and confession is like Zelda's computation and her paper submission to her teacher. Second, like Zelda's qualified and competent teacher, the qualified and competent Augustinian jury must proceed to discover, by checking Augustine's confessed akratic computation, that his submission is, in fact, a correct solution to his vexing problem. Again, this is not in any way to say that the Augustinian jury's assessment makes Augustine's submission be correct. Rather, the sage jury certifies, confirms, or otherwise signals its well-founded acknowledgment that, even if Augustine was dubious of his achievement, his doubt was unfounded. Like Zelda, he got it right too. Just like Zelda, Augustine achieved his goal because both steps necessary for his achievement were taken—the first by him, the second by his jury. And thus, if they complete their goal, neither Augustine nor his jury can rightly claim success in the first-person singular although both the defendant and jury can claim it in the first-person plural. For, once again, their *we* gets the project done.

In order to reach their objective verdict, the Augustinians read Augustine's mind. Being empathetic, they simulate the very way in which, with his conflicted wills, Augustine akratically and regretfully acts. Thus, Augustinians are apt practically to reason as did Augustine. For the psychology—presumably Spinozan—that governs him also governs them. So, Augustinians all—including both the confessee and confessors—are similarly apt to resist the control of their common psychology. Hence, if Augustine is leeway free, so also are Augustinians. Their assessment of him applies by precedent to all of them. Hence freedom does proliferate even in a Spinozan world should there be Augustinians, those among us who would charitably assess Augustine's will. Should you too hope to be leeway free if the world proves to be Spinozan? Well, membership in the Augustinians is always open. One need only be empathetic to Augustine automatically to be admitted. Indeed, you may already be a member. For recall that one's social identity can covertly dodge self-awareness since proclivity to detect and affirm it is cognitively penetrable.

As I see it, Augustinians so assess Augustine's will as to consider him a trendsetter to emulate. Their assessment carries the aim of undertaking to deliberate as he would on occasions of conflicted—akratic—willing. Their endorsement involves resolving to resist psychological processes that would contravene the formation of well-reasoned preferences and disrupt them prior to the point of their execution in choice. Put differently, Augustinians cleave to cognitive norms that require resisting tempting and tempestuous desires that, if determinative, would preclude acting as well-reasoned preference would have it. Augustinians recognize, as Augustine's akrasia demonstrates, that our governing psychology so rules us that occasionally reason is doomed to lose to desire. Nonetheless, the Augustinian assessment is that doomed rational resistance against overwhelming desire is required by the norms of their social group, as set by that group's confessed trendsetter. Far better that, say Augustinians, than to be wanton.

What Augustine, as a trendsetter, models for his fellow travelers is how to deal with the imperious ways in which human psychology, especially if Spinozan, tends to tear us in two. Though he long ago could not have known what contemporary developmental psychology has since demonstrated, he may have intuitively appreciated its point. From our youngest days forward our presumably necessitarian psychology inclines us to both see the world and ourselves through morality's lens and also to act in the way it brings into focus. Recall in this context the discoveries of psychologists whose research resonates with that of Wynn and Bloom. The unindoctrinated child sees both nice and nasty puppets respectively help or hinder another puppet (Hamlin, Wynn, and Bloom 2007; Wynn and Bloom 2013; P. Bloom 2010; Hamlin 2015; Wynn et al. 2018; Marshall, Wynn, and P. Bloom 2020). Typically, the mind-reading child reacts by recognizing the helpers and hinderers *as such*. And she adjusts her own behavior toward those whose attitudes and actions she has assessed so as to set right, in the little ways she can, what—in the light of her moral bias—she sees as shockingly wrong. The point to be seized is that from the start, our psychology evidently imposes upon us an aptitude to think, feel, and act in recognizably moral ways (Schroeder, Roskies, and Nichols 2010; Sinnott-Armstrong, Young, and Cushman 2010; Rosati 2016). The child who thinks ill of the hindering puppet thinks of it both as able not to hinder and as obliged not to hinder. If that is how she thinks of the puppet, she evidently thinks similarly of herself, as able and as obliged to act otherwise upon occasions of her own nasty behavior. Yet, though the child's moral psychology may be developmentally early if not innate, her psychology also occasionally induces her to hinder rather than help. So, it seeds in the innocent child the weed of akrasia. For, as she undergoes the psychological process that shall eventuate in her hindering on an occasion, her moral module must be promoting that she not hinder, that she aim to be able to act otherwise than to hinder. Her psychology so rules that she be conflicted. The laws of the mind determine that she be like akratic Augustine. For she too must travel the Sisyphean curve toward the possibility of not doing what she inevitably does. From infancy forward we are driven to be moral and that drives us to be able to act otherwise when we are not what we naturally aspire to be. Augustine confesses to Augustinians the way in which he struggles with this inescapably human problem. He submits his solution to his assessors as his contribution to their common two-step project. And being wise and fair jurors, they recognize that doing one's just so best when psychologically conflicted is almost doing enough ideally to resolve the conflict. Thus, to complete their step in the shared process, his sapient jurors objectively judge that in such cases almost enough is plenty enough.

Notice now the analogies, tuned to social psychology and its ontology, waiting to be noticed. Augustine, Parks, and Mazeroski were each trendsetting members of their respective social groups. Parks and Mazeroski each did something that enabled their respective groups collectively to achieve their respective goals. By resisting the oppression of segregation, Parks enabled the civil rights movement collectively to achieve its victory. By resisting the opposing pitcher, Mazeroski enabled the social conjunction of his team and its fans collectively to achieve its victory. And, so, you won't be surprised that by resisting Spinozan psychology, Augustine enabled his social group— the Augustinians—collectively to achieve its victory, leeway freedom for them all. Each of our three individual agents did something remarkably important by way of enabling the collective achievement of her or his group. Yet since the achievements were collective, none of the three heroes may have rightly said, "I achieved it!" Nonetheless, each member of their respective groups may gratefully say "We achieved it!" Leeway freedom is a collective achievement, a collective victory over Spinozan determinism against impossible odds.

To the victors go the spoils. Help yourself!

## NOTES

1. Lurking in the background here is the question of the motivational character of normative attitudes. To be clear, I am not advocating for a particular conception of the motivational character of normative judgments. Rather, what I am claiming is that we are apt to resist action-inducing practical attitudes that, introspectively, seem to cut against our sense of autonomy. To dip your toe into the large and complex issues about normative motivation, see Rosati (2016).

2. Perhaps this softly echoes something better described by Camus's rendition of the plight of mythic Sisyphus (Camus 2012, 41).

3. While acknowledging that Nagel doubts that we might be the ultimate authors of any of our actions, Kane elliptically quotes Nagel's influential expression of the conception of ultimacy in play, as follows (Kane, 1999-03-18, pp. 79–80):

> The sense that we are the authors of our own actions is not just a feeling, but a belief; and we can't come to regard it as pure appearance without giving it up altogether. But what belief is it? . . . Although many of the external and internal conditions of choice are inevitably fixed by the world and not under my control, some range of . . . possibilities is generally presented to me on an occasion of action—and when acting I make one of these possibilities . . . actual, the final explanation . . . is given by the intentional explanation of

my action. . . . My reason for doing it is the *whole* reason why it happened, and no further explanation is either necessary or possible. (Nagel, 1989, pp. 114–15)

4. See the debate between Fodor and Paul Churchland regarding the encapsulation of visual experience (Fodor 1984; Paul Churchland 1988).

5. This is why Augustine is certainly no wanton despite the fact that his behavior may be prompted by urges and desires that he cannot overcome. For his indecisiveness satisfies conditions on self-reflection that wantons fail to meet (Frankfurt 1971). There is something that we recognize in Augustine's akratic failure to live up to his own—but too weakly willed—standards that invites us to forgive him for the ways in which he may wrong himself or others, including ourselves. See Calhoun (2016).

6. If the judge's contextually tuned verdict should be correct, it locates Augustine's freedom to act otherwise in those of his efficacious reactive attitudes constitutive of his resentful resistance to nature's governance. Perhaps this, or something like it complements Holliday's remark upon concluding his argument for incompatibilism. "For those who regard the traditional debate about the freedom to do otherwise as resolved in favor of incompatibilism, it is time to consider the other kinds of control that we wield over the natural world, including ourselves as parts of it. We may yet find a form of inner freedom that is possible even in a deterministic world" (Holliday 2012, 206).

7. On the contextual character of our assessment of Augustine, compare Nichols (2015, 11): "I argue that while people believe in indeterminism, that belief is grounded in faulty inference and should be regarded as unjustified. However, even if determinism is true, it's a further substantive question whether that means that free will doesn't exist. I argue that, because of the flexibility of reference, there is no single answer to this question. In some contexts, it will be true to say 'free will exists'; in other contexts, it will be false to say that. With this substantive background in place, I argue for a pragmatic approach to prescriptive issues. In some contexts, the prevailing practical considerations suggest that we should deny the existence of free will and moral responsibility; in other contexts the practical considerations suggest that we should affirm free will and moral responsibility."

8. See Sherif (1956); Velleman (1997), Gilbert (1989, 2004 and 2010); Searle (1990, 1995); Bratman (1993, 1999); Tuomela (2000 chaps. 1–4, 2007 chaps. 1, 2, 5 and 6, 2013), Ellemers, Spears, and Doosje (2002); Thomasson (2003, 2014 chaps. 3, 6 and 9, and 2019), Greenwood (2003); Turner and Reynolds (2003, 2011); Appiah (2005); Hornsey (2008); Miller (2010); List and Pettit (2011); Doris and Nichols (2012); Goldman (2013 pts. I and II, and 2014), Lackey (2014a and 2014b); Bird (2014); Pettit (2014), Ludwig (2016 pt. II); and Bicchieri (2017, chaps. 1 and 5).

9. See Ludwig (2016 pt. II) and Miller (2010) for critical assessments of Gilbert's conception of a plural self.

10. Representing what is central to the social psychology of social groups, Thomasson penetratingly writes, "the social groups that are most important to us in our lives together have a shared normative structure. Yet we can note this commonality while still respecting important differences across different kinds of social groups. We can also identify what distinguishes all of these social groups from arbitrary assemblages of people, or groups of people who merely share some physical characteristic(s).

There are no governing norms for how Genghis Khan and I are both to be treated, nor (in our culture) for how people with a longer second toe, or hazel eyes, are to be treated, or are to act. There are, unfortunately, such norms for how people of color, and women, are to act and be treated. As participants in the social world, we can be blind to these norms and fail to recognize the social groups (which is in part a matter of recognizing or reacting understandingly to the norms) only at our own peril—peril of sanctions, ostracism, or worse. (Girls with autism spectrum disorders—who have far more difficulty recognizing social norms—are also far more likely to be sexually abused.)

   "Membership in such social groups has normative significance: significance for how people (group insiders and/or outsiders) are to behave towards, regard, and treat group members, and/or for how the members themselves are to behave, to regard themselves and others. . . . Arbitrary mereological sums or sets of people (or people, worlds, and times) will generally carry no such significance. Similarly, groups of people that involve merely shared characteristics (a longer second toe, hazel eyes, sufferers of mitochondrial disease) do not constitute groups of *social significance* unless or until these groups are linked to norms: for how members of the group are to behave, or for how others are to regard or treat them. Left-handed people are not currently subject to such shared norms, in this country, but they might be—or might have been—in societies in which left-handedness was taken as a sign of being 'sinister,' in league with the devil, marking out left-handed people as to be treated in certain ways differently from their right-handed counterparts. To be part of one of these social groups that plays a central role in our lives together is to be part of a group that is significant for how you are to act and to regard yourself (it may be part of your social 'identity') and/or for how others are to behave towards and regard you" (Thomasson 2019, 480). In a footnote to this passage, Thomasson adds, "This account of social groups fits reasonably well with the notion employed by social identity theories of norms—which hold that group norms are obeyed because one identifies with being a member of the group. For this to have any plausibility (even as a partial account of norms) the groups in question must be governed by internal and/or structuring norms: mere belonging in a group of people with a longer second toe intuitively does not affect one's feelings of identification, and doesn't bring with it any norms to comply with. In short, social identity theorists about norms must think of social groups as normatively structured (though more specifically, as having internal and/or structuring norms—not just external norms)."

   11. Of course, even if one accepts the existence of social groups within one's preferred ontological scheme, their exact status remains curious. Are they, as old-fashioned idealists and contemporary deconstructionists maintain, creatures born from the ways in which we happen to think of ourselves and our surroundings? That is, are all social groups ultimately aligned with the likes of *fashionable cocktail attire* and, thus ontologically dependent on the vagaries of the ways in which we find ourselves communicating? Or are at least some social groups rightly allied with the likes of planetary systems, namely kinds or categories of systems of things that, because of the objective relations among their constituents, are the systems they are regardless of the ways in which we happen to speak of, or cognitively represent, what we

encounter? For an illuminating discussion of this, see Mallon and Stich (2000) and Mallon (2016).

12. See Epstein (2019) and Ritchie (2013 and 2015) for accounts of social groups in general.

13. Doris and Nichols argue that our capacity to reason is fundamentally social— i.e., that individuals deprived of normal social interactions tend to exhibit defec- tive—often crippling—patterns of reasoning (Doris and Nichols 2012). If they and the persuasive empirical literature they cite are correct, it would seem likely that one's capacity to reason presupposes that one self-categorize and self-identify as a member of various social groups.

14. For discussion of non-summative conceptions of collective action, compare Goldman (2014), Bird (2014), and Lackey (2014b).

15. But there are tricky cases. Suppose members of the board discover that their fellow member is a devout Catholic, a member of a group opposed to Planned Parent- hood. So, they change their attitudes toward the Catholic member sufficient for her expulsion. But assume that the Catholic remains steadfast in her attitudes that enable her board membership. Is that person in or out of that social group? See Epstein (2019) and Ritchie (2013 and 2015) for their sophisticated theories of social groups.

16. Lexical priming is to be distinguished from behavioral or social priming. The former's long-standing scientific credentials are not diminished by the problems recently afflicting social priming (Open Science Collaboration 2015; Daniel Gilbert et al. 2016; Anderson et al. 2016; Camerer et al. 2018).

17. To exemplify trendsetters, Bicchieri points to the civil rights leaders in the 1960s in some of the American south as trendsetters for the social groups subject to discrimination (Bicchieri 2017, 164–65).

18. In referring to a representation's centrality in an agent's Mentalese autobiog- raphy, I hope to echo Quine's conception of the centrality of expensive-to-eliminate, but in principle eliminable, particular beliefs within one's pragmatically adopted web of belief or overall conceptual scheme (Quine 1951, 39ff.).

19. Recall Gilbert's notion of a plural subject (or agent) of a collective action and her complementary conception of pooled wills (Gilbert 1989, 5 and 14–32, chap. IV (regarding plural subjects); and 30 and 210–34 (regarding pooled wills)). Also note Gilbert's notion of collective intention—i.e., *we-intention* (Gilbert 2010) and compare Tuomela (2013) and Miller (2010). Also see Velleman's account of shared intention (Velleman 1997, 38). Additionally, notice Mathiesen's (2005) discussion of a con- scious collective subject and her notion (2003) of *the first-person plural perspective* in the service of her account of *collective identity*. Tuomela provides a detailed account of group or social identity and collective action (2013, chaps. 1, 2, 5 and 6).

20. Regarding the significance of one's identifying oneself with a group—i.e., categorizing oneself as a group participant, Turner and Reynolds write: "The social identity perspective is explicitly and specifically addressed to reference groups. It uses the term 'category,' not in the sense of sociological categories, but in the sense of self-categories. Such 'categories' are psychological representations in the mind; they are cognitive structures which people use *to define themselves* and to change their behavior. The point of SCT is to explain how a sociological group becomes a

psychological group, how a membership group becomes a reference group. The idea is that people create cognitive categories to represent themselves as a higher-order entity and that, insofar as they represent themselves in terms of such categories, in terms of psychological concepts which become part of their mental functioning, they are able to transform their relationships to each other. As one moves from the 'I' to the 'we,' we transform our behavioral and psychological relationships to each other so that we can now act in terms of a higher-order, emergent entity called a psychological group" (Turner and Reynolds 2003, 137).

21. "I admit that there is a quite peculiar obstacle in the way of an understanding with my reader. By a kind of necessity of language my expressions, taken literally, sometimes miss my thought. . . . I fully realize that in such cases I was relying upon a reader who would be ready to meet me halfway—who does not begrudge a pinch of salt" (Frege, Gottlob, and Geach 1951, 179).

# Chapter 4

# Akratic Compatibilism
# Tried but Acquitted

Thank you, beyond-patient jurors, for persisting to this point in the trial of akratic compatibilism! You have been more than just to my thesis in the pages past. But in the mercifully few leaves ahead perhaps you'll want to consider the closing statements of the prosecution and defense.

## MANIPULATION

We do not know whether the laws of nature are necessary or contingent. Neither do we know whether the past is immutably fixed. Humeans contend that the laws are contingent and the past plastic. Spinozans maintain the contrary. I do not know whether the friends of Hume are right or whether Spinozans are on the mark. But I do ask whether freedom of the will might be compatible with determinism under the worrisome provisional assumption that the laws and history are Spinozan rather than Humean. I have argued that free will is compatible with Spinozan determinism. My rendition of compatibilism— akratic compatibilism—begins with the unapologetic hunch that Spinoza was right where Hume went wrong. Akratic compatibilism aims to procure leeway in action, and hence freedom of the will, by appealing to the way in which an agent engages in practical reasoning in psychologically tormenting circumstances. Thus, the doctrine looks to the cognitive source of an action to secure the leeway it wants. Compatibilism, if of the akratic brand I preach, is ecumenical insofar as it aims to accommodate the central insights of those two kinds of standard compatibilists that, in chapter 1, I respectively called *sopranos*—those who sing of leeway in action—and *contraltos*—those who cantillate of an action's psychological source. Having provisionally assumed that nature is Spinozan, akratic compatibilism trusts to the way in which an agent akratically, albeit inevitably, reasons her way toward action. The leading idea is that this peculiar psychological source of an action settles whether the willful action is free by ensuring that, situated as she is, she could have acted otherwise. The central thought is that the agent's characteristic relevant cognitive processes involve the resolution of an internal volitional conflict brewing within her. Like Augustine, Augustina wants to do something, say, to eat the vanilla ice cream, but she also wants not to do that. The conflicted actor's psychic struggle is one in which she asymptotically approaches a decision to act in one way—not to eat the treat. But, because Augustina's approach not to have the ice cream is only asymptotic, her governing Spinozan psychology ultimately dictates that she does eat the alluring sweet. Akratic compatibilism holds that, in virtue of the conflicted cognitive process serving as Augustina's asymptotic approach not to have the ice cream, she almost acts so as to be able not to do what she actually does. Although Augustina almost is able not eat the ice cream, she certainly does eat it. In light of the psychological facts, akratic compatibilism asserts that since Augustina almost was able not to eat the ice cream—*in her circumstances*—she was able not to eat it. However, we saw in chapter 2 that, thanks to the peculiar logic of "almost," in some contexts almost enough is indeed enough. So, always relative to her prevailing situation, Augustina was in fact able to act otherwise. She had just the sort of leeway in action required by soprano compatibilists who insist upon an agent's ability to act otherwise. And she achieved her leeway by conforming to the contraltos' song. For, *in eius situ*, Augustina had an open, but never traveled, possible path in the sequence of actions that constitute her way through life. She went for the ice cream exactly when she could have veered away from the irresistible delight. That is why, though the laws of nature be necessary, Augustina freely ate the ice cream. Yes, she ate it, but—as a fair and wise assessment of her willing ought to conclude, she could have foregone it. For she did what she did because of its akratic psychological source. She achieved leeway freedom on the occasion by having recruited her akratic psychological decision process.

Hence, akratic compatibilism is at once a distinctive edition of both leeway and source compatibilism. Such standard conceptions of compatibilism admit of various formulations, but they typically would sprout free will from some rationally virtuous way in which an agent deliberates. Baldly put, akratic compatibilism contrastively asserts that it suffices for an agent's will to be free that she reason like Augustine, akratically, rather than in some unconflicted or happily harmonious fashion. The human will, if free, is free because it is all too human. Augustina achieves her liberating leeway by cognitively resisting irresistible temptation, by deliberating in something like conflicted Augustine's weakly willed way. He too feebly wills to act one way—morally—while he strongly wills to act in an antagonistic way—immorally.

Under the assumption that the laws of nature necessitate an agent's actions, Augustine's immoral action that results from his tormented practical reasoning is inevitable. His resistance to acting immorally, though itself also necessitated by Spinozan psychology, is bound to fail. Nevertheless, it is supposedly the most in the way of reasoned resistance that Augustine—being only human—can fairly be expected to muster. And akratic compatibilism deems that level of resistance—since almost enough—to be good enough in his prevailing context for imperfect Augustine to be able to act otherwise. If so, then—according to akratic compatibilism—Augustine is free and, hence, responsible—relative to his overall situation. Much the same applies, of course, to Augustina. The only noteworthy difference that separates them is that he, but not she, is morally conflicted. And that difference, though often important, is irrelevant to the question of the freedom of their wills. So, source and leeway compatibilism, each in a new key and as a duet, may sing of akratic compatibilism.

Leeway and source accounts of responsibility and freedom are typically liable to *manipulation arguments*. These fanciful objections are presented as would-be counterexamples involving imagined agents whose supposed peculiar misfortune makes them manipulated dupes of either some crafty conniver or wily nature. Such objections invite us to suppose, for example, that Jack and Jill are psychological twins (Putnam 1975; Burge 1979). Each, we are told, thinks the same as the other in a particular situation. When, in that situation, they deliberate, their streams of mental representations, since indistinguishable, are to be syntactically the same. If Jack should will to eat his vanilla ice cream by volitionally tokening *I WILL TO EAT MY VANILLA ICE CREAM!*, *then, as his psychic twin, so too does Jill*. However, by hypothesis, their psychological histories are to differ. Thus, the explanations of his and her attitudes enabled by their coincident representations respectively differ and that difference, the objection says, undermines the chance that either twin's will be free.

In some incantations, manipulation arguments assume that, by his luck and for better or worse, Jack is apt to deliberate as he does because, in the obscure past and unbeknownst to Jack, a nearly omnipotent and omniscient conniver put in motion a remarkable chain of events. Long story short, that chain ensures that Jack deliberates precisely as he does, that his stream of mental representations is exactly what it is and always as the conniver wants and knows it to be. So, an adequate explanation of Jack's way of willing must cite the role of his manipulator.[1] However, Jill, happily, is nobody's stooge. Her psychological representations and powers of reasoning characteristically arise within her in the normal course of human development and experience (Pereboom 1995, 2001, and 2014; Mele 2006; McKenna 2004 and 2014). Having indulged in this fantasy of the possible, the critic of compatibilism invites us to consider a case in which a psychologically astute observer of Jack and Jill catches them in similar but separate circumstances as each decides what to do. Since the fully informed observer completely understands human psychology, he easily "reads" their synchronized minds. It is as if the observer were to view the identical streams of Mentalese representations respectively encoded in Jack and Jill that realize within each of them their processes of practical reasoning. Having witnessed the streams, the observer concludes that Jack and Jill reason the same, that they have the same practical attitudes.[2] The observer then judges that Jill acts upon virtuously deliberating in conformity with the preferred specifications of source compatibilism. So, her will should be free and, thus, she should be responsible for her action. So, the same should apply to Jack who reasons and behaves the same as Jill. But, the critic claims, Jack is not free nor is he responsible for what he does since he is the manipulator's puppet. Hence, Jack's will is not free although it is realized by the same sort of practical reasoning as is Jill's. So, the source of Jill's action, since the same as Jack's, does not suffice for the freedom of her will after all. If so, editions of source compatibilism generally fail. In that case, akratic compatibilism should stumble too. For should the conniver arrange Augustine's easily imagined twin, perhaps Augustina, to reason in Augustine's indecisive akratic way, the troubles of Jack and Jill would trouble Augustine and Augustina too.

## Manipulation Dodged

Analytical philosophy's allegiance to counterexamples predicated on undisciplined imagination is an enduring philosophical fashion, but it should have been a fashion foregone. It takes the following suspect form: A philosophical thesis, $\Psi$, is proposed to hold with necessity of some typically unspecified sort. The quick critic pounces on $\Psi$'s modality—first—by claiming to imagine or conceive of a situation, $\Phi$, inconsistent with $\Psi$. Second, the critic infers the possibility of $\Phi$ from the presumption of having imagined or conceived $\Phi$. Supposedly, what is imagined or conceived is possible. In that case, bingo, $\Psi$ would need be falsified by the absurdity of a possible world in which $\Psi$ and $\Phi$ obtain. How could $\Psi$ be necessary if its contrary, $\Phi$, is possible? That's the formal structure of the above complaint against source accounts of free will.

### Fallible Imagination

Philosophical counterexamples often rightly presuppose the necessity of the thesis they aim to contradict. But I hope that it is plain that akratic compatibilism does not presume to hold with any sort of necessity. It is offered as an abductive hypothesis as to how, under the provisional assumption of

Spinozan determinism, we might nevertheless be free relative to our particular circumstances—that is able to act otherwise than we do. Akratic compatibilism is on all fours with modally neutral theses regarding facts that obtain in the actual world as it is. The hypothesis that Jupiter is bigger than Earth is, I suppose, simply true and among the theses properly enshrined in astronomy. I guess that one might imagine or conceive each of the planets differently sized, that, imaginatively, Earth is bigger than Jupiter. And perhaps it is even possible that Earth be bigger than Jupiter. But although it should be possible that Earth be bigger than Jupiter, that would not diminish Jupiter's girth or augment Earth's. So, I think akratic compatibilism is unthreatened by arguments that would mistakenly burden it with a beefier modality than it bears. And even if akratic compatibilism should be construed as a thesis on modal par with the *a posteriori* hypothesis that water is $H_2O$—a true hunch couched in nomic necessity regarding what it rigidly names—neither thesis would be falsified by a critic's claim to have imagined either the will or water to be other than whatever and wherever they are (Kripke 1980).

Anyway, there are at least three other reasons to demur with akratic compatibilism's critic who complains of manipulation. *First,* is the critic's initial claim to imagine or conceive $\Phi$—now the supposed contrary to akratic compatibilism—correct? Conception and imagination, like belief, are evidently fallible modes of fallibly attributable mental representation. A critic's assertion to have imagined or conceived $\Phi$ is certainly defeasible. Suppose I've not previously heard of anyone named "Abraham." However, I hurry past the open door to the lecture hall where you are delivering your popular course on American artists during the nation's Civil War. I overhear you say to your students, "Abraham Lincoln was the president during the Civil War." The following day, while you and some of your students are touring the art museum and, by chance, then looking at Rembrandt's *Abraham and Isaac*, I again wander past. I notice you, and eavesdrop again as you say, "There's Abraham with a knife ready to sacrifice his son Isaac to appease God." Shocked, I too then look at Rembrandt's painting, and say, "Wow, imagine that! There's President Lincoln ready to kill his son!" Although I have sincerely asserted that I have conceived or imagined President Lincoln ready to kill his son, my assertion is certainly false. I haven't *imagined* or *merely conceived* anything at all. Rather, I've *seen* the painting and falsely *believed* that it depicts the president and his son. My facile assertion to have imagined Lincoln and his son mistakes, by misstating, my mental state's type. I've not imagined at all and, hence, not imagined Lincoln poised to murder anyone. Rather, I have innocently misdescribed my occurrent psychological status. I've not engaged imagination; and neither have I, in the manner of mere conception or contemplation, non-doxastically adopted a mental representation. Rather, I've confused my coincident perception and belief for an instance of imagination or epistemically neutral conception. Moreover, my report of my psychological state at the moment I observe the painting errs if it implies that I then think in any way *of* President Lincoln or any *of* his three sons.[3] For, as a matter of fact, I am actually visually thinking *of* biblical Abraham, not Abraham Lincoln. So, although while I wander the museum, I insist that I am imagining or conceiving Lincoln as killing his son, my confused assertion is simply false. Contrary to my assertion, I am not imagining at all. And I am thinking of someone not Lincoln.

Granted the above, a critic of compatibilism fallibly faults accounts of free will by sincerely claiming to imagine or conceive a situation in which a conniver manipulates one of a pair of psychological twins. When the critic aims to refer to such a potent conniver, his aim may well fail just as my words uttered in the museum fail to refer to Abraham Lincoln. For there does not exist anyone who is both depicted by Rembrandt and an American president. The sincere critic is liable to make a mistake like mine in the museum. For the critic may mistake his question begging *belief* that it is possible that there exists a conniving conniver for the psychological state he would be in were he to imagine such a conniver. After all, how could he imagine such a conniver unless—as his belief begs—there possibly is one? Certainly, by parallel reasoning, no one really can *imagine* or indeed conceive that π, the irrational ratio of a circle's circumference to its diameter, plays the tuba. For it is impossible that any number, rational or not, play the tuba. Were that possible, maybe one could imagine it. But one surely can't legitimately claim to have imagined an irrational number to play the tuba as part of a proof to prove the possibility of that silly impossibility. Though one might nonsensically assert, "π plays the tuba," such a vacuous utterance falls far short of demonstrating an instance of imagination and shorter still of proving the possibility of anything. So too, whether one can really imagine or conceive of conniving connivers depends in part on whether those would-be connivers are in the same boat with tuba-tooting irrationals. And the odds do seem to put such connivers in that same sinking ship. For so far as sound science can see, it is nomically impossible that connivers connive as cleverly as do the complex laws of nature in their partnership with the past. To pull off such a miracle, a conniving conniver would need be nearly divine, and no one not already divine could be near enough.

## Conceivability and Possibility

The *second* reason to wave off the critic of akratic compatibilism who would recruit a possible miraculous manipulator is that it is dubious, as such arguments require, that unrestricted conceivability implies possibility. With apology for redundancy, I rehearse an argument (by *reductio ad absurdum* buried in endnote 4 to chapter 2) against the implication from conceivability to possibility. As before, $\Diamond$ and $\Box$ are respectively the familiar *S5* modal operators for possibility and necessity as applied to (nominalized) sentences or propositions:

(a) You conceive that p (Fixed assumption that conception is unrestricted)
(b) Therefore, $\Diamond$p (From (a) and the thesis for *reductio*: conceivability implies possibility)
(c) I conceive that $\Box$~p (Assumption that conception is unrestricted)
(d) Therefore, $\Diamond\Box$~p (From (c) and thesis for reductio: conceivability implies possibility)
(e) Therefore, $\Box$~p (From (d) and S5)
(f) Therefore, ~$\Diamond$~~p (From (e) and S5)
(g) Therefore, ~$\Diamond$p (From (f) and S5)
(h) Therefore, $\Diamond$p and ~$\Diamond$p (From (b) and (g))

Therefore, the thesis for reductio is false (From (h) and *reductio ad absurdum*).

## Wily Nature

Our first two replies above to manipulation arguments against versions of compatibilism—including akratic compatibilism—address cases in which a conniver supposedly dupes a psychological twin. I have argued that these cases ought to be ignored considering their dubious presuppositions. However, a *third* way to run a sort of manipulation argument remains in which wily nature credibly replaces the incredible manipulator. In the incredible case, the supposed conniver is to manipulate one of two psychological twins, both of whom are akratic although the manipulated one lacks free will. The proffered, but suspect, conclusion is that being akratic in the fashion favored by akratic compatibilism fails to suffice for free will. However, might potent nature manage credibly to do what the impossible conniver can't? Might nature so manipulate psychological twins that both satisfy akratic compatibilism's requirements on free will while one of them clearly fails to be free? If so, then akratic compatibilism would have failed to find a sufficient condition for leeway liberty. I contend that nature is ill suited to manipulate in the supposed manner of the would-be manipulator.

Mother Nature is certainly crafty enough apparently to secure a common effect from different causes. Mother Nature may already have arranged that, at their histories' start, designated intact twin vases are liable so to break that, though the causes of their fractures should differ, the fractures would seem to be the same. One vase might be accidentally dropped onto a marble floor, while its twin's fate is to be the victim of a vandal's iron hammer. However, the broken pieces of each fractured vase might be, piece by piece, similar and all isomorphically scattered. If so, might nature causally suffice for psychological twins, Jack and Jill, to start their story the same? But might they then be just so buffered by different causes that they each end up in apparently similar akratic states? And might those states be of the sort akratic compatibilism would have suffice for leeway free will? And yet, with an eye on the causes of their common akrasia, might it be plain that Jack so fails to be free as to preclude Jill's freedom? That would scuttle akratic compatibilism should the psychological twins really be as they might appear.

Suppose that Jack and Jill start the same and apparently both end up akratically the same. If Jack fails to be free owing to the way of his will, then neither would Jill be free although akratic compatibilism would have her so. Might psychology have multiple ways to ensure that different agents akratically will the same but such that they differ with respect to freedom of the will? That is to ask whether one of nature's ways of inducing akrasia might be tantamount to a manipulator's ways, a way that by precluding one twin's freedom of the will, precludes it in the other? This kind of "natural" incarnation of the standard "unnatural" manipulation argument would, if cogent, suggest that at most only some—lucky—akratic episodes might suffice for producing actions that signal an agent's achievement of free will. But other—perhaps unlucky—ways might result in the same sort of episode, with bad luck bleeding away any claim to achievement of free will at all.[4]

Nature is wily in the ways it employs causation as our twin vases reveal. Similar fragile vases are nomically apt to break either if dropped onto a marble floor or if hit with an iron hammer. Causation can get the job done in apparently different ways. The laws of physics so govern similar vases that correct explanations of their breakings may sometimes cite marble floors, but other times blame iron hammers by vandals swung. Probably, most broken vases break because they are accidentally dropped; few are victims of hammering vandals. Acknowledging this fact, we might well say that the typical or normal cause of a broken vase is a hard, but innocent, floor rather than a vandal's hard, but guilty, hammer. And so, we may say that the dropped vase is *normally broken*, but that the hammered vase is *abnormally broken*. Thus, a pair of broken twin vases might be differently broken: one normally, the other abnormally. Suppose our twin vases each begin intact and end in isomorphic patterns of scattered pieces of similar sizes. Nevertheless, the patterns, though isomorphic, might differ historically in that one was broken normally while the other was broken abnormally. And such historical differences might matter. The owner of both vases might have insured them each against being broken by crime but neither by accident. In that case a knowledgeable insurance adjuster would be apt to assess the status of the twin vases differently, with one, but not the other, meriting compensation. The broken vases might look the same but yet be deeply different, different in the fully informed eyes of the adjuster. With this in mind, let's turn to Jack and Jill.

Suppose that it is Monday and that every Monday Jack and Jill are each offered vanilla ice cream. Suppose that the necessitarian, and hence inviolable, laws of nature conjoined to the fixity of the past should entail that, upon the occasion of being visually presented with Monday's vanilla ice cream, Jack naturally tokens this perceptual Mentalese representation:

(A) *HERE IS MY VANILLA ICE CREAM.*

However, he seems to be akratically conflicted. He wills too weakly, albeit asymptotically, to refrain from the ice cream, but succumbs because he strongly wills to eat it. For simplicity, we model his conflict of wills as his tokening a sequence of conflicting volitional Mentalese representations—that is

(B) *<I, WILL TO EAT MY VANILLA ICE CREAM!, I, WILL NOT TO EAT MY VANILLA ICE CREAM!>.*

Thus, according to akratic compatibilism, Jack eats the vanilla ice cream of his own free will.

Being his twin, Jill, like Jack, starts her cognitive process by visually tokening:

(C) *HERE IS MY VANILLA ICE CREAM,*

and, still mirroring Jack, she proceeds to token

(D) *<I, WILL TO EAT MY VANILLA ICE CREAM!, I, WILL NOT TO EAT MY VANILLA ICE CREAM!>.*

Since she mirrors Jack, Jill succumbs too. According to akratic compatibilism, Jack eats the ice cream of his own free will if and only if Jill does too.

Insofar as Jack and Jill respectively token *(A)* and *(C)*, they are analogous to our two intact similar vases prior to being broken. Like the intact vases, Jack and Jill start their stories the same: by respectively tokening *(A)* and *(C)*, each perceives the ice cream seen. Although the vases start the same and appear to be the same at the end, their apparent final congruence masks a deep and crucial difference. One, but not the other, broken vase is in a state that, thanks to its history, ensures its insurance. For the explanations of the similar breakings significantly differ. One explanation cites a normal accident, the other an abnormal crime. And, thus, the way in which the ultimate situations of the vases ought to be evaluated for insurance purposes does indeed differ. From the perspective of a knowledgeable insurance adjuster the broken vases differ in kind despite being physically isomorphic. Now, consider *(B)* and *(D)*. In the story of Jack and Jill, these two instances of syntactically isomorphic psychological states are the terminal conditions of Jack and Jill respectively. *(B)* and *(D)* are like the isomorphic scatterings of the broken vases. The explanations of the similar looking scatterings differ significantly with respect to how the situations of the broken vases are to be assessed. Suppose that the correct explanations of *(B)* and *(D)* should differ by the way in which they cite the psychological histories of Jack and Jill. In order that the stewing manipulation-by-nature objection gel, nature need so to have manipulated one twin, say, Jack, as to preclude his will being free despite his apparent volitional similarity to Jill, as flagged by the congruence of *(B)* and *(D)*. What might nature have done to Jack to render him, but not Jill, its dupe? Well, the laws of nature that apply to Jack and Jill are the same. Hence, if the explanation of Jack's psychological situation is to differ from Jill's, then—like the explanation of the broken vases—it must be due to a difference in their human histories. If nature is to have rendered Jack its dupe, his peculiar history would need to include something weird in the way of bad luck. His past would need include something analogous, say, to strange operant conditioning. Perhaps nature has so arranged his history of reinforced responses to selected stimuli as to suffice for his being conditioned akratically to will when presented with vanilla ice cream on Mondays. Skinner's oddly trained pigeon, having been effectively reinforced, weirdly pecks when and only when the red light flashes. And so too it might be that Jack tokens the likes of *(B)* when and only when it is Monday. On other days of the week, since he is chronically indifferent to all sweets, he would not then token the first element of *(B)* and, thus, not will in the manner of *(B)*. In contrast, Jill would akratically will whenever presented with vanilla ice cream because, unlike Jack, she always desires it intensely despite knowing herself to be hyper allergic to it. Evidently, Jill's akrasia is predicated on her suffering a desire that she knows full well to be harmful if satisfied. Jill's akratic conflict is what one would expect of a normal person in her situation. But Jack's mind on Monday is not at all normal. She is normal; he is not. How would one who is apt to assess the wills of others in a Strawsonian fashion assess Jack and Jill upon knowing their histories? Surely, such a Strawsonian assessor would be apt rightly to assess their wills differently. Such an assessor would empathetically credit Jill, but not Jack, for doing her best to deal with a naturally difficult situation. Jill akratically wills in a way that a Strawsonian assessor would empathetically approve. Yet, the same assessor would be hard pressed to empathize with Jack's queer way of eating vanilla ice cream on Mondays. Their assessor, if wise and just, would be positioned differently to assess the freedom of Jack's and Jill's wills. The assessor of wills is, in a sense, like a wise and just insurance adjuster. Assume that the adjuster knows the histories of, and policies for, the two broken vases. Then the adjuster accordingly assesses the vases with an eye on their histories. The one vase, but not the other, qualifies for compensation. And so too should a knowledgeable Strawsonian assessor, mindful of their different histories, differently assess the wills of Jack and Jill. Abnormal Jack is as he is by his past bad luck. Of course, Jill is lucky too. It is her good luck not to have had Jack's bad luck, not to have a history like his. The hammered vase is to be rightly recognized by a competent insurance adjuster as qualifying for compensation by the historical fact of its insurance. Analogously, Jill is to be rightly recognized by a wise and fair Strawsonian assessor as qualifying for free will by the historical fact of her normal development. Even in a Spinozan world where history is immutably fixed, all of us have whatever luck our histories bequeath us. After all, what is luck if not inescapable history. So, yes, whether one achieves freedom, as akratic compatibilism would have it, is at least in part a matter of luck. But that is true of every human achievement. Jill is lucky to have free will. But though lucky, she achieved it. Jack may be unlucky should he lack free will, unlucky that its achievement is beyond his reach. Wilt Chamberlin, though lucky to be talented and tall, achieved his league's record for most points scored per game (Nozick, 2013). By my bad luck I am untalented and far shy of Wilt's stature. But my bad luck does not dull his achievement. He has the record that I could never match. No matter how loudly I cuss or carp, my complaints don't dent his achievement. Should Jack complain and curse along with me, that would not dent Jill's achievement of free will. So, given their histories, Jack and Jill end up in different, though isomorphic, volitional states when each twin eats ice cream on Monday. Jack's will is not free; Jill's is. Nature may have tried to manipulate Jack into a volitional state like Jill's by arranging that he tokens *(B)* while she tokens *(D)*. But that does not suffice to equate their wills in the sight of a fair and right-minded assessor of wills.

Here is an alternative way of appreciating the psychological difference that separates Jack and Jill: *(B)* pertains to Jack. It includes his mental representations on Monday's episode in which he eats his vanilla ice cream. *(B)* includes Jack's token of *I, WILL TO EAT MY VANILLA ICE CREAM!* However, that tokened mental representation in Jack is not the realization of a real instance of willing. For its history disqualifies it. By our prevailing assumption of functionalism, mental states are type identified by their typical causal roles. Were Jack's targeted token a kosher case of his willing, a token of its type would be apt to recur within him on presentations of vanilla ice cream on days other than Monday. But that's not how Jack's psychic system works. A genuine willing, as exemplified by Jill's willing, is apt to recur on similar occasions. Give her the opportunity to have vanilla ice cream on any day of the week, and she is apt to token *I, WILL TO EAT MY VANILLA ICE CREAM!*. In Jill, *I, WILL TO*

*EAT MY VANILLA ICE CREAM!* is normal but in Jack it is not.[5] For Jack's history of conditioning is how Mother Nature has found a way of encoding in Jack a mental misrepresentation, an illusory willing. We know that Mother Nature has devised various ways of encoding within all of us false mental representations. For example, she has made most of us chronically liable to encode false representations in persistently illusory visual situations. Though I know the truth about the Müller-Lyer illusions, their parallel lines persist in seeming to me to differ in length. And in Jack's odd case, Mother Nature has relied on conditioning to encode pseudo willings on Mondays. As it turns out, although Jack and Jill appear to be psychological twins, they are not. Jill is genuinely akratic; Jack is not. For their histories psychologically distinguish them in ways masked by the syntactic congruence of their streaming mental representations.[6] Their Monday mental states are states of different types despite their congruent structure, just as the broken states of our two vases are states of different types despite their congruent structure. History matters. Think of Jack's situation this way. As a child in elementary school, I stood each morning with my right hand on my chest while saying, "I pledge allegiance to the flag of the United States of America!" Whether my statement on successive Mondays actually was my pledge depends upon whether I was apt to state the same on other school days. Were I not so apt—were I apt instead to refrain on other days—my Monday statement would certainly not be a genuine pledge. And that is much the situation of Jack. He is apt to token *I, WILL TO EAT MY VANILLA ICE CREAM!* only on Monday. That he is so rarely and so unusually apt renders false the hunch that his Monday token is an instance of his willing. At best his token is counterfeit coin, whereas Jill's token of *I, WILL TO EAT MY VANILLA ICE CREAM!* is real cognitive currency. It is the history of their productions that distinguish counterfeit from genuine coins. And much the same applies to the distinction between authentic and faux willings. Jill's is authentic; Jack's is faux.

## ADDICTION

Addiction is nature's cruelest manipulation. But, properly understood, it need not undermine akratic compatibilism. The reluctant addict is unable to resist the terrible substance that manipulates him when his body gravitates to the potent stuff. Being reluctant, the addict might indecisively fret, when in the drug's gravitational grip, whether then to inject. But, being addicted, he inevitably succumbs to the drug's irresistible pull. He too weakly wills not to inject but cannot do otherwise than succumb. Addicted as he is, the addict's action is not free when he takes hit after hit of the too attractive stuff.

The critic of akratic compatibilism is entitled to ask whether the addict and Augustine are alike and, if so, whether Augustine's will—like the addict's—is not free. After all, each confronts what, by hypothesis, is irresistible. The drug pulls the addict to indulge—though he too weakly wills otherwise. And the occasion to sin pulls Augustine to indulge—though he also too weakly wills otherwise. If the reluctant addict's will is not free when he irresistibly injects, how can akratic compatibilism have Augustine's will be free when—and indeed since—he irresistibly indulges?

Although the addict's addictive act is not free, Augustine's peccant act may yet be free owing to the difference in their proper explanations. For Augustine's, but not the addict's, act is caused by the agent's will. The addictive substance wields a power over the addict analogous to the gravitational power of the Earth over its moon. The moon circumvents the Earth not by volition but, of course, by gravity. Gravity, we are told, is a force of nature that works on all bodies, including those like ours that embody minds. Consider the unfortunate stoic's plight as she accidentally plunges off the high cliff and falls to her rocky fate far below. She has ample time as she travels from top to bottom to reflect on her problem. At first, she is distressed, wanting not to fall. She wills to escape her peril—flaps her arms and screams—but all to no avail. Still, she is a good stoic, and, so, after screaming, is distressed with herself for being distressed. To restore her equanimity and ensure her happiness, she decides not merely to acquiesce to her impending misfortune but indeed to embrace it. So, before it is too late, she wills that she fall exactly as she does on her way to her doom. In the end, things turn out for her exactly as her last chance at willing would ultimately have it. From a formal perspective, it seems that the psychology of the free-falling stoic is parallel to tempted Augustine's akratic deliberation. For given akratic compatibilism, upon falling into temptation Augustine initially, but weakly, wills not to succumb to his irresistible fate. So, yes, early on in their formally parallel dilemmas Augustine and the stoic correspondingly engage in practical reasoning. But in the end their psychological situations fundamentally differ. Augustine is akratic whereas the stoic is not. For, by his own correct admission, the explanation of how and why he succumbs to sin is that he himself ultimately willed it. His will not to sin was operant but too weak. So alluring was his temptation that, in the course of indecision, he came strongly and effectively to will in favor of the forbidden fruit. His ultimately willing what was irresistible is what caused him to do what was done. Were he not so to have willed, what actually happened would not have happened. His weak will would have won. But the same is not true of the stoic. She, like Augustine, ultimately willed what would be done. However, her final fling at willing is not what caused what was ultimately done. What caused her to meet the fate that she met was not her irrelevant willing that she end just so but rather the Newtonian gravity of her grave situation. It is gravity, not psychology, that figures in the right explanation of the stoic's fate. It was the massive mass of Earth working on the modest mass of her body that explains her situation. But it was psychology, not gravity, that explains Augustine's. He did what he did because he willed it. She did what she did because gravity had its way.

Addiction is like gravity. The moon and Earth are gravitationally attracted because they are commonly contained in the system of space-time. So too, an addict and his additive substance are two bodies linked by a force that pulls the one to the other within the common system within which they move. While it is true that the attracted addict engages in practical reason to secure his next hit, that he takes that hit is not because he willed it but rather because the drug, like the Earth, is attractive. Not long ago when we misunderstood addiction, perhaps we were—and still remain—too quick mistakenly to judge the addict akratic. Ill-informed, we may have thought that what caused the addict to inject was his ultimately so willing. Probably he did ultimately will it. But that willing may be like the stoic's causally idle and entirely ineffective willing to fall. She finally willed to fall. But that is not what caused her to fall. Gravity—the mass of the earth tugging on the mass of the stoic—was the causal culprit. The right explanation of her fall makes no mention of her psychology in general or her volition in particular. So too, the reluctant addict might conflictedly will on his way toward ultimately willing to inject. But that conclusive volition need not be what really causes him to inject. His injecting, rightly conceived, may be independent of his volition. Addiction—the chemical mass of the drug tugging on the chemical mass of his body—would be the causal culprit. Our lingering inclination to cite the addict's will as the cause of his injecting is likely prompted by a bad bit of the false part of folk psychology. Yes, he sees the drug. Yes, he desires it. And yes, he wills to inject it. That he sees it and that he desires it certainly are both to be cited in the full explanation of his habitual injection. But his willing to inject need not figure in that explanation. Perhaps habit does. But what is habit if not behavior that expeditiously bypasses full dress deliberation suffused with volition? Our unflinching endorsement of folk psychology biases our intuitive judgments regarding the disheveled guy in the gutter with the needle in his arm. We now nearly know better: that we ourselves would be in that gutter too were our bodies, like his, within a drug's gravitational grip. Were my body's mass of molecules more like his than they luckily are, I too would be in the chemical bound of a substance so small but so massive as to be pulled down into the gutter alongside him. But not because I would have willed it and not because the drug may have caused me to will it. God, no! But rather because that's what some drugs do to some bodies, not because embodied wills will it for their bodies.

## ACHIEVEMENT

Akratic compatibilism maintains that freedom of the will is an achievement, both personal and social. Augustine personally achieves freedom of his will in the context of his climactic episode of *akrasia* in which he resentfully resists the dictates of Spinozan psychology. Should your will be similarly free, then that you too are free is your achievement rather than a drab metaphysical fact indifferently imposed upon you by the sheer way of the world. And akratic compatibilism adds that such personal achievement is communal too since it proliferates within the Augustinian social circle. Among the many yet unmentioned objections a persistent fair critic might understandably voice against akratic compatibilism are these final two: One would reject the idea that freedom of the will is a personal achievement, the other that it is a social achievement.

## Personal Achievement

A stream that falls with a spectacular splash over the cliff on its course achieves nothing by way of its splashy splash. For—granted necessitarianism—water necessarily falls as it does, given the laws of gravity and the slope down which the creek does run. The nomic necessity of the stream's cascading precludes crediting the witless water with achievement for its spectacle. It could not help but fall with just such a splash; it could not fall in a fashion other than splashy. Hence, the stream achieves nothing by necessarily splashing. Tipped to this, a critic of akratic compatibilism might complain that since the hypothesis presupposes necessitarian psychology, it must treat Augustine's splashy *akrasia* the same as the stream's splashy fall. Each, being an episode of nomic necessitation, is no achievement at all. If Newtonian law bars the stream from *achieving* its splash, then so too should Cartesian psychology enjoin Augustine from personally *achieving* freedom of his will.

The critic is right to deny achievement to the stream but wrong to refuse it to Augustine. That something is done is one thing; how it is done is another thing still. And whether it's an achievement depends crucially upon how it was done. That the stream makes a splash is not an achievement because its splash is not an action—that is the result of practical reason. That Augustine makes his will be free is an achievement partly because it is the result of his akratic practical reason. The expert archer whose arrows repeatedly find the distant bull's-eye on a windy day has surely achieved something even if the laws of nature conjoined with history should entail that her arrows satisfy her aim with necessity. For her skill is a function of her long days of practice. Though the wind blows hard east to west, she has learned how best to point her arrow and how she ought to temper the tension of her bow to compensate for whatever circumstances prevail. Of course, what we call her practice is how, despite the steep opportunity cost of dissatisfying many desires, she transforms herself with expensive effort birthed by her practical reason. She persistently practices because, unlike lazy me, she prefers the prospect of a better tomorrow to a good today. Only by deciding at personal cost tirelessly to repeat the tedious process of sending arrows toward targets does she hone the skill that explains why her arrows crowd the bull's-eye. Over many arduous episodes of practice, the confluence of the principles of perception, habituation, and physiology have their way with the result that on the windy day her expert arrows, but not inexpert mine, concentrate in the target's center. Her success and my failure are largely, though not entirely, explained by reference to our different histories of practical attitudes. She practiced although it was hard, but I did not, because our practical attitudes, inclusive of our settled preferences, differed. That her arrows repeatedly hit the bull's eye while mine never do is inadequately explained without reference to her practical reasoning regardless of its nomic modality. It is an action's roots in practical reason, not that reason's contingency or necessity, which matters for achievement's chance. In contrast to the expert archer's achievement, the stream's impressive splash is fully explained without any reference to practical thinking at all. Achievement is possible when what is well done is intentional action not easily done. So, yes, the critic is right to say that if psychology is Spinozan, then, in a way, Augustine's thinking akratically is like the stream's splashing. His thought and its splash are both necessary. But that similarity does not cross the gap that separates physics from psychology. Augustine achieves free will by acting in virtue of thinking as he does, while the stream achieves nothing for not having thought at all. Gravity suffices for the stream impressively to splash, but it is akratic practical reason that suffices for Augustine freely to will.

## A Little More on Luck and Achievement

We are all lucky, lucky to have been born. Improbable though it was, the zygote from which I developed was the one that won the existential lottery that my parents enabled. What is the chance that the sperm and egg from whose marriage any person arises managed to marry? Zero! Yet, as Nozick influentially reminds us, that we are each lucky to exist is no bar to our individually different achievements. Wilt, mentioned above, was lucky to have been tall and able to dunk. It is my bad luck to be shy of seventy-two inches and incapable of dribbling except when I drool. Lucky Wilt earned fame and fortune; unlucky me not so. Nevertheless, Wilt, by pairing his fortunate physique with his *effort, determination, and commitment* earned and deserved our applause, our voluntary acknowledgement of his achievements on the court. With this in mind and if you should be susceptible to philosophical thought experiments, pretend that St. Augustine had a brother, St. Lucky. Lucky was lucky in that, unlike Augustine, he never suffered temptation and, so, that saint never sinned. Throughout his life, whenever Lucky found himself with the opportunity to fall off his high moral horse, he simply never suffered the inclination or temptation to let loose the reins. Because he was always inclined (perhaps owing to Spinozan psychology) to prefer the good over the bad, he always chose the better over the worse. Thus, Lucky met St. Peter at the pearly gates without a single demerit and was admitted to the heavenly host immediately upon application. Augustine was not so lucky. I suspect that he too got past St. Peter and into the celestial choir. But his application confessed lots of demerits. However, unlike Lucky, when Augustine occasionally managed to do what he ought—rather than what he was sorely tempted—to do, his good behavior was the result of the character he developed as the result of his history of resistance to temptation. Were you in St. Peter's chair, how would you comparatively judge the two applicants? Wouldn't you assign Augustine a better seat for the show than you assign Lucky? And wouldn't your wise assessment recognize that Augustine achieved what he did whereas Lucky did not? Admittedly, Augustine was not without luck. He was lucky to be born and—granted that psychology is Spinozan—he was lucky that it so governed him that he developed the character that he did. But, like Wilt, developing that character required Augustine's *effort, determination, and commitment*. It is that fact, as it applies to each, that ensures that Wilt and Augustine each achieved what luck made possible but did not ensure. Wilt achieved superstar status. Augustine achieved freedom of his will. Had Wilt not been as lucky as he was, he would not have achieved what he did. And had Augustine not been as lucky as he was, he would not have achieved what he did. However, Lucky did not achieve his sainthood because, unlike Wilt and Augustine, he was only lucky. Luck, achievement, and even desert are compatible with akratic compatibilism (Schmidtz, 2002).

## Collective Achievement

Undaunted, the critic who concedes Augustine's personal achievement might balk at the idea that the achievement is, as akratic compatibilism claims, also a collective achievement in which all Augustinians participate. There are two parts to this objection; one part denies the existence of Augustinians—that is the social group I have previously described; the other part denies that Augustine's achievement proliferates. Let's take these parts in turn.

Is there actually such a social group as the Augustinians? Well, recall that one way of discerning the existence of a social group is by attending to the ways in which individuals are apt to self-classify and self-identify. If asked, Fred and Ginger each is apt authoritatively to self-classify and self-identify as members of their particular duet. Also, that they are that duet explains why each of them dances exactly so. Similarly, that some people are prone to classify themselves as fans of the Pittsburgh Pirates and that they are apt to self-identify as such is evidence of the existence of the social group known as the

Pirates fans. Were those in the bleachers not mostly Pirates fans, why were so many folks in the bleachers cheering in unison when Mazeroski hit his pitch? The individual dancers and the individual fans respectively coordinate their behavior with selected others all by being apt to adopt mutually complementary practical attitudes. Much the same applies to many who know Augustine's writings or witness his struggles. In the way in which we primates are both apt and competent to assess the wills and attitudes of our conspecifics, those knowing of Augustine *read his mind* (Goldman 2006 and 2013; Stich and Nichols 1992; Goldman 2006 and 2013; Gopnik 2009a and 2009b; Siegel 2010 and 2017; Zeimbekis and Raftopoulos 2015; Mole 2015). They tend empathetically to understand as well as one might the ways in which his conflicting practical attitudes evolve into his ultimate decisions and actions. His admirers do recognize him as a *trendsetter* acting in ways that invite them to amend their own practical attitudes to think and act in ways reflective of his (Bicchieri 2017). It is reasonable to conjecture that by admiring him and amending their own ways, readers of his mind implicitly self-classify as his posse and self-identify as such. Were it not for those facts, why would they communicate among themselves as they do and conduct themselves similarly? They recommend to each other reading what Augustine wrote and they exhort others to learn about the life he so effectively modeled. The thoughts and actions of Fred and Ginger, on the one hand, and the attitudes and actions of those who root for the Pirates, on the other hand, suffice to reify the duet and fans, respectively. And so too that some of those knowledgeable of Augustine amend their practical attitudes in ways that complement his suffices for the existence of Augustinians. T-shirts with logos are not required.

Once we recognize the reality of the Augustinians, we get for free the proliferation of freedom of the will regardless of whether the achievement is collectively secured for all by the singular action of any one person.[7] For at this point in the dialectic, the critic concedes that one's resentful resistance (if like Augustine's) of Spinozan psychology ensures that one's individual will be free. Add to that concession that Augustinians are those who are apt to adopt aptitudes for practical reason modeled on Augustine's aptitudes. So, Augustinians are, like Augustine, apt resentfully to resist Spinozan psychology. Recall our discussion many pages back of our apparent inclination to prefer personal autonomy to dictation. There, we supposed that our Spinozan psychology determines that we are natively inclined to resist its overwhelming inclination to act contrary to ways in which our governing psychology introspectively seems to undermine autonomy. So, all such Augustinians have free will if Augustine does. Free will does proliferate.

But how widely and how long does free will proliferate? How long does this achievement last? Fred and Ginger dance only until the orchestra stops, and once it ends so does their elegant achievement along with their minimal social group. A team that wins one day might lose the next and disband. On the one day, all on the team are winners, but on the next day all are losers or no longer members at all. Whether the achievement of Augustinian free will be personal or collective, how enduring is it? Might one have free will one day but not the next and nevermore? Is free will sporadic?

Augustinian freedom may be an achievement at risk, just as the objection suggests. Such freedom presupposes that our Spinozan psychology continues to ensure, as it has at least until now, that we remain apt to replicate Augustine's akratic practical reasoning. Although it is entirely reasonable to suppose that the laws of nature, and hence psychology, persist forever unchanged, none of us can know what the constant laws entail for tomorrow. I guess, and so might you, that meteorology is invariant over time. But it's no state secret of science that our epistemic limitations render our weather forecasts, in particular, and our *a posteriori* forecasts, in general, always uncertain and never better than probable. Probably, tomorrow will be like today here in the beautiful Sonoran Desert. So, I guess the sun will shine as bright tomorrow as today. But it might not. None of us can know for sure one way or the other. Weather forecasting is tricky. That's our fallible fault, not meteorology's. But let's move on.

Probably tomorrow will be like today here in me. So, I guess my hope for the Pittsburgh Pirates will be as bright in my heart tomorrow as it is today. But it might not. None of us can know for sure one way or the other. Weather forecasting is tricky, but psychological forecasting is trickier still. That too is our fallible fault, not psychology's. But let's move on.

Probably tomorrow will be like today in all of us. So, I guess that our aptitude resentfully to resist our governing psychology, if Spinozan, will burn as bright in our hearts tomorrow as it might today. But it might not. None of us can know for sure one way or the other. Weather forecasting is tricky, psychological forecasting is trickier still, but philosophical forecasting is for philosophers better at it than this one in the desert. But I'm not worried. For should the philosophical forecast finally be right, that would be a collective achievement. If you should get it right, then we all would get it right. Turns out that we philosophers are all in the same game together. And that's no fault at all.

## NOTES

1. Recall from chapter 1 that Lehrer (forthcoming) makes this point about explanations of manipulated agents.

2. The inference from syntactic to semantic sameness is perilous at best. It presumes a sort of internalism regarding the content of mental states in opposition to

externalism of the sort originally proposed by Putnam (1975) and Burge (1979) and thereafter adopted by Stich (1983) and others. The externalist idea is that mental representations that are formally or syntactically the same can differ in their meaning or content depending upon the environments which their hosting cognizers inhabit. Thus, if a conniver's presence and odd contribution to Jack's cognitive processes differentiates his overall situation from Jill's, then it is an open question as to whether these twins think the same thoughts or reason in the same practical way.

3. Mine is certainly not the first, and surely not the last, word on how the reference of words figures in our thoughts. The diverse literature on this is large and unlikely soon to be settled (Michaelson and Reimer 2019).

4. Mele offers a raft of instructive examples of how luck bears upon the notion of responsibility as the child of free will. See Mele and Moser (1997) and Mele (2006 and 2014).

5. The sophisticated semantics of imperatives is relevant here. In the context of assessing the semantic value of a volition I use 'normal' and its negation merely as surrogates to label whatever may be the appropriate—presumably bivalent—semantic values proper to nonindicative representations in the family of imperatives and prescriptions. See Hare (1952 and 1981), Sosa (1967), Castañeda (1975), and Vranas (2008).

6. For opposition to this sort of externalism (per endnote 2 for this chapter), see Horgan, Tienson, and Graham (2004) and Horgan (2011).

7. A wise referee has made me see what to others must be obvious and perhaps problematic with my appeal to collective action and achievement. Consider a group of which I am a member. Let it be true that the group acts collectively. Suppose that I am a Pirates fan when they win the World Series. So, I am entitled to say, "We won!" But suppose the team should engage in some sort of deeply evil behavior. Imagine that the team were to be guilty of a terrible crime against an innocent child. If I rightly say, "We won!", must I also admit complicity in the team's crime? Am I obliged to admit, "We are criminally guilty"? And what if I should be a member of two groups, one of which is criminally culpable, the other innocent of the same. Am I bound to admit to both guilt and innocence? I do not know how to answer these questions. But I do fret that variations on them may haunt akratic compatibilism. For it allows that I may be free thanks to my membership in a group like the Augustinians. Yet might not it also allow that I never be free because it turns out that I am a member of a group of Anti-Augustinians, namely a group centered on Anti-Augustine, whose conflictive psychology is such that he always asymptotically approaches impossibly acting otherwise? Although I am unconfident about how to think about this nasty nest of problems, I suspect that there may be a helpful asymmetry in play. The winning behavior of the Pirates proliferates among the fans because they need only cheer (or be apt to cheer) the team's on-field to participate in the victory. But the evil that team does proliferates among the fans only if they do something more than cheer the team's on-field play' perhaps such as cheering for the evil done as such. So too for unwitting members of the Anti-Augustinians.

# Bibliography

Anderson, Christopher J., Stepán Bahník, Michael Barnett-Cowan, Frank A. Bosco, Jesse Chandler, Christopher R. Chartier, Felix Cheung et al. 2016. "Response to Comment estimating the reproducibility of psychological science." *Science* 351: 1037.

Annas, Julia. 2011. *Intelligent Virtue.* Oxford: Oxford University Press.

Appiah, Kwame Anthony. 2005. *The Ethics of Identity.* Princeton, NJ: Princeton University Press.

Armstrong, David M. 1978. *A Theory of Universals.* Vol. 2 of *Universals and Scientific Realism.* Cambridge: Cambridge University Press.

Armstrong, David M. 1983. *What is a Law of Nature?* Cambridge: Cambridge University Press.

Augustine of Hippo. 1991. *St. Augustine: Confessions.* Translated with an introduction by Henry Chadwick. New York: Oxford University Press.

Austin, John L. 1975. *How to Do Things with Words*, 2nd ed. In Marina Sbisà and James Opie Urmson (eds.). Oxford: Oxford University Press.

Austin, J. L., J. O. Urmson, and G. J. Warnock. 1979-03-06a. "Truth." In J. O. Urmson, and G. J. Warnock (eds.). *J. L. Austin: Philosophical Papers*, 3d ed. Oxford: Oxford University Press, 1979. Oxford Scholarship Online, 2003. Accessed August 16, 2021. https://oxford.universitypressscholarship.com/view/10.1093/019283021X.001.0001/acprof-9780192830210-chapter-5.

Austin, J. L., J. O. Urmson, and G. J. Warnock. 1979-03-06b. "Ifs and Cans." In J. O. Urmson and G. J. Warnock (eds.). *J. L. Austin: Philosophical Papers*, 3d ed. Oxford: Oxford University Press, 1979. Oxford Scholarship Online, 2003. Accessed July 23, 2020. https://www.oxfordscholarship.com/view/10.1093/019283021X.001.0001/acprof-9780192830210-chapter-9.

Bach, Kent, and Robert M. Harnish. 1979. *Linguistic Communication and Speech Acts.* Cambridge, MA: MIT Press.

Bach, Kent and Robert M. Harnish. 1992. "How performatives really work: A reply to Searle." *Linguistics and Philosophy* 15: 93–110.

Baker, L. R. 1987. *Saving Belief.* Princeton, NJ: Princeton University Press.

Baker, L. R. 2016. "Making sense of ourselves: Self-narratives and personal identity." *Phenomenology and the Cognitive Sciences* 15: 7–15. https://doi.org/10.1007/s11097-014-9358-y.

Barwise, Jon, and John Perry. 1983. *Situations and Attitudes.* Cambridge, MA: MIT Press.

Bechtel, William, and Abrahamsen, Adele A. 2002. *Connectionism and the Mind: Parallel Processing, Dynamics, and Evolution in Networks,* 2d ed. Oxford: Basil Blackwell.

Beebee, Helen. 2003. "Local miracle compatibilism." *Noûs* 37: 258–77.

Beebee, Helen, and Alfred Mele. 2002. "Humean compatibilism." *Mind* 111, no. 442 (April 2002): 201–24. https://doi-org.ezproxy1.library.arizona.edu/10.1093/mind/111.442.201.

Bernstein, S. 2015. "The Metaphysics of omissions." *Philosophy Compass*, 10, pages 208–18, doi: 10.1111/phc3.12206.

Bicchieri, Cristina. 2017-02-23. *Norms in the Wild: How to Diagnose, Measure, and Change Social Norms.* Oxford: Oxford University Press. Accessed August 25, 2021. https://oxford.universitypressscholarship.com/view/10.1093/acprof:oso/9780190622046.001.0001/acprof-9780190622046.

Bigelow, John, Brian Ellis and Caroline Lieres. 2004. "The world as one of a kind: Natural necessity and the laws of nature." In John Carroll (ed.). *Readings on Laws of Nature.* Pittsburgh: University of Pittsburgh Press, pp. 141–60.

Bird, Alexander. 2014-11-20. "When is there a group that knows? Distributed cognition, scientific knowledge, and the social epistemic subject." In Jennifer Lackey (ed.). *Essays in Collective Epistemology.* Oxford: Oxford University Press. Oxford Scholarship Online 2015. Accessed September 29, 2021. https://oxford.universitypressscholarship.com/view/10.1093/acprof:oso/9780199665792.001.0001/acprof-9780199665792-chapter-3.

Block, Ned. 1980a. "What is functionalism?" In his *Readings in the Philosophy of Psychology,* vol. 1, 171–84. Cambridge, MA: Harvard University Press.

Block, Ned. 1980b. "Troubles with functionalism." In his *Readings in the Philosophy of Psychology,* vol. 1, 268–305. Cambridge, MA: Harvard University Press.

Block, Ned. 1986. "Advertisement for semantics for psychology." *Midwest Studies in Philosophy* 10: 615–78.

Block, Ned. 1998. "Conceptual role semantics." In Edward Craig (ed.). *The Routledge Encyclopedia of Philosophy.* London and New York: Routledge, pp. 242–56.

Block, Ned. 2001. "Functional role semantics." In R. A. Wilson and F. C. Keil (eds.). *The MIT Encyclopedia of the Cognitive Sciences.* Cambridge, MA: MIT Press, pp. 331–32.

Block, Ned. 2007. "Consciousness, accessibility, and the mesh between psychology and neuroscience." *Behavioral and Brain Sciences* 30: 481–548.

Block, Ned, and J. A. Fodor. 1972. "What psychological states are not." *The Philosophical Review* 81 (2): 159–81. https://doi.org/10.2307/2183991.

Bloom, Paul. 2010. "The moral life of babies." *New York Times,* 9 May 2010, Sunday magazine. https://www.nytimes.com/2010/05/09/magazine/09babies-t.html.

Bloom, Paul. 2013. *Just Babies: The Origins of Good and Evil*. New York: Crown Publishing.

BonJour, Laurence. 1985. *The Structure of Empirical Knowledge*. Cambridge, MA: Harvard University Press.

Bratman, Michael. 1993. "Shared intention." *Ethics* 104 (1): 97–113. Accessed August 25, 2021. http://www.jstor.org/stable/2381695.

Bratman, Michael. 1999. *Faces of Intention: Selected Essays on Intention and Agency*. New York: Cambridge University Press.

Bratman, Michael. 2000. "Reflection, planning, and temporally extended agency." *The Philosophical Review* 109 (1): 35–61. https://doi.org/10.2307/2693554.

Bratman, Michael. 2007-01-18. "Valuing and the will." In his *Structures of Agency*: *Essays*. New York: Oxford University Press. Oxford Scholarship Online, 2011. Accessed August 25, 2021. https://oxford.universitypressscholarship.com/view /10.1093/acprof:oso/9780195187717.001.0001/acprof-9780195187717-chapter-3.

Brewer, Bill. 2011. Perception and Its Objects. Oxford: Oxford University Press.

Bromberger, Sylvain. 1965. "An approach to explanation." In Ronald J. Butler (ed.). *Analytical Philosophy* (v. 2), Oxford: Basil Blackwell (pp. 72–105).

Bromberger, Sylvain. 1993. *On What We Know We Don't: Explanation, Theory, Linguistics, and How Questions Shape Them*. Chicago: University of Chicago Press.

Broome, John. 2021. "Reasoning with preferences?" in his *Normativity, Rationality and Reasoning: Selected Essays*. Oxford, online edn, Oxford Academic, 21 Oct. 2021, https://doi-org.ezproxy4.library.arizona.edu/10.1093/oso/9780198824848 .003.0011, accessed 10 Sept. 2022.

Burge, Tyler. 1979. "Individualism and the mental." *Midwest Studies in Philosophy* 4: 73–112.

Byrne, Alex, and Heather Logue. 2009. *Disjunctivism*. Cambridge, MA: MIT Press.

Calhoun, Cheshire. 2016-01-01. "Changing one's heart." In her *Moral Aims: Essays on the Importance of Getting It Right and Practicing Morality with Others*. New York: Oxford University Press. Oxford Scholarship Online, 2015. Accessed October 6, 2021. https://oxford.universitypressscholarship.com/view/10.1093/acprof :oso/9780199328796.001.0001/acprof-9780199328796-chapter-10.

Camerer, Colin F., Anna Dreber, Felix Holzmeister, Teck-Hua Ho, Jürgen Huber, Magnus Johannesson, Michael Kirchler et al. 2018. "Evaluating the replicability of social science experiments in *Nature* and *Science* between 2010 and 2015." *Nature Human Behaviour* 2: 637–44.

Campbell, Joe, and Keith Lehrer. 2018. "Keith Lehrer on compatibilism." *Journal of Ethics* 22: 225. https://doi-org.ezproxy1.library.arizona.edu/10.1007/s10892-018-9269-1.

Camus, Albert. 2012. *The Myth of Sisyphus and Other Essays*. New York: Knopf Doubleday Publishing Group. ProQuest Ebook Central.

Carnap, Rudolf. 1950. "Empiricism, semantics and ontology." *Revue International de Philosophie* 4: 20–40.

Carroll, John W. 1987. "Ontology and the laws of nature." *Australasian Journal of Philosophy* 65: 3, 261–76. https://doi.org/10.1080/00048408712342931.

Carroll, John W. 1994. *Laws of Nature*. Cambridge Studies in Philosophy. Cambridge: Cambridge University Press.

Carroll, John W. 2004. *Readings on Laws of Nature*. Pittsburgh: University of Pittsburgh Press.

Carruthers, Peter. 2005. *Consciousness: Essays from a Higher-Order Perspective*. Oxford: Oxford University Press.

Carruthers, Peter. 2006. *The Architecture of the Mind*. Oxford: Oxford University Press.

Cartwright, Nancy. 1980. "Do the laws of physics state the facts?" *Pacific Philosophical Quarterly* 61: 75–84.

Castañeda, Hector-Neri. 1975. *Thinking and Doing*. Dordrecht: D. Reidel.

Chemero, Anthony. 2009. *Radical Embodied Cognitive Science*. Cambridge, MA: MIT Press.

Cherniak, Christopher. 1986. *Minimal Rationality*. Cambridge, MA. The MIT Press.

Chisholm, Roderick. 1966. "Freedom and action." In Keith Lehrer (ed.). *Freedom and Determinism*. New York: Random House, pp. 11–44.

Chisholm, Roderick. 1967. "He could have done otherwise." *Journal of Philosophy* 4: 409–17.

Chisholm, Roderick. 1976. *Person and Object: A Metaphysical Study*. La Salle, IL: Open Court.

Chisholm, Roderick. 1989. "Human freedom and the self." Reprint of his 1964 Lindley Lecture in his *On Metaphysics*, 5–15. Minneapolis: University of Minnesota Press.

Churchland, Patricia Smith. 1989. *Neurophilosophy: Toward a Unified Science of the Mind-Brain*. Cambridge, MA: MIT Press.

Churchland, Paul. 1979. *Scientific Realism and the Plasticity of Mind*. Cambridge, MA: Cambridge University Press.

Churchland, Paul. 1988. "Perceptual plasticity and theoretical neutrality: A reply to Jerry Fodor." *Philosophy of Science* 55: 167–87.

Churchland, Paul. 1992. *A Neurocomputational Perspective: The Nature of Mind and the Structure of Science*. Cambridge, MA: MIT Press.

Clark, Andy, and David J. Chalmers. 1998. "The extended mind." *Analysis* 58: 7–19.

Clark, Romane. 1970. "Concerning the logic of predicate modifiers." *Noûs* 4: 311–35.

Clark, Romane. 1993. "Seeing and inferring." *Philosophical Papers* 22 (2): 81–96. https://doi.org/10.1080/05568649309506396.

Clarke, Randolph. 2003-10-30. *Libertarian Accounts of Free Will*. New York: Oxford University Press. Oxford Scholarship Online, 2005. Accessed July 8, 2020. https://doi.org/10.1093/019515987X.001.0001.

Clarke, Randolph. 2014. *Omissions: Agency, Metaphysics, and Responsibility*. New York: Oxford University Press, online edn, Oxford Academic https://doi-org.ezproxy4.library.arizona.edu/10.1093/acprof:oso/9780199347520.001.0001, accessed 7 Oct. 2022.

Clarke, Randolph, Michael McKenna, and Angela M. Smith. 2015. "Introduction." In Randolph Clarke, Michael McKenna, and Angela M. Smith (eds). *The Nature of Moral Responsibility: New Essays*. New York: online edn, Oxford Academic, 18 June 2015, https://doi-org.ezproxy1.library.arizona.edu/10.1093/acprof:oso/9780199998074.003.0001, accessed 13 Sept. 2022.

Cohen, Stewart. 1986. "Knowledge and context." *Journal of Philosophy* 83 (10): 574-583. Access August 15, 2019. https://www.jstor.org/stable/2026434.

Cohen, Stewart. 2013. "Contextualism defended." In Matthias Steup et al. (eds.). *Contemporary Debates in Epistemology*, 2nd ed. Hoboken, NJ: John Wiley & Sons, pp. 56–61.

Coltheart, M. 1980. "Iconic memory and visible persistence." *Perception and Psychophysics* 27 (3): 183–228.

Conee, Earl. 2013. "Contextualism Contested." In Matthias Steup et al. (eds). *Contemporary Debates in Epistemology*. Hoboken, NJ: John Wiley & Sons, pp. 60–69.

Cowling, Sam. 2012. "Haecceitism for modal realists." *Erkenntnis* 77 (3): 399–417. Accessed September 10, 2021. http://www.jstor.org/stable/23356774.

Davidson, Donald. 1973. "On the very idea of a conceptual scheme." In *Proceedings and Addresses of the American Philosophical Association* 47: 5–20. https://doi.org/10.2307/3129898.

Davidson, Donald. 1980. "How is weakness of the will possible?" In his *Essays on Actions and Events*, 21–42. Oxford: Clarendon Press.

Davidson, Donald. 2001a. "Actions, reasons and causes." In his *Essays on Actions and Events*, 2nd ed. Oxford: Oxford University Press. Oxford Scholarship Online, 2003. Accessed June 30, 2020. https://doi.org/10.1093/0199246270.003.0001.

Davidson, Donald. 2001b. "Mental events." In his *Essays on Actions and Events*, 2nd ed. Oxford: Oxford University Press. Oxford Scholarship Online, 2003. Accessed June 30, 2020. https://doi.org/10.1093/0199246270.003.0011.

Davidson, Donald. 2001c. "Psychology as philosophy." In his *Essays on Actions and Events*, 2nd ed. Oxford: Oxford University Press. Oxford Scholarship Online, 2003. Accessed July 10, 2020. https://doi.org/10.1093/0199246270.003.0012.

Davidson, Donald. 2002. "Intending." In his *Essays on Actions and Events*, 2nd ed, 83–102. Oxford: Oxford University Press.

Della Rocca, Michael. 2008. *Spinoza*. New York: Routledge. Accessed May 8, 2020. https://search-ebscohost-com.ezproxy2.library.arizona.edu/login.aspx?direct=true&db=e025xna&AN=232636&site=ehost-live.

Dennett, Daniel C. 1975. "Brain writing and mind reading." *Minnesota Studies in the Philosophy of Science* 7: 403–15.

Dennett, Daniel C. 1978a. "A cure for the common code." In his *Brainstorms: Philosophical Essays on Mind and Psychology*. Montgomery, VT: Bradford Books, pp. 90–108.

Dennett, Daniel C. 1978b. "Artificial intelligence as philosophy and psychology." In his *Brainstorms: Philosophical Essays on Mind and Psychology*. Montgomery, VT: Bradford Books, 109–28. http://cognet.mit.edu/pdfviewer/book/9780262271509/chap7.

Dennett, Daniel C. 1983. "Intentional systems in cognitive ethology: The 'Panglossian paradigm' defended." *Behavioral and Brain Sciences* 6 (3): 343–55. https://doi.org/10.1017/S0140525X00016393.

Dennett, Daniel C. 1984. *Elbow Room: The Varieties of Free Will Worth Wanting*. Cambridge, MA: MIT Press/Bradford Books.

Dennett, Daniel C. 1987. *The Intentional Stance*. Cambridge, MA: MIT Press.

Dennett, Daniel C. 1991. "Real patterns." *Journal of Philosophy* 88 (1): 27–51.

Dennett, Daniel C. 1992. "The self as a center of narrative gravity." In F. Kessel, P. Cole, and D. Johnson (eds). *Self and Consciousness: Multiple Perspectives.* Hillsdale, NJ: Erlbaum.

Dennett, Daniel C. 1996. *Darwin's Dangerous Idea: Evolution and the Meanings of Life.* New York: Simon & Schuster. ProQuest Ebook Central.

Dennett, Daniel C. 2003. *Freedom Evolves.* New York: Viking Press.

Dennett, Daniel C. 2006. "Cognitive wheels: The frame problem of AI." In J. L. Bermúdez (ed.). *Philosophy of Psychology: Contemporary Readings.* New York: Routledge, pp. 433–54.

Dennett, Daniel, and Marcel Kinsbourne. 1992. "Time and the observer: The where and when of consciousness in the brain." *Behavior and Brain Sciences* 15: 234–47. https://doi.org/10.1017/S0140525X00068527.

DeRose, Keith. 1992. "Contextualism and knowledge attributions." *Philosophy and Phenomenological Research* 52.4: 913–29.

DeRose, Keith. 1999. "Contextualism: An explanation and defense." In John Greco and Ernest Sosa, (eds.). *The Blackwell Guide to Epistemology.* Oxford: Blackwell, 185–203.

Desimone, Robert, and John Duncan. 1995. "Neural mechanisms of selective visual attention." *Annual Review of Neuroscience* 18: 1, 193–222.

Doris, John M. 2002. *Lack of Character: Personality and Moral Behavior.* Cambridge, MA: Cambridge University Press. https://doi.org/10.1017/CBO9781139878364.

Doris, John, and Shaun Nichols. 2012. "Broad-minded: Sociality and the cognitive science of morality." In Eric Margolis, Richard Samuels, and Stephen P. Stich (eds.). *The Oxford Handbook of the Philosophy of Cognitive Science.* https://doi.org/10.1093/oxfordhb/9780195309799.013.0018.

Dretske, Fred. 1977. "Laws of nature." *Philosophy of Science* 44: 248–68.

Dretske, Fred. 1981a. "The pragmatic dimension of knowledge." *Philosophical Studies* 40: 363–78.

Dretske, Fred. 1981b. *Knowledge and the Flow of Information.* Cambridge, MA: MIT Press.

Dretske, Fred. 1988. *Explaining Behavior: Reasons in a World of Causes.* Cambridge, MA: MIT Press/Bradford Books.

Dretske, Fred. 1995. *Naturalizing the Mind.* Cambridge, MA: MIT Press.

Ekstrom, Laura. 2010. "Volition and the will." In Timothy O'Connor and Constantine Sandis (eds.). *A Companion to the Philosophy of Action.* Hoboken, NJ: Wiley-Blackwell, pp. 99–107.

Ellemers, Naomi, Russell Spears, and Bertjan Doosje. 2002. "Self and social identity." *Annual Review of Psychology* 53: 161–86. https://link.gale.com/apps/doc/A83789644/AONE?u=uarizona_main&sid=bookmark-AONE&xid=5a10273c.

Ellemers, Naomi, and S. Alexander Haslam. 2011. "Social identity theory." In P. A. M. Van Lange, A. W. Kruglanksi, and E. T. Higgins (eds.). *Handbook of Theories of Social Psychology.* ProQuest Ebook Central, 379–98.

Epstein, Brian. 2019. "What are social groups? Their metaphysics and how to classify them." *Synthese* 196: 4899–932. https://doi.org/10.1007/s11229-017-1387-y.

Evans, Gareth. 1982. *The Varieties of Reference.* Oxford: Oxford University Press.

Fales, Evan. 1990. *Causation and Universals*. London and New York: Routledge.

Fales, Evan. 1993. "Are causal laws contingent?" In John Bacon, Keith Campbell and Lloyd Reinhardt (eds.). *Ontology, Causality and Mind: Essays in Honour of D. M. Armstrong*. New York: Cambridge University Press, pp. 121–51.

Fine, Kit. 2002. "Varieties of necessity." In Tamar Szabo Gendler and John Hawthorne (eds.). *Conceivability and Possibility*. New York: Oxford University Press, pp. 253–81.

Fischer, John Martin. 1994. *The Metaphysics of Free Will: An Essay on Control*. Oxford: Blackwell.

Fischer, John Martin. 2009. "Stories and the meaning of life." In his *Our Stories: Essays on Life, Death and Free Will,* chap. 10. New York: Oxford University Press.

Fischer, John Martin, and Mark Ravizza. 1998. *Responsibility and Control: A Theory of Moral Responsibility*. Cambridge Studies in Philosophy and Law. Oxford: Cambridge University Press.

Fodor, Jerry. 1974. "Special sciences, or the disunity of science as a working hypothesis." *Synthese* 28: 97–115.

Fodor, Jerry. 1975. *The Language of Thought*. Cambridge, MA: Harvard University Press/Crowell.

Fodor, Jerry. 1978. "Propositional attitudes." *The Monist* 61: 501–23.

Fodor, Jerry. 1980. "Methodological solipsism considered as a research strategy in cognitive psychology." *Behavioral and Brain Sciences* 80: 63–109.

Fodor, Jerry. 1983. *The Modularity of Mind.* Cambridge, MA: MIT Press.

Fodor, Jerry. 1984. "Observation reconsidered." *Philosophy of Science* 51: 23–43.

Fodor, Jerry. 1987. *Psychosemantics*. Cambridge, MA: MIT Press.

Fodor, Jerry. 1991. "You can fool some of the people all of the time, everything else being equal: Hedged laws and psychological explanations." *Mind* 100: 19–34.

Fodor, Jerry. 1997. "Special sciences: Still autonomous after all these years." *Philosophical Perspectives* 11: 149–63.

Fodor, Jerry. 2001. *The Mind Doesn't Work That Way: The Scope and Limits of Computational Psychology*. Cambridge, MA: MIT Press/Bradford Books.

Fodor, Jerry. 2008. *LOT 2: The Language of Thought Revisited*. Oxford: Oxford University Press.

Frankfurt, Harry. 1969. "Alternate possibilities and moral responsibility." *Journal of Philosophy* 66: 829–39.

Frankfurt, Harry. 1971. "Freedom of the will and the concept of a person." *Journal of Philosophy* 68 (1): 5–20. Accessed August 19, 2021. https://doi.org/10.2307/2024717.

Frankfurt, Harry. 1982. "The importance of what we care about." *Synthese* 53 (2): 257–72.

Frankfurt, Harry. 1988. "Identification and externality." In his *Importance of What We Care About,* 80–94. New York: Cambridge University Press.

Frege, Gottlob, and Peter Thomas Geach. 1951. "On concept and object." Translated by Max Black. *Mind* 60 (238): 168–80. https://www.jstor.org/stable/2251430.

Gallese, Vittorio, and Alvin Goldman. 1998. "Mirror neurons and the simulation theory of mind-reading." *Trends in Cognitive Sciences* 2: 493–501.

Gallie, W. B., W. J. H. Sprott, and C. A. Mace. 1947. "Does psychology study mental acts or dispositions?" *Aristotelian Society Supplementary Volume* 21 (1): 134–74.

Published by Oxford University Press on behalf of the Aristotelian Society. https://www.jstor.com/stable/4106539.

Garrett, Don. 2018-09-03. "Spinoza's necessitarianism." In his *Necessity and Nature in Spinoza's Philosophy*. Oxford: Oxford University Press. Oxford Scholarship Online, 2018. Accessed March 13, 2020. https://doi.org/10.1093/oso/9780195307771.003.0007.

Gaus, Gerald, and Shaun Nichols. 2017. "Moral learning in the open society: The theory and practice of natural liberty." *Social Philosophy and Policy* 34 (1): 79–101. https://doi.org/10.1017/S0265052517000048.

Geach, Peter. 1957. *Mental Acts: Their Contents and Objects*. New York: The Humanities Press.

Geach, Peter. 1967. "Identity." *The Review of Metaphysics* 21: 3–12. Accessed August 17, 2019. https://www.jstor.org/stable/20124493.

Geach, Peter. 1980, *Reference and Generality* (third edition). Ithaca: Cornell University Press.

Giere, Ronald N. 1988. *Explaining Science: A Cognitive Approach*. University of Chicago Press. *ProQuest Ebook Central*, https://ebookcentral.proquest.com/lib/uaz/detail.action?docID=648132.

Gibson, James J. 1966. *The Senses Considered as Perceptual Systems*. Boston: Houghton Mifflin.

Gibson, James J. 2015. *The Ecological Approach to Visual Perception*. New York: Taylor & Francis/Psychology Press.

Gigerenzer, Gerd. 2001. "What is the role of culture in bounded rationality?" In Gerd Gigerenzer and Reinhard Selten (eds.). *Bounded Rationality: The Adaptive Toolbox*. Cambridge, MA: MIT Press, pp. 343–59.

Gigerenzer, Gerd. 2001. "The adaptive toolbox." In Gerd Gigerenzer and Reinhard Selten (eds.). *Bounded Rationality: The Adaptive Toolbox*. Cambridge, MA: MIT Press, pp. 37–50.

Gigerenzer, Gerd, and Reinhard Selten, eds. 2001. *Bounded Rationality: The Adaptive Toolbox*. Cambridge, MA: MIT Press.

Gilbert, Daniel, Gary King, Stephen Pettigrew, and Timothy Wilson. 2016. "Comment on 'Estimating the reproducibility of psychological science.'" *Science* 351 (6277): 1037a–1038a.

Gilbert, Margaret. 1989. *On Social Facts*. New York and London: Routledge.

Gilbert, Margaret. 2004. "Collective epistemology." *Episteme* 1: 95–107.

Gilbert, Margaret. 2010. "Collective action." In Timothy O'Connor and Constantine Sandis (eds.). *A Companion to the Philosophy of Action*. Hoboken, NJ: Wiley-Blackwell, pp. 67–73.

Ginet, Carl. 1966. "Might we have no choice?" In Keith Lehrer (ed.). *Freedom and Determinism*. New York: Random House, pp. 87–104.

Ginet, C. 1990. *"On action." Cambridge Studies in Philosophy*. Cambridge: Cambridge University Press. doi:10.1017/CBO9781139173780

Goldman, Alvin I. 1970. *Theory of Human Action*. Princeton, NJ: Princeton University Press.

Goldman, Alvin I. 2006. *Simulating Minds: The Philosophy, Psychology, and Neuroscience of Mindreading.* New York: Oxford University Press.

Goldman, Alvin I. 2013. *Joint Ventures: Mindreading, Mirroring and Embodied Cognition.* New York: Oxford University Press.

Goldman, Alvin I. 2014-11-20. "Social process reliabilism: Solving justification problems in collective epistemology." In Jennifer Lackey (ed). *Essays in Collective Epistemology.* Oxford: Oxford University Press. Oxford Scholarship Online, 2015. Accessed September 29, 2021. https://doi.org/10.1093/acprof:oso/9780199665792.003.0002.

Goodale, Melvyn, and David Milner. 2013-06-27. *Sight Unseen: An Exploration of Conscious and Unconscious Vision.* Oxford: Oxford University Press. Oxford Scholarship Online, 2013. Accessed September 18, 2021. https://doi.org/10.1093/acprof:oso/9780199596966.001.0001.

Goodman, Nelson. 1983. *Fact, fiction, and forecast*, 4th ed. Boston: Harvard University Press.

Gopnik, Alison. 2009a. *The Philosophical Baby: What Children Teach Us About Truth, Love and the Meaning of Life.* New York: Farrar, Straus and Giroux.

Gopnik, Alison. 2009b. "Reading other minds: How infants come to understand others." *Zero to Three* 30: 28–32.

Graham, George, and Terry Horgan. "Southern fundamentalism and the end of philosophy." *Philosophical Issues* 5 (1994): 219–47. Accessed September 9, 2021. https://doi.org/10.2307/1522881.

Greenberg, Gabriel. 2013. "Beyond resemblance." *Philosophical Review* 122: 215–87.

Greenwood, John D. 2003. "Social facts, social groups and social explanation." *Noûs* 37 (1) 93–112. https://doi-org.ezproxy1.library.arizona.edu/10.1111/1468-0068.00430.

Grice, Paul. 1989. *Studies in the Way of Words.* Cambridge, MA: Harvard University Press.

Grice, H. Paul, and Peter F. Strawson. 1956. "In defense of a dogma." *The Philosophical Review* 65 (2): 141–58. https://www.jstor.org/stable/2182828.

Griffin, Nicholas. 1977. *Relative Identity.* Oxford: Oxford University Press.

Halpin, John F. 1999. "Nomic necessity and empiricism." *Noûs* 33 (4): 630–43. https://doi-org.ezproxy4.library.arizona.edu/10.1111/0029-4624.00197.

Hamlin, J. K. 2015. "The case for social evaluation in preverbal infants: Gazing toward one's goal drives infants' preferences for helpers over hinderers in the hill paradigm." *Frontiers in Psychology* 5: 1563. https://doi.org/10.3389/fpsyg.2014.01563.

Hamlin, J. Kiley, Karen Wynn, and Paul Bloom. 2007. "Social evaluation by preverbal infants." *Nature* 450: 557–59. https://doi.org/10.1038/nature06288.

Hare, R. M. 1952. *The Language of Morals.* Oxford: Clarendon Press.

Hare, R. M., "Backsliding," *Freedom and Reason* (Oxford, 1965; online edn, Oxford Academic, 1 Nov. 2003), https://doi-org.ezproxy4.library.arizona.edu/10.1093/019881092X.003.0005, accessed 20 Mar. 2023.

Hare, R. M. 1981. *Moral Thinking: Its Levels, Method and Point.* Oxford: Clarendon Press.

Harman, Gilbert. 1973. *Thought.* Princeton, NJ: Princeton University Press.

Harman, Gilbert. 1982. "Conceptual role semantics." *Notre Dame J. Formal Logic* 23 (2): 242–56. doi:10.1305/ndjfl/1093883628.

Harman, Gilbert. 1999. "Moral philosophy meets social psychology: Virtue ethics and the fundamental attribution error." *Proceedings of the Aristotelian Society* 99: 315–31. Accessed June 29, 2020. https://www.jstor.org/stable/4545312.

Harman, Gilbert. 2000. "The nonexistence of character traits." *Proceedings of the Aristotelian Society* 100: 223–26. Accessed June 29, 2020. https://www.jstor.org/stable/4545327.

Haug, Matthew C., ed. 2014. *Philosophical Methodology: The Armchair or the Laboratory?* New York: Routledge.

Hausman, D. 2011. *Preference, Value, Choice, and Welfare.* Cambridge: Cambridge University Press. doi:10.1017/CBO9781139058537.

Henrich, J., Wulf Albers, Robert Boyd, Kevin McCabe, Gerd Gigerenzer, H. Peyton Young, and Axel Ockenfels. 2001. "What Is the Role of Culture in Bounded Rationality?" In *Bounded Rationality: The Adaptive Toolbox*, edited by Gerd Gigerenzer and Reinhard Selten, 343–59. Cambridge, MA: MIT Press.

Holliday, Wesley. 2012. "Freedom and the fixity of the past." The *Philosophical Review* 121 (2): 179–207. https://doi-org.ezproxy1.library.arizona.edu/10.1215/00318108-1539080.

Holton, Richard. 2009a. "Strength of will." In his *Willing, Wanting, Waiting,* chap. 6. Oxford: Oxford University Press. Oxford Scholarship Online, 2009. Accessed September 5, 2021. https://doi.org/10.1093/acprof:oso/9780199214570.003.0006.

Holton, Richard. 2009b. "Weakness of will." In his *Willing, Wanting, Waiting,* chap. 4. Oxford: Oxford University Press. Oxford Scholarship Online, 2009. Accessed September 5, 2021. https://doi.org/10.1093/acprof:oso/9780199214570.003.0004.

Horgan, Terence. 1985. "Compatibilism and the consequence argument." *Philosophical Studies* 47 (3): 339–56. https://doi-org.ezproxy1.library.arizona.edu/10.1007/BF00355208.

Horgan, Terence. 1993. "From supervenience to superdupervenience: Meeting the demands of a material world." *Mind* 102 (408): 555–86.

Horgan, Terry. 2011. "From agentive phenomenology to cognitive phenomenology: A guide for the perplexed." In Tim Bayne, and Michelle Montague (eds). *Cognitive Phenomenology.* Oxford, online edn, Oxford Academic, 19 Jan. 2012, https://doi-org.ezproxy3.library.arizona.edu/10.1093/acprof:oso/9780199579938.003.0003, accessed 3 Oct. 2022.

Horgan, Terence, and James Woodward. 1985. "Folk psychology is here to stay." *Philosophical Review* 94 (April): 197–226. Accessed September 9, 2021. https://www.jstor.org/stable/2185428.

Horgan, Terence, and George Graham. 1991. "In defense of southern fundamentalism." *Philosophical Studies* 62, no. 2 (May): 107–134. Accessed September 9, 2021. http://www.jstor.org/stable/4320199.

Horgan, Terence, John Tienson, and George Graham. 2004. "Phenomenal intentionality and the brain in a vat." In R. Schantz (ed.). *The Externalist Challenge: New Studies on Cognition and Intentionality.* Amsterdam: de Gruyter pp. 297–318.

Hornsey, M. J. 2008. "Social identity theory and self-categorization theory: A historical review." *Social and Personality Psychology Compass* 2/1: 204-2–22. https://doi.org/10.1111/j.1751-9004.2007.00066.x.

Ismael, Jenann. 2007. *The Situated Self.* New York: Oxford University Press.

Ismael, Jenann. 2016-03-01. *How Physics Makes Us Free.* New York: Oxford University Press. Oxford Scholarship Online, 2016. Accessed May 19, 2020. https://doi.org/10.1093/acprof:oso/9780190269449.001.0001.

Jackson, Frank. 2000-03-09. *From Metaphysics to Ethics: A Defence of Conceptual Analysis.* Oxford: Oxford University Press. Oxford Scholarship Online, 2003. Accessed September 7, 2021. https:// doi.org/10.1093/0198250614.001.0001.

James, William. 1890/1905. *The Principles of Psychology,* vols. I and II. New York: Henry Holt and Company.

Kahneman, Daniel, and Amos Tversky. 1979. "Prospect theory: An analysis of decision under risk." *Econometrica* 47 (2): 263–91. https://doi.org/10.2307/1914185.

Kahneman, Daniel, Paul Slovic, and Amos Tversky, eds. 1982a. *Judgment Under Uncertainty Heuristics and Biases.* Cambridge: Cambridge University Press.

Kahneman, Daniel, and Amos Tversky. 1982b. "The psychology of preferences." *Scientific American,* vol. 246, no. 1, 1982, pp. 160–73. *JSTOR,* http://www.jstor.org/stable/24966506. Accessed 2 Sep. 2022.

Kaiserman, Alex. 2020. "Reasons-sensitivity and degrees of free will." *Philosophy and Phenomenological Research.* https://doi.org/10.1111/phpr.12738.

Kamtekar, Rachana. 2004. "Situationism and virtue ethics on the content of our character." *Ethics* 114 (3): 458–91.

Kane, Robert. 1999-03-18. *The Significance of Free Will.* Oxford: Oxford University Press. Oxford Scholarship, 2003. Accessed August 27, 2021. https:/doi.org/10.1093/0195126564.001.0001.

Kane, Robert. 1999. "Responsibility, luck, and chance: Reflections on free will and indeterminism." *Journal of Philosophy* 96 (5): 217–40. https://doi.org/10.2307/2564666.

Kapitan, Tomis. 2000. "Autonomy and manipulated freedom." *Philosophical Perspectives* 14: 81–104.

Kaplan, David. 1989. "Demonstratives." In Joseph Almog, John Perry, and Howard Wettstein (eds.). *Themes from Kaplan.* Oxford: Oxford University Press, pp. 481–563.

Kim, Jaegwon. 1990. "Supervenience as a philosophical concept." *Metaphilosophy* 21 (1/2): 1–27. Accessed August 15, 2021. http://www.jstor.org/stable/24436754.

Kim, Jaegwon. 1992. "Multiple realization and the metaphysics of reduction." *Philosophy and Phenomenological Research* 52 (1): 1–26. https://doi.org/10.2307/2107741.

Kitcher, Philip. 2001. "Real realism: The Galilean strategy." *The Philosophical Review* 110 (2): 151–97. https://doi.org/10.2307/2693674.

Kitcher, Philip, and Wesley C. Salmon (eds.). 1962. *Scientific Explanation.* University of Minnesota Press. *ProQuest Ebook Central,* https://ebookcentral.proquest.com/lib/uaz/detail.action?docID=310140.

Kneale, William. 1950. "Natural laws and contrary-to-fact conditionals." *Analysis* 10 (6), 121–25. https://doi.org/10.2307/3326480.

*Bibliography*

Kripke, Saul A. 1980. *Naming and Necessity.* Cambridge, MA: Harvard University Press.

Kuhn, Thomas. 1962. *The Structure of Scientific Revolutions.* Chicago: University of Chicago Press.

Lackey, Jennifer, ed. 2014a-11-20. *Essays in Collective Epistemology.* Oxford: Oxford University Press. Oxford Scholarship Online, 2015. Accessed September 29, 2021. https://doi.org/10.1093/acprof:oso/9780199665792.001.0001.

Lackey, Jennifer. 2014b-11-20. "A deflationary account of group testimony." In Jennifer Lackey (ed). *Essays in Collective Epistemology.* Oxford: Oxford University Press. Oxford Scholarship Online, 2015. Accessed September 29, 2021. https://doi.org/10.1093/acprof:oso/9780199665792.003.0004.

Lackner, J. R., and M. F. Garrett. 1972. "Resolving ambiguity: Effects of biasing context in the unattended ear." *Cognition* 1: 359–72.

Lehrer, Keith. 1960. "Can we know that we have free will by introspection?" *Journal of Philosophy* 57 (March): 145–56. Accessed January 21, 2020. https://www.jstor.org/stable/2022533.

Lehrer, Keith. 1970. *Knowledge.* Oxford: Clarendon Press.

Lehrer, Keith. 1980. "Preferences, conditionals and freedom." In Peter van Inwagen (ed.). *Time and Cause: Essays Presented to Richard Taylor.* Philosophical Studies Series in Philosophy 19. Dordrecht: Springer. https://doi.org/10.1007/978-94-017-3528-5_11.

Lehrer, Keith. 1990-06-14. (Originally reprinted in 1980.) "Preferences, conditionals and freedom in Keith Lehrer's *Metamind.*" Oxford: Oxford University Press. Accessed January 24, 2020. https://www-oxfordscholarship-com.ezproxy3.library.arizona.edu/view/10.1093/acprof:oso/9780198248507.001.0001/acprof-9780198248507. Reprint, with an introductory chapter.

Lehrer, Keith. 2004. "Freedom and the power of preference." In Joseph Keim Campbell, Michael O'Rourke, and David Shier (eds.). *Freedom and Determinism.* Cambridge, MA: MIT Press/Bradford Books, pp. 47–69.

Lehrer, Keith. 2011. "Stories, exemplars and freedom." *Social Theory and Practice* 11: 1–17. https://www.jstor.org/stable/23562581.

Lehrer, Keith. 2016. "Freedom and preference: A defense of compatibilism." *Journal of Ethics* 20: 35–46.

Lehrer, Keith. 2020. "Ultimate preference and explanation," *Grazer Philosophisce Studien*, 97: 600–15.

Lehrer, Keith. Forthcoming in 2023. *Ultimate Freedom: Beyond Free Will.* New York: Oxford University Press.

Lewis, David. 1973. *Counterfactuals.* Cambridge, MA: Harvard University Press.

Lewis, David. 1981. "Are we free to break the laws?" *Theoria* 47 (3): 113–21. Reprinted in David Lewis. 1987. *Philosophical Papers Volume II.* New York: Oxford University Press. Published online November 2003. Oxford Scholarship Online. Accessed July 23, 2020. http://dx.doi.org/10.1093/0195036468.003.0010.

Lewis, David. 1983a-08-18. "An argument for the identity theory." In his *Philosophical Papers Volume I.* New York: Oxford University Press. Oxford Scholarship Online, 2003. Accessed May 18, 2020. https://doi.org/10.1093/0195032047.003.0007.

Lewis, David. 1983b-08-18. "Mad pain and Martian pain." In his *Philosophical Papers Volume I*. New York: Oxford University Press. Oxford Scholarship Online, 2003. Accessed December 4, 2019. https://doi.org/10.1093/0195032047.003.0009.

Lewis, David. 1983c-08-18. "Scorekeeping in a language game." In his *Philosophical Papers Volume I*. New York: Oxford University Press. Oxford Scholarship Online, 2003. Accessed September 9, 2021. https://doi.org/10.1093/0195032047 .003.0013.

Lewis, David. 1983d. "New work for a theory of universals." *Australasian Journal of Philosophy* 61: 343-377.

Lewis, David. 1987. "A subjectivist's guide to objective chance." In his *Philosophical Papers Volume II*. New York: Oxford University Press. Published online November 2003. Oxford Scholarship Online. Accessed June 26, 2020. https:// oxford.universitypressscholarship.com/view/10.1093/0195036468.001.0001/ acprof-9780195036466-chapter-4.

Libet, Benjamin. 1985. "Unconscious cerebral initiative and the role of conscious will in voluntary action." *Behavioral and Brain Sciences* 8: 529–39.

List, Christian, and Philip Pettit. 2011. *Group Agency: The Possibility, Design and Status of Corporate Agents*. Oxford: Oxford University Press.

Locke, John. 2004. (Last updated 2017. Originally published 1690.) *An Essay Concerning Humane Understanding, Volume I*. Urbana, IL: Project Gutenberg. www .gutenberg.org/ebooks/10615.

Loewer, Barry. 2004. (Originally published 1996.) "Humean supervenience." Reprinted in John Carroll (ed). *Readings on Laws of Nature*. Pittsburgh, PA: University of Pittsburgh Press, pp. 176–206.

Loewer, Barry. 2012. "Two accounts of laws and time." *Philosophical Studies* 160 (1): 115–37.

Ludwig, Kirk. 2016-09-29. *From Individual to Plural Agency: Collective Action I*. Oxford: Oxford University Press. Oxford Scholarship Online, 2016. Accessed September 20, 2021. https://doi.org/10.1093/acprof:oso/9780198755623.001.0001.

Mallon, Ron. 2016-08-18. *The Construction of Human Kinds*. Oxford: Oxford University Press. Oxford Scholarship Online, 2016. Accessed September 14, 2021. https://doi.org/10.1093/acprof:oso/9780198755678.001.0001.

Mallon, Ron, and Stephen P. Stich. 2000. "The odd couple: The compatibility of social construction and evolutionary psychology." *Philosophy of Science* 67 (1): 133–54. http://www.jstor.org/stable/188617.

Maloney, J. Christopher. 1987. *The Mundane Matter of the Mental Language*. New York: Cambridge University Press.

Maloney, J. Christopher. 2013. "Context operationalized." *International Review of Pragmatics,* 5 (2): 233-252. https://doi.org/10.1163/18773109-13050205.

Maloney, J. Christopher. 2018. *What It Is Like to Perceive*. New York: Oxford University Press.

Marr, David. 1982. *Vision*. San Francisco: Freeman.

Marshall, Julia, Karen Wynn, and Paul Bloom. 2020. "Do children and adults take social relationship into account when evaluating people's actions?" *Child Development* 91: e1082-e1100. https://doi.org/10.1111/cdev.13390.

Massimi, Michaela. 2016-07-01. "Bringing real realism back home: A perspectival slant." In Mark Couch and Jessica Pfeifer (eds.), *The Philosophy of Philip Kitcher*. New York: Oxford University Press, 980120. Oxford Scholarship Online, 2016. Accessed September 22, 2021. https://doi.org/10.1093/acprof:oso/9780199381357.003.0005.

Mathiesen, Kay. 2003. "On collective identity." *Protosociology* 18: 66–86.

Mathiesen, Kay. 2005-10-06. "Collective consciousness." In David Woodruff Smith and Amie L. Thomasson (eds.). *Phenomenology and Philosophy of Mind*, 235–52. Oxford: Oxford University Press. Oxford Scholarship Online, 2010. Accessed September 15, 2021. https://doi.org/10.1093/acprof:oso/9780199272457.003.0012.

Mathiesen, Kay. 2006. "We're all in this together: Responsibility of collective agents and their members." *Midwest Studies in Philosophy* 30 (1): 240–55. https://doi-org.ezproxy3.library.arizona.edu/10.1111/j.1475-4975.2006.00137.x.

McKenna, Michael S. 2001. "Source incompatibilism, ultimacy, and the transfer of non-responsibility." *American Philosophical Quarterly* 38 (1): 37–51. Accessed May 4, 2020. www.jstor.org/stable/20010021.

McKenna, Michael. 2004. "Responsibility and globally manipulated agents." *Philosophical Topics* 32 (1/2): 169–92. http://www.jstor.org/stable/43154434.

McKenna, Michael. 2012-03-28. *Conversation and Responsibility*. Oxford: Oxford University Press. Oxford Scholarship Online, 2012. Accessed July 6, 2020. https://doi.org/10.1093/acprof:oso/9780199740031.001.0001.

McKenna, Michael. 2013. "Reasons-responsiveness, agents, and mechanisms." In David Shoemaker (ed.). *Oxford Studies in Agency and Responsibility*, vol. 1. Oxford: Oxford University Press, pp. 151–84.

McKenna, Michael. 2014. "Resisting the manipulation argument: A hard-liner takes it on the chin." *Philosophy and Phenomenological Research* 89 (2): 467–84. https://doi.org/10.1111/phpr.12076.

McKenna, Michael, and Derk Pereboom. 2016. *Free Will: A Contemporary Introduction*. New York: Routledge.

Mele, Alfred R. 1987. *Irrationality: An Essay on* Akrasia, *Self-Deception, and Self-Control*. New York: Oxford University Press.

Mele, Alfred R. 1992. *Springs of Action: Understanding Intentional Behavior*. New York: Oxford University Press.

Mele, Alfred R. 2006. *Free Will and Luck*. New York: Oxford University Press.

Mele, Alfred R. 2012-06-01. *Backsliding: Understanding Weakness of Will*. New York: Oxford University Press. Oxford Scholarship Online, 2012. Accessed July 14, 2020. https://doi.org/10.1093/acprof:oso/9780199896134.001.0001.

Mele, Alfred R. 2014. "Luck and free will." *Metaphilosophy* 45 (4/5): 543–57 http://www.jstor.org/stable/24441754.

Mele, Alfred R. 2017. "Actions, explanations, and causes." in his *Aspects of Agency: Decisions, Abilities, Explanations, and Free Will*. New York, online edn, Oxford Academic, 18 May 2017, https://doi.org/10.1093/acprof:oso/9780190659974.003.0003, accessed 8 Sept. 2022.

Mele, Alfred R. 2019-05-30. *Manipulated Agents: A Window to Moral Responsibility*. New York: Oxford University Press. Oxford Scholarship Online, 2019. Accessed July 6, 2020. https://doi.org/10.1093/oso/9780190927967.001.0001.

Mele, Alfred R., and Paul K. Moser. 1997. "Intentional action." In Alfred Mele (ed.). *The Philosophy of Action.* New York: Oxford University Press, pp. 223–55.

Menary, Richard, ed. 2010. *The Extended Mind.* Cambridge, MA: MIT Press.

Menzies, Peter. 2017-06-15. "The consequence argument disarmed: An interventionist perspective." In Helen Beebee, Christopher Hitchcock, and Huw Price. (eds.). *Making a Difference: Essays on the Philosophy of Causation.* Oxford: Oxford University Press. Oxford Scholarship Online, 2017. Accessed May 14, 2020. https://doi.org/10.1093/oso/9780198746911.003.0016.

Michaelson, Eliot, and Marga Reimer. 2019. "Reference." In Edward N. Zalta (ed.). *The Stanford Encyclopedia of Philosophy,* Spring 2019, URL https://plato.stanford.edu/archives/spr2019/entries/reference/.

Miller, Seumas. 2010. *The Moral Foundations of Social Institutions: A Philosophical Study.* New York: Cambridge University Press. https://search-ebscohost-com.ezproxy3.library.arizona.edu/login.aspx?direct=true&db=e025xna&AN=312520&site=ehost-live.

Milner, A. David, and Mel Goodale. 1995. *The Visual Brain in Action.* Oxford: Oxford University Press.

Mole, Christopher. 2015-08-01. "Attention and cognitive penetration." In John Zeimbekis and Athanassios Raftopolous (eds.). *The Cognitive Penetrability of Perception: New Philosophical Perspectives.* Oxford: Oxford University Press. Oxford Scholarship Online, 2015. Accessed September 16, 2021. https://doi.org/10.1093/acprof:oso/9780198738916.003.0010.

Moore, G. E., and William H. Shaw. 2005-08-25. *Ethics: and "The Nature of Moral Philosophy."* Oxford: Oxford University Press. Oxford Scholarship Online, 2006. Accessed May 6, 2020. https://doi.org/10.1093/0199272018.001.0001.

Moore, Tirim, and Marc Zirnsak. 2017. "Neural mechanisms of selective visual attention." *Annual Review of Psychology* 68: 1, 47–72.

Muraven, Mark, Dianne M. Tice, and Roy F. Baumeister. 1998. "Self-control as a limited resource: Regulatory depletion patterns." *Journal of Personality and Social Psychology* 74 (3): 774–89.

Muraven, Mark, and Roy F. Baumeister. 2000. "Self-regulation and depletion of limited resources: Does self-control resemble a muscle?" *Psychological Bulletin* 126 (2): 247–59.

Nadel, Lynn, and Walter P. Sinnott-Armstrong, eds. 2012. *Memory and Law.* New York: Oxford University Press. Oxford Scholarship Online, 2013. Accessed August 14, 2016. https://doi.org/10.1093/acprof:oso/9780199920754.001.0001.

Nagel, Thomas. 1989. *The View from Nowhere.* New York: Oxford University Press. ProQuest Ebook Central.

Neisser, Ulric. 1967. *Cognitive Psychology.* Englewood Cliffs, NJ: Prentice-Hall.

Nelkin, Dana Kay. 2011-07-01. *Making Sense of Freedom and Responsibility.* Oxford: Oxford University Press. Oxford Scholarship Online, 2011. Accessed August 11, 2020. https://doi.org/10.1093/acprof:oso/9780199608560.001.0001.

Newman, John Henry. 2006. Last updated 2013. (Originally published in 1864.) *Apologia Pro Vita Sua: A Reply to a Pamphlet.* Urbana, IL: Project Gutenberg. www.gutenberg.org/ebooks/19690.

Nichols, Shaun. 2015-01-08. Introduction to his *Bound: Essays on Free Will and Responsibility*. Oxford: Oxford University Press. Oxford Scholarship Online, 2015. Accessed August 26, 2021. https://doi.org/10.1093/acprof:oso/9780199291847 .003.0001.

Nozick, Robert. *Anarchy, State, and Utopia*. 2013. Basic Books. *ProQuest Ebook Central*, https://ebookcentral.proquest.com/lib/uaz/detail.action?docID =894945.

O'Connor, Timothy. 2002-11-28. *Persons and Causes: The Metaphysics of Free Will*. New York: Oxford University Press. Oxford Scholarship Online, 2003. Accessed September 10, 2021. https://doi.org/10.1093/019515374X.001.0001.

Open Science Collaboration. 2015. "Estimating the reproducibility of psychological science." *Science* 349, no. 6251 (Aug 28). https://doi.org/10.1126/science.aac4716.

O'Shaughnessy, Brian. 1973. "Trying (as the Mental 'Pineal Gland')." *Journal of Philosophy* 70: 365–86.

Papineau, David. 2009. "The poverty of analysis." *Aristotelian Society Supplementary Volume* 83, no. 1 (June): 1–30. https://doi-org.ezproxy3.library.arizona.edu/10 .1111/j.1467-8349.2009.00170.x.

Peacocke, Christopher. 2001. "Does perception have a nonconceptual content?" *Journal of Philosophy* 98: 239–64.

Pereboom, Derk. 1995. "Determinism *al dente*." *Noûs* 29: 21–45. Accessed February 13, 2020. https://www.jstor.org/stable/2215725.

Pereboom, Derk. 2001. *Living Without Free Will*. Cambridge Studies in Philosophy. Cambridge: Cambridge University Press. Accessed February 18, 2020. https:// search-ebscohost-com.ezproxy3.library.arizona.edu/login.aspx?direct=true&db =nlebk&AN=72802&site=ehost-live.

Pereboom, Derk. 2014-02-27. "A manipulation argument against compatibilism." In his *Free Will, Agency, and Meaning in Life*. Oxford: Oxford University Press. Oxford Scholarship Online, 2014. Accessed July 24, 2020. https://doi.org/10.1093 /acprof:oso/9780199685516.003.0005.

Pereboom, Derk. 2018. "On Carolina Sartorio's *Causation and Free Will*." *Philosophical Studies* 175: 1535–43.

Perry, John. 2004. "Compatibilist options." In Joseph Keim Campbell, Michael O'Rourke, and David Shier (eds.). *Freedom and Determinism*. Cambridge, MA: MIT Press, pp. 231–54.

Pettit, Philip. 2014-11-20. "How to tell if a group is an agent." In Jennifer Lackey (ed.). *Essays in Collective Epistemology*, 97–121. Oxford: Oxford University Press. Oxford Scholarship Online, 2015. Accessed September 29, 2021. https://doi .org/10.1093/acprof:oso/9780199665792.003.0005.

Phillips, Ian B. 2011. "Perception and iconic memory: What Sperling doesn't show." *Mind and Language* 26: 381–411.

Pollock, John. 1995. *Cognitive Carpentry*. Cambridge, MA: MIT Press.

Pollock, John L. and Jenann Ismael. 2006. "So you think you exist?" In Thomas M. Crisp, Matthew Davidson, and David Vander Laan (eds.). *Knowledge and Reality: Essays in Honor of Alvin Plantinga*. Philosophical Studies Series 103. Dordrecht: Springer, pp, 35–62.

Powell, L. J., and Elizabeth Spelke. 2013. "Preverbal infants expect social group members to act alike." *Proceedings of the National Academy of Sciences* 110 (41): E3965-E3972. https://doi.org/10.1073/pnas.1304326110.

Putnam, Hilary. 1960. "Minds and machines." In Sidney Hook (ed.). *Dimensions of Minds.* New York: New York University Press, pp. 138–64.

Putnam, Hilary. 1967. "Psychological predicates." In W. H. Capitan and D. D. Merrill (eds.). *Art, Mind, and Religion.* Pittsburgh: University of Pittsburgh Press, pp. 37–48.

Putnam, Hilary. 1975. "The meaning of 'meaning'." In K. Gunderson (ed.) *Language, Mind, and Knowledge*, pp. 131–93. *Minnesota Studies in the Philosophy of Science* 7. Minneapolis: University of Minnesota Press.

Pylyshyn, Zenon. 1984. *Computation and Cognition.* Cambridge, MA: MIT Press/ Bradford Books.

Pylyshyn, Zenon. 1987. *The Robot's Dilemma: The Frame Problem in Artificial Intelligence.* Norwood, NJ: Ablex Publishing.

Pylyshyn, Zenon. 1999. "Is vision continuous with cognition? The case for cognitive impenetrability of visual perception." *Behavioral and Brain Sciences* 22: 341–65.

Quine, Willard Van Orman. 1951. "Two dogmas of empiricism." *Philosophical Review* 60: 20–43.

Recanati, François. 2010. *Truth-Conditional Pragmatics.* Oxford: Oxford University Press.

Reid, Thomas. 1785. *Essays on the Intellectual Powers of Man.* Printed for John Bell, Parliament Square, and G. G. J. & J. Robinson, London. https://link.gale.com /apps/doc/CW0107462279/ECCO?u=uarizona_main&sid=bookmark-ECCO&xid =8b50be92&pg=77.

Rey, Georges. 1995. "A not 'merely empirical' argument for a language of thought." *Philosophical Perspectives* 9: 201–22.

Rey, Georges. 1997. *Contemporary Philosophy of Mind: A Contentiously Classical Approach.* Oxford: Blackwell.

Ritchie, Katherine. 2013. "What are groups?" *Philosophical Studies* 166 (2): 257–72. http://www.jstor.org/stable/42920268.

Ritchie, Katherine. 2015. "The metaphysics of social groups." *Philosophy Compass* 10 (5): 310–21. https://doi.org/10.1111/phc3.12213.

Rhodes M. 2012. "Naïve theories of social groups." *Child Development.* 83(6): 1900–16. doi: 10.1111/j.1467-8624.2012.01835.x. Epub 2012 Aug 20. PMID: 22906078.

Rosati, Connie S. 2016. "Moral motivation." In Edward N. Zalta (ed.). *The Stanford Encyclopedia of Philosophy.* Winter 2016, URL https://plato.stanford.edu/archives /win2016/entries/moral-motivation/.

Rosenberg, Alexander. 1994. *Instrumental Biology, or the Disunity of Science.* Chicago: University of Chicago Press.

Rowlands, Mark. 2010. *The New Science of the Mind: From Extended Mind to Embodied Phenomenology.* Cambridge, MA: MIT Press/ Bradford Book. https:// doi.org/10.7551/mitpress/9780262014557.001.0001.

Rumelhart, David E., and James L. McClelland. 1986. *Parallel Distributed Processing*, vol. I. Cambridge, MA: MIT Press/ Bradford Book.

Rupert, Robert D. 2009. *Cognitive Systems and the Extended Mind.* New York: Oxford University Press. Oxford Scholarship Online, 2009. https://doi.org/10.1093 /acprof:oso/9780195379457.001.0001.

Russell, Daniel C. 2009. *Practical Intelligence and the Virtues.* Oxford: Clarendon Press.

Rysiew, Patrick. 2002. "The context-sensitivity of knowledge attributions." *Noûs* 35 (4): 477–514. https://doi:10.1111/0029-4624.00349.

Sartorio, Carolina. 2016. *Causation and Free Will.* Oxford: Oxford University Press.

Sartorio, Carolina. 2021. "Responsibility and the metaphysics of Omissions." In Sara Bernstein and Tyron Goldschmidt (eds). *Non-Being: New Essays on the Metaphysics of Nonexistence.* Oxford, online edn, Oxford Academic, 22 Apr. 2021, https://doi-org.ezproxy4.library.arizona.edu/10.1093/oso/9780198846222 .003.0016, accessed 8 Oct. 2022.

Schacter, Daniel. 2001. *The Seven Sins of Memory: How the Mind Forgets and Remembers.* New York: Houghton Mifflin.

Schaffer, Jonathan. 2005. "Quiddistic knowledge." *Philosophical Studies* 123 (1/2): 1–32. Accessed July 11, 2020. www.jstor.org/stable/4321570.

Schiffer, Stephen. 1991. "Ceteris paribus laws." *Mind,* 100: 1–17.

Schmidtz, D. 2002. "How to deserve." *Political Theory* 30(6), 774–99. http://www .jstor.org/stable/3072566.

Schroeder, Timothy, Adina L. Roskies, and Shaun Nichols. 2010-06-10. "Moral motivation." In John M. Doris and the Moral Psychology Research Group (eds.). *The Moral Psychology Handbook,* 72–110. Oxford: Oxford University Press. Oxford Scholarship Online, 2010. Accessed October 4, 2021. https://doi.org/10 .1093/acprof:oso/9780199582143.003.0004.

Searle, John R. 1969. *Speech Acts: An Essay in the Philosophy of Language.* Cambridge: Cambridge University Press.

Searle, John R. 1980. "Minds, brains, and programs." *Behavioral and Brain Sciences* 3 (3): 417–57.

Searle, John. 1989. "How performatives work," *Linguistics and Philosophy,* 12: 535–58.

Searle, John R. 1990. "Collective intentions and actions." In Philip R. Cohen, Jerry Morgan, and Martha Pollack (eds.). *Intentions in Communication.* Boston: MIT Press, pp. 401–15.

Searle, John R. 1995. *The Construction of Social Reality.* New York: The Free Press.

Shepard, Roger N., and Lynn A. Cooper. 1982. *Mental Images and Their Transformations.* Cambridge, MA: MIT Press.

Sherif, Muzafer. 1956. "Experiments in group conflict." *Scientific American* 195 (5): 54–59. http://www.jstor.org/stable/24941808.

Shoemaker, David W. 2003. "Caring, identification, and agency." *Ethics* 114: 88–118.

Shoemaker, David. 2015. "Ecumenical attributability." In Randolph Clarke, Michael McKenna, and Angela M. Smith (eds.). *The Nature of Moral Responsibility: New Essays.* New York: Oxford University Press, pp. 115–40.

Shoemaker, Sydney. 1981. "Some varieties of functionalism." *Philosophical Topics* 12 (1): 93–119.

Shoemaker, Sydney. 1998. "Causal and metaphysical necessity." *Pacific Philosophical Quarterly* 79: 59–77. https://doi.org/10.1111/1468-0114.00050.

Sider, Theodore. 2011-11-24. *Writing the Book of the World.* Oxford: Oxford University Press. Oxford Scholarship Online, 2012. Accessed September 19, 2021. https://doi.org/10.1093/acprof:oso/9780199697908.001.0001.

Siegel, Susanna. 2010. *The Contents of Visual Experience.* New York: Oxford University Press.

Siegel, Susanna. 2017-01-05. *The Rationality of Perception.* Oxford: Oxford University Press. Oxford Scholarship Online, 2017. Accessed September 16, 2021. https://doi.org/10.1093/acprof:oso/9780198797081.001.0001.

Simon, Herbert. 1957. *Models of Man,* New York: John Wiley.

Sinnott- Armstrong, Walter, Liane Young, and Fiery Cushman. 2010-06-10. "Moral intuitions." In John M. Doris and the Moral Psychology Research Group (eds.). *The Moral Psychology Handbook,* pp. 246–72. Oxford: Oxford University Press. Oxford Scholarship Online, 2010. Accessed October 4, 2021. https://doi.org/10.1093/acprof:oso/9780199582143.003.0008.

Slote, Michael. 1980. "Understanding free will." *Journal of Philosophy* 77: 136–51.

Slote, Michael. 1982. "Selective necessity and the free will problem." *Journal of Philosophy* 79: 5–24.

Smith, Michael. 2003-09-04. "Rational capacities, or: How to distinguish recklessness, weakness, and compulsion." In Sarah Stroud and Christine Tappolet (eds.). *Weakness of Will and Practical Irrationality.* pp 17–38. Oxford: Oxford University Press. Oxford Scholarship Online, 2005. Accessed May 4, 2020. https://doi.org/10.1093/0199257361.003.0002.

Smith, Stephanie M., and Ian Krajbich. 2019. "Gaze amplifies value in decision making." *Psychological Scienc*e 30 (1): 116–28. https://doi.org/10.1177/0956797618810521.

Smolensky, Paul. 1988. "On the proper treatment of connectionism." *Behavioral and Brain Sciences* 11: 1–74.

Sosa, E. 1967. "The semantics of imperatives." *American Philosophical Quarterly,* 4(1), 57–64. http://www.jstor.org/stable/20009227.

Sosa, Ernest. 2000. "Skepticism and contextualism." *Philosophical Issues* 10: 1–18. Accessed August 3, 2020. www.jstor.org/stable/3050558.

Sosa, Ernest. 2007. *A Virtue Epistemology: Apt Belief and Reflective Knowledge, Volume I.* Oxford, online edn., Oxford Academic, 1 Sept. 2007. https://doi-org.ezproxy2.library.arizona.edu/10.1093/acprof:oso/9780199297023.001.0001, accessed 1 Sept. 2022.

Sperling, G. 1960. "The information available in brief visual presentations." *Psychological Monographs* 74: 1–29.

Sterba, James P., and Janet A. Kourany. 1981. "How to complete the compatibilist account of free action." *Philosophy and Phenomenological Research* 41 (4): 508–23. https://doi.org/10.2307/2107254.

Stich, Stephen. 1983. *From Folk Psychology to Cognitive Science: The Case Against Belief.* Cambridge, MA: MIT Press.

Stich, Stephen. 1990. *Fragmentation of Reason: Preface to a Pragmatic Theory of Cognitive Evaluation.* Cambridge, MA: MIT Press/Bradford Books.

Stich, Stephen, and Shaun Nichols. 1992. "Folk psychology: Simulation or tacit theory?" *Mind & Language* 7 (1–2): 35–71.

Strauss, Barry. 2009. *The Spartacus War.* New York: Simon and Schuster. https://archive.org/details/spartacuswar00stra/page/n5/mode/2up.

Strawson, Galen J. 1994. "The impossibility of moral responsibility." *Philosophical Studies* 75 (1/2): 5–24. Accessed February 18, 2020. www.jstor.org/stable/4320507.

Strawson, Galen. 2005. "Free will." In E. Craig (ed.). *Shorter Routledge Encyclopedia of Philosophy.* London: Routledge. pp. 286–94.

Strawson, Peter. 1962. "Freedom and resentment." *Proceedings of the British Academy* 48: 187–211.

Sussman, Steve, Pallav Pokhrel, Richard D. Ashmore, and B. Bradford Brown. 2007. "Adolescent peer group identification and characteristics: A review of the literature." *Addictive Behaviors* 32 (8): 1602–27.

Swoyer, Chris. 1982. "The nature of natural laws." *Australasian Journal of Philosophy* 60: 203–23.

Tassone, Biagio G. 2012. *From Psychology to Phenomenology: Franz Brentano's 'Psychology from an Empirical Standpoint' and Contemporary Philosophy of Mind.* London: Palgrave Macmillan. https://doi-org.ezproxy3.library.arizona.edu/10.1057/9781137029225.

Thagard, P. 2007. Coherence, truth, and the development of scientific knowledge. *Philosophy of Science* 74(1), 28–47. https://doi.org/10.1086/520941.

Thomasson, Amie L. 2003. "Foundations for a social ontology." *Protosociology* 18/19, Understanding the Social II: Philosophy of Sociality: 269–90.

Thomasson, Amie L. 2014-11-28. *Ontology Made Easy.* New York: Oxford University Press. Oxford Scholarship Online, 2014. Accessed September 19, 2021. https://doi.org/10.1093/acprof:oso/9780199385119.001.0001.

Thomasson, Amie. 2019. "The ontology of social groups." *Synthese* 196 (12): 4829–45.

Tooby, John, and Leda Cosmides. 2015. "Conceptual foundations of evolutionary psychology." In David M. Buss (ed.). *The Handbook of Evolutionary Psychology,* 2nd ed, 5–67. Hoboken, NJ: Wiley. https://doi-org.ezproxy1.library.arizona.edu/10.1002/9780470939376.ch1.

Tooley, Michael. 1977. "The nature of laws." *Canadian Journal of Philosophy* 7 (4): 667–98.

Tuomela, Raimo. 2000. *Cooperation: A Philosophical Study,* Philosophical Studies Series 82. Dordrecht: Kluwer.

Tuomela, Raimo. 2007-09-01. *The Philosophy of Sociality: The Shared Point of View.* New York: Oxford University Press. Oxford Scholarship Online, 2007. Accessed September 15, 2021. https://doi.org/10.1093/acprof:oso/9780195313390.001.0001.

Tuomela, Raimo. 2013-09-16. *Social Ontology: Collective Intentionality and Group Agents.* New York: Oxford University Press. Oxford Scholarship Online, 2013.

Accessed September 20, 2021. https://doi.org/10.1093/acprof:oso/9780199978267 .001.0001.

Turing, Alan M. 1950. "Computing machinery and intelligence." *Mind* 59: 433–60.

Turner, John C., and Katherine J. Reynolds. 2003. "The social identity perspective in intergroup relations: Theories, themes, and controversies." In Rupert Brown and Samuel L. Gaertner (eds.). *The Blackwell Handbook of Social Psychology: Intergroup Processes*, chap. 7. Oxford: Blackwell Publishing. https://doi-org.ezproxy4 .library.arizona.edu/10.1002/9780470693421.ch7.

Turner, John C., and Katherine J. Reynolds. 2011. "Self-categorization theory." In Paul A. M. van Lange, Arie W. Kruglanski, and E. Tory Higgins (eds.). *The Handbook of Theories of Social Psychology: Collection*, vols. 1 and 2, chap. 46. London: Sage Publications. ProQuest Ebook Central.

Tversky, Amos, and Daniel Kahneman. 1974. "Judgment under uncertainty: Heuristics and biases." *Science* 185 (4157): 1124–31. Accessed June 29, 2020. www.jstor .org/stable/1738360.

Tye, Michael. 2009. *Consciousness Revisited: Materialism without Phenomenal Concepts*. Cambridge, MA: MIT Press.

Unger, Peter. 1971. "A defense of skepticism." *Philosophical Review* 80: 198–219.

Unger, Peter. 1975. *Ignorance: A Case for Scepticism*. New York: Oxford University Press.

van Inwagen, Peter. 1975. "The incompatibility of free will and determinism." *Philosophical Studies* 27: 185–99.

van Inwagen, Peter. 1983. *An Essay on Free Will*. New York: Oxford University Press.

van Inwagen, Peter. 2008. "How to think about the problem of free will." *Journal of Ethics* 12 (3/4): 327–41.

Velleman, J. David. 1997. "How to share an intention." *Philosophy and Phenomenological Research* 57 (1): 29–50. https://doi.org/10.2307/2953776.

Velleman, James David. 2000. *The Possibility of Practical Reason*. New York: Clarendon Press, Oxford University Press.

Velleman, J. David. 2006. "The self as narrator." In his *Self to Self: Selected Essays*, 203–23. Cambridge: Cambridge University Press. https://doi.org/10.1017/ CBO9780511498862.009.

Vihvelin, Kadri. 2013. *Causes, Laws, and Free Will: Why Determinism Doesn't Matter*. New York: Oxford University Press. online edn, https://doi-org.ezproxy3 .library.arizona.edu/10.1093/acprof:oso/9780199795185.001.0001, accessed 12 Aug. 2022.

von Wright, G. H. 1972. "The logic of preference reconsidered." *Theory and Decision* 3, 140–69. https://doi-org.ezproxy1.library.arizona.edu/10.1007/BF00141053.

Vranas, Peter B. M. 2008. "New foundations for imperative logic I: Logical connectives, consistency, and quantifiers." *Noûs* 42 (4): 529–72.

Wason, P. C. 1968. "Reasoning about a rule." *Quarterly Journal of Experimental Psychology* 20: 273–81.

Watson, Gary. 2003. *Free Will*. New York. Oxford University Press.

Weiskrantz, Lawrence. 2009. *Blindsight: A case study spanning 35 years and new developments,* 2nd ed. Oxford: Oxford University Press.

Wilson, Alastair. 2013. "Schaffer on laws of nature." *Philosophical Studies: An International Journal for Philosophy in the Analytic Tradition* 164 (3): 653–67. Accessed July 11, 2020. www.jstor.org/stable/41932752.

Wolf, Susan. 1990. *Freedom within Reason.* New York: Oxford University Press.

Woodward, James. 2016-07-01. "Unificationism, explanatory internalism, and autonomy." In Mark Couch and Jessica Pfeifer (eds.). *The Philosophy of Philip Kitcher,* New York: Oxford University Press. Oxford Scholarship Online, 2016. Accessed September 22, 2021. https://doi.org/10.1093/acprof:oso/9780199381357 .003.0006.

Woodward, James and Lauren Ross. 2021. "Scientific explanation," *The Stanford Encyclopedia of Philosophy* (Summer 2021 Edition), Edward N. Zalta (ed.), URL = <https://plato.stanford.edu/archives/sum2021/entries/scientific-explanation/>.

Wynn, Karen, and Paul Bloom. 2013. "The moral baby." In Melanie Killen and Judith G. Smetana (eds.). *The Handbook of Moral Development,* 435–53. New York. Taylor & Francis Group. ProQuest Ebook Central.

Wynn, Karen, Paul Bloom, Ashley Jordan, Julia Marshall, and Mark Sheskin. 2018. "Not noble savages after all: Limits to early altruism." *Current Directions in Psychological Science* 27 (1): 3–8. https://doi.org/10.1177/0963721417734875.

Zagzebski, L. 1996. In *Virtues of the Mind: An Inquiry into the Nature of Virtue and the Ethical Foundations of Knowledge.* Cambridge: Cambridge University Press. doi:10.1017/CBO9781139174763.005.

Zeimbekis, John, and Athanassios Raftopoulos, eds. 2015-08-01. *The Cognitive Penetrability of Perception: New Philosophical Perspectives.* Oxford: Oxford University Press. Oxford Scholarship Online, 2015. Accessed September 16, 2021. https://doi.org/10.1093/acprof:oso/9780198738916.001.0001.

# Index

Abelard, Peter, 77

abnormal choice-controlling preference, 44–45

achievement, 144; collective, 147–49; luck and, 146–47; personal, 145–46

action: collective, 102, 129n19; free, 6, 112; freedom of, 51, 53n10; Humean psychology and, 4; immoral, 133; intentional, 18, 21, 50

act psychology, 12

Adderley, Cannonball, 108

addiction: akratic compatibilism and, 142; Augustine and, 142–43; folk psychology on, 144; manipulation and, 142–44

*The Adventures of Huckleberry Finn* (Twain), 73

*akrasia*, 89, 91; achievement and, 144–45; Augustine and, 94, 120–22, 125, 145; literature on, 55; nature and, 138; necessitarianism and, 65

akratic compatibilism, 6; achievement and, 144–45; addiction and, 142; of Augustine, 99, 124; collective achievement and, 147; confessed, 63–68; fallible imagination and, 134–35; luck and, 141; manipulation and, 131–44; possibility and, 136; source compatibilism and, 134. *See also specific topics*

"almost," 132; cognitive context and, 80–81; determinism and, 64; logic of, 75; mathematical context and, 81–83; phenomenal context and, 79–80; social context and, 78–79

analyticity, 76

*apologia pro vita*, 88

*apologia pro vita sua*, 94, 120

approximation, 63; asymptotic, 97

arguments: Consequence Argument, 65, 66; manipulation, 133–34

Aristotle, 43, 60n44

Armstrong, David M., 4, 65

artifacts, social, 79

assessment, charitable, of Augustine, 95–99

asymmetry, 35

asymptotic approximation, 97

Augustine (Saint), 7, 101, 103, 110, 118, 123, 147; achievement and, 144; addiction and, 142–43; *akrasia* and, 94, 120–22, 125, 145; akratic compatibilism of, 99, 124; charitable assessment of, 95–99; *Confessions*, 6, 100, 120, 121; immoral action of, 133; necessitarianism and, 95; self-reflection by, 127n5; Spinozan psychology and, 95, 99–100, 124–25; Strawson and, 97–99; as trendsetter, 124–25, 148

# About the Author

**J. Christopher Maloney** is professor emeritus of philosophy and cognitive science at the University of Arizona, where he was on the faculty beginning in 1988. His research centers on the philosophy of mind, the philosophical foundations of cognitive science, and how that science variously bears upon some of the perennial problems in philosophy.

In addition to *Akratic Compatibilism and All Too Human Psychology: Almost Enough Is Free Will Enough*, he is the author of two other books: *What it is Like to Perceive: Direct Realism and the Phenomenal Character of Perception* (Oxford University Press, 2018) and *The Mundane Matter of the Mental Language* (Cambridge University Press, 1989).

Ingram Content Group UK Ltd.
Milton Keynes UK
UKHW010618010523
421006UK00003B/19

9 781666 919486